CREATIVITY
IN THE EARLY YEARS

CREATIVITY
IN THE EARLY YEARS

Engaging Children Aged 0-5

SIMON TAYLOR

S Sage

1 Oliver's Yard
55 City Road
London EC1Y 1SP

2455 Teller Road
Thousand Oaks
California 91320

Unit No 323-333, Third Floor, F-Block
International Trade Tower
Nehru Place, New Delhi 110 019

8 Marina View Suite 43-053
Asia Square Tower 1
Singapore 018960

Library of Congress Control Number: 2023945487

British Library Cataloguing in Publication data

A catalogue record for this book is available from the British Library

Editor: Delayna Spencer
Editorial assistant: Harry Dixon
Production editor: Nicola Marshall
Copyeditor: Ritika Sharma
Indexer: TNQ Tech Pvt. Ltd.
Marketing manager: Lorna Patkai
Cover design: Sheila Tong
Typeset by: TNQ Tech Pvt. Ltd.
Printed in the UK

ISBN 978-1-5297-4366-1
ISBN 978-1-5297-4365-4 (pbk)

Contents

This book is dedicated to the memory of a good friend, artist, arts manager, director and cultural fundraiser - Laura Pottinger (1970–2023), who did so much throughout her life and work to support an inclusive approach to the arts and creativity.

About the Author

Simon Taylor is a Senior Lecturer with the Department for Education and Inclusion at the University of Worcester. Prior to this he worked in the arts and cultural sector for many years; as Head of Learning for Birmingham's Ikon Gallery (2011–2015) and Education and Community Outreach Manager for The Making (2004–2011), an arts development agency based in Hampshire.

Originally a graduate of the University of Brighton, Simon started his career as a professional artist in the South East, teaching in a range of settings including Special schools, Children's Centres, Prisons and FE colleges, and working with a diverse range of learners from adults to young people at risk from exclusion, children with special needs, prisoners and young offenders.

Simon is married with two 'grown up' children, is a keen drummer, loves live music and is hoping his potter's wheel is still waiting for him somewhere buried in the garage…

About the Contributors

Janet Harvell is a Senior Lecturer at the Department for Children and Families, University of Worcester. She has worked in the Early Years sector for 28 years with experience as a child-minder, pre-school supervisor, nursery manager and registered Ofsted HM Inspector. Janet's research interests are focused on international approaches, including extensive experience in China and a collaborative learning and teaching project linked to refugee children and their families in Calais.

Nicola Watson is a Senior Lecturer at the Department for Children and Families, University of Worcester. She has worked as an educator in the early years, primary and higher education sectors for over 20 years. Prior to this, Nicola was a family lawyer and mediator. Her professional interests include creativity and social pedagogy. Nicola is passionate about social and environmental justice and exploring creative ways of promoting the interests of the least powerful in society, including human and non-human animals.

Acknowledgements

My sincere thanks go to my contributors and esteemed colleagues from the University of Worcester, Nicola Watson and Janet Harvell, I have certainly benefitted from your experience and wealth of knowledge. To my editors at SAGE, Delayna Spencer and Catriona McMullen, thank you for all your encouragement and support, and also, to my writing 'mentors' Maggi Savin-Baden and Janette Kelly-Ware, for all their generosity with their time, expertise and insight.

Most importantly, thanks must go to my family; my wife Dion, and sons Luke and Toby, for their patience and understanding, their inspiration and creativity.

Thank you!

INTRODUCTION

My own varied career over the last 30 years has given me wonderful insights into the power of creativity in a wide range of educational settings; from the early days as a hands-on artist-educator, dragging bags of clay and my potter's wheel into schools in the South East of England, to commissioning artists to collaborate with the newly established Sure Start Children's Centres that emerged whilst I was working as a community arts manager in Hampshire. My subsequent move into museum and gallery education in the West Midlands gave me real insights into the innovative work that is taking place in terms of early years practice outside of the classroom. More recently I have had the privilege of teaching undergraduates studying education and early childhood courses at university level and this has opened my eyes to a multitude of new theories, concepts and research from around the world.

On a more personal level, from my own experience of having two children go through nursery and pre-school in England and seeing the amazing work taking place, it is my firm belief that early years practitioners are in a unique position to encourage the value of creativity: they can support children's agency and enable their voice to be heard in the world. However, I am also aware that many early childhood professionals lack confidence in their skills or abilities, or struggle with outside expectations and worry about how to make the case for new or more innovative approaches.

It is also true to say that the field of creativity itself is vast and ever-evolving, and so this book cannot claim to be comprehensive and can only ever be a 'snapshot' of this particular moment in time. What I have attempted to do is include all those practical ideas, theories, philosophies and approaches that I have seen to be so effective over the years, with the caveat, of course, that new ones are emerging all the time and every educator has their own personal philosophy and set of values.

My sincere hope is that this book will provide an inspirational and practical, research-based resource for all those involved in this sector whatever your role, whether you are a student, artist-educator, academic, parent, practitioner, support staff or nursery manager. Collectively, we can become real advocates for creativity, creative thinking, teaching and leading for creativity in the early years.

Simon Taylor

SECTION I
DEFINING CREATIVITY

1

WHAT IS CREATIVITY? DEFINITIONS AND DEBATES...

One of the most important questions of child psychology and pedagogy is the question about creativity in children, its development and its significance for the general development of the child. Lev Vygotsky (1967)

━━━━━━━━━━ **Chapter overview** ━━━━━━━━━━

The main purpose of this opening chapter is to put creativity in context and begin the debate, exploring different definitions and contested ideas around creativity. The discussion is wide-ranging, and many of these ideas and theories will be examined in more depth in subsequent chapters. Readers will be encouraged to develop their own definition of creativity and reflect on how this might evolve and change over time in the light of experience and a deeper understanding of the literature.

Creativity in context

Why is creativity important? In the words of Lev Vygotsky 'one of the most important questions of child psychology and pedagogy is the question about creativity in children, its development and its significance for the general development of the child' (Vygotsky, 1967). This is indeed true, but I would argue we need to go beyond questions of child development and advocate for a rights-based approach to creative education and an inclusive approach to creativity in the early years. Why is this significant? Even before the impact of coronavirus disease 2019 (COVID-19), we have experienced a decade of austerity in the UK and have seen a widespread rise in economic insecurity, persistent levels of child poverty and widening attainment gaps for children from the poorest areas. According to the Children's Commissioner for England (2020), these differences in school attainment emerge as development gaps even before the age of five. Educational settings, especially those specialising in early years are on the front line in this battle to tackle disadvantage and inequality in our society. This issue will become more pressing over the next decade and could be said to be a matter of social justice.

It is important for practitioners and those aspiring to work in this context that they understand the complexity of children's lives and the many challenges families face, whatever their social background or status. Issues of social mobility and unequal access to opportunities persist. This book explores an inclusive pedagogy and the importance of providing children access to the arts, culture and creativity and the many and varied benefits that this access can provide.

In 2019, the Durham Commission published a report on the value of creativity in education, saying 'The evidence shows that teaching for creativity confers personal, economic and social advantage. As a matter of social justice and national interest it should be available to all young people, not only to those who can afford it' (2019, p.9). Whilst many of these issues will be explored in more depth in subsequent sections, this chapter will offer different perspectives so the reader can start to form their own personal view about the value of creativity in education.

Views of creativity

In this section, we will explore seemingly opposing views of creativity: the elite view versus the democratic view. These two views may appear mutually exclusive, but it is a mistake to consider this an 'either/or' question in my opinion. A more useful approach is to perhaps consider the strengths and weaknesses of each argument. The democratic view is that 'everyone is creative' and that creativity manifests itself as curiosity, imagination and divergent thinking in young children – the ability to think of multiple alternatives to any given question or scenario (Robinson, 2016). The late Ken Robinson, educationalist and inspirational speaker, was a passionate advocate for children's innate creative ability and considered it part of a life-long process of 'finding your element' or natural talent (2010). Early Years expert Tina Bruce also believed this, stating that, 'creativity is part of the process through which children begin to find out they have something unique to "say", in words or dance, music, or hatching out their theory' (Bruce, 2011, p.12).

This idea of creativity enabling a child's 'agency' is something we will explore in later sections of this book. Some writers and commentators make the case that children are fundamentally 'born creative' (Tims, 2010) and that every child can be considered to have creative potential and to be capable of creative expression. English author and former Children's Laureate, Michael Rosen, is passionate about the potential of every child and the importance of supporting creativity to enable real learning. He is also very clear about the complexity of this process,

> . . .learning is complex. It isn't a piece of one-dimensional travel along one axis. We make advances and retreats. The retreats may well be in the long run advances;

some advances may be cul-de-sacs. These free-flowing processes can be inhibited in many ways, one of which comes from giving people a fear of failure. If you are afraid to travel about in the multidimensions of learning, you will be prevented from getting to the next step. (Michael Rosen, 2010, p.12)

What is the fundamental role of creativity in this process? Rosen firmly believes it is the ability to be 'open to receiving ideas, processes, sensations and feelings' (2010, p.12) and then being allowed to respond by being given a sense that there are many ways of getting things 'right', rather than a simple binary of 'right or wrong'. Also important is having time to reflect on any 'product' or simply the process itself, and perhaps doing so in co-operation with others. In this way, we make personal meaning and true learning can take place (see Chapter 5: Art and children's drawings: making meaning and visual literacy). Rosen also suggests we use the following 'checklist' for creativity, asking: are we investigating? discovering? inventing and co-operating? and in an ideal world, doing all four of these at the same time? (2010, p.13). Using these definitions, we might consider that all people are capable of creative achievement in some area of activity, provided the conditions are right and they have acquired the relevant knowledge and skills. Moreover, a democratic society should provide opportunities for everyone to succeed according to their own strengths and abilities.

Others hold what might be called a more 'elite' view: that only very rare people are creative and that creativity involves unusual talents. Historically, the literature on creativity often tends to focus on the great men (and sometimes women) who have produced or made ground-breaking compositions, paintings, inventions or theories. Often referred to as 'geniuses', these people, it is sometimes said, make their mark without special help and may even gain strength from educational failure. For both reasons, it is assumed that there is limited scope and little point in trying to educate for creativity. Obviously, there are many people with exceptional creative talents, but the elite conception of creativity is important because it only really focuses attention on creative achievements which are of historical originality, which push back the frontiers of human knowledge and understanding.

Bearing all this in mind, the following case study is of particular interest in the fact that it subverts this either/or debate and provides an example of a creative activity which is both at the same time, 'elite' and 'democratic'...

■■■■■■■■ Case study – Musicadoodledo ■■■■■■■■

Cheng has been attending a series of family-friendly drawing-based activities organised by a contemporary music group at a local art gallery in Birmingham. They take the form of collaborative community workshops in local libraries and art galleries that cleverly combine participatory elements for children with 'elite' classically trained musicians in an informal learning context.

(Continued)

(Continued)

During the workshop, Cheng draws large doodles spontaneously on the walls and floor, and these form graphic scores for the musicians to play on their instruments live in the moment. The experience (combining sight, sound and touch) has been profound and will stay with him for a long time. However, there was no 'final product' or final performance and the experience now exists only in Cheng's memory, and in the material form of photographs and audio-visual recordings kept by the gallery.

Reflective questions

- What aspects of creativity are being explored here?
- Why do you think it is such a memorable experience for Cheng?
- Which elements had to be planned in advance? and which were spontaneous do you think?

Figure 1.1 Musicadoodledo – Birmingham Contemporary Music Group's early years project, mixing listening, adult-framed and child-initiated music play

Source: Image courtesy Simon Taylor.

Knowledge, skills or imagination?

Having laid out these two quite different concepts of creativity, it is worth looking at other, perhaps more nuanced assessments to see how they might help to inform our own under-standing. Some people view creativity as being based on acquiring skills in literacy, numeracy and fundamental subject knowledge which manifests itself as expertise that makes a difference in the world (Leunig, 2016), whilst others take a more inclusive approach, noting the difference between 'everyday creativity, specialist creativity and world-shaking creativity' (Bruce, 2011). This term 'everyday creativity' might encompass such banal activities as choosing your outfit in the morning, cooking a meal with new ingredients, or even putting together a playlist for your daily exercise routine. As Bateson notes, denying everyday creativity 'deprives us of a range of models for the creative process' (1999, p.153).

In an educational context, however, encouraging creativity is not without its own problems and dilemmas, practical and theoretical, psychological and pedagogical. Craft (2006) has highlighted several of these tensions, from the assumption that creativity is universal in nature and always a 'good thing' in the classroom, to the more pragmatic relationship between knowledge, the curriculum and creativity. These tensions are explored further in subsequent chapters. Also, viewing creativity as solely or mainly the domain of 'creative' subjects such as art, drama or music is unhelpful according to some, because it can lead to a denial of the role of creativity in other areas, such as science and mathematics. Indeed, creativity is not subject-specific and if we see it as a way of approaching problem-solving then it can be utilised in different domains. It does not take place in a vacuum and the way in which children express creativity will be different in different curriculum areas (Sharp, 2004) (see also Chapter 11: Children as researchers: Supporting children's natural curiosity through science, technology, the arts and mathematics). Breakthroughs in science and theoretical physics for example are often due to creative people who like 'adventures with ideas' (Bruce, 2011, p.13). If, therefore, using one's imagination is a critical cognitive skill that is used throughout life, then it is important to encourage imagination in childhood. Possibly, the most famous scientist of them all, Albert Einstein, is quoted as saying:

> Imagination is more important than knowledge. For while knowledge defines all we currently know and understand, imagination points to all we might yet discover and create. (Albert Einstein, cited in Bower, 2005, p.3)

━━━━━━━━━━ **Reflective questions** ━━━━━━━━━━

- To what extent do you agree with Einstein?
- Is imagination more important than knowledge in your view?
- What might happen if we have one without the other?

Cultural understandings

Some might question these assumptions and take the position that it is our different cultural and social readings of society that determine what we value about creativity. On the one hand, we might have a structural, institutional and highly formalised vision of culture, based on the passive reception of a traditional 'canon' and the work of great creative 'genius' (think-national museums, opera, ballet, literature and classical music) whilst on the other hand, we can hold a vision of culture that is open, active, dynamic and filled with the everyday productions of ordinary people and communities (think-local festivals, bedroom DJs, murals/street art/graffiti, etc.) (Glăveanu, 2011).

Those who believe in the former vision, or 'cultural lens', might ask if children have ever added to a culturally significant body of knowledge. This might seem like a simplistic provocation, but it could be argued that it is legitimate to ask these questions. Should adult and child creativity be seen as different, distinct and valued accordingly? Psychologist Mihaly Csikszentmihalyi certainly thinks so and asserts '...children often appear to adults to be original, imaginative, or nonconforming. One could just as well interpret such behaviour as ignorance of rules, or inability to follow them' (Csikszentmihalyi in Sawyer et al., 2003, p.220). He goes on to state that what children produce does not relate to notions of adult creativity as we might understand them, that is to say, 'an original response that is socially valued and brought to fruition' (2003, p.220). He does, however, acknowledge that children's productions can be 'valuable' to parents and teachers but maintains that they remain 'peripheral to every culture' and as a result 'not very relevant' (2003, p.220).

Some would argue that children cannot produce 'great creations' because they lack the intention or ability to plan and do not have mastery of a skill that meets the '10-year' or '10,000 hour rule': the minimum time it is believed that is needed to reach the level of an expert in a particular field (Gardner, 1982). Gardner's critique draws our attention to the child's lack of control or intention and an inability to select from among alternatives, 'from this point of view, children's *apparently* imaginative activities are best written off as happy accidents' (Gardner, 1982, p.169). It could be argued that these critiques, despite their seeming disregard for small and mundane acts of creation, relate back to Tina Bruce's (2011) concepts of 'everyday creativity, specialist creativity and world-shaking creativity', distinctions that we explored earlier in this chapter. Anna Craft talks about 'little c creativity' extensively in her work and the 'resourcefulness and agency of ordinary people' (Craft, 2001, p.49), but that is not to say that 'ordinary' creativity cannot have 'extraordinary' effects, amongst them the maintenance and continual re-generation of human culture (Glăveanu, 2011). It could be argued that this also reveals the false dichotomy or apparent divide between 'high culture' and 'low' or 'popular culture', when in reality, one informs the other in a symbiotic and mutually beneficial relationship.

Psychological perspectives

Some commentators have looked into the psychology of creativity and have asked if it is merely an act of 'rediscovery' of what has gone before in a particular culture, 'discovery for others' (e.g., scientific or artistic breakthroughs) or 'discovery for oneself' (i.e., subjective novelty)? (Kudryavtsev, 2011). Vladimir Kudryavtsev, from the Vygotsky Institute of Psychology in Moscow, goes on to acknowledge that 'childhood is almost the only part of a person's life where creative work is a universal and natural way of existence' (Kudryavtsev, 2011, p.46).

What is the role of the adult as a key influence in this important period of a child's life? Again, psychologist Kudryavtsev claims it is as a result of the combination of children's and adult's imagination working together that the children's imagination is activated (Kudryavtsev, 2011, p.49). This idea has been developed into a pedagogical approach within the early years known as 'sustained shared thinking' and is explored in greater depth in Chapter 2.

Some have questioned if our ideas about children's creativity are perhaps influenced by our ideological convictions and cultural beliefs as much as they are based on observation (Bruner, 1996). In this way, creativity and culture appear intimately linked,

> …for everyone, creative achievement always draws from the ideas and achievements of other people: from the books, theories, poems, music, architecture, design and the rest that mark the trails of other people's creative journeys. Just as different modes of thinking interact in a single mind, individual creativity is affected by dialogue with others. In these ways, creative development is intimately related to cultural development. NACCCE (1999)

It could also be argued that the classroom context is a cultural system in itself, comparable to the artist's studio, the scientist's laboratory or the inventor's test space (Engel, 1993). If that is the case then it is essential that we recognise the characteristics of creativity and then do our best to facilitate the creative process, that is to say, 'teaching for creativity'. This is explored in greater detail later in this chapter.

Characteristics of creativity

If defining creativity is challenging, or even impossible in some people's eyes, then it might be argued that it is more productive to look at the characteristics of the creative process or creative thinking, that is to say, 'What does creativity look like in practice?'

It is not possible to produce an exhaustive list of these characteristics, but as a starting point we might consider:

- Imagining
- Deep engagement
- Enquiring
- Exploring ideas and possibilities
- Tolerating ambiguity

- Risk-taking
- Self-expression
- Playfulness
- Making connections
- Composing
- Curating
- Expressing
- Responding to an aesthetic (a sensory experience)

Some commentators, like the late Ken Robinson, have usefully defined the creative process as 'producing original ideas that have value' (Robinson, 2010). Others, such as Caroline Sharp from the National Foundation for Educational Research, have considered evidence from research and theory and concluded that the process involves key components (Sharp, 2004), most often:

- Imagination
- Originality
- Productivity (divergent thinking)
- Problem-solving
- The ability to produce an outcome of value and worth

Sharp also identifies some common myths about developing young children's creativity; that it is limited to arts subjects (see previous discussion and Chapter 11), that the creative process is 'fun' and should not be taken too seriously (in reality, it requires concentration, persistence and determination and may be a frustrating and difficult process), that free play and unstructured activities are sufficient creative experience (this can become routine and repetitive, children need stimulation and creative problems to solve), that it does not require knowledge or skill (these are fundamental to creativity, people cannot fully express their creativity without the necessary skills or understanding of the area) and that children find it easy to transfer learning from one domain to another (children can struggle with context-specific knowledge so adults should help children to make connections) (Sharp, 2004).

Can we measure creativity?

We live in an age of testing, standardisation and measurement, for good or ill, and some have asked if we can test for creativity? It is important to state here that creativity is distinct from intelligence, indeed children that score highly on intelligence quota (IQ) tests are not necessarily highly creative (Sharp, 2004). Since the 1960s, educational psychologists have been looking at the different traits of divergent thinking. To this end, Torrance Tests were developed by Dr. Paul Torrance in the 1960s to identify key characteristics of creativity. These were refined to include novelty and value, divergence from previously accepted ideas and persistence (Torrance, 1969). Most notable for Early Childhood Practitioners is Torrance's recognition that 'the creative behaviour of preschool children is characterised by wonder and magic' (Bracken, 2004, p.352). However, it has also been noted that this high level of creativity is not necessarily maintained throughout childhood and into adulthood. Evidence from the United States has shown that creativity (measured by divergent thinking tests) declines when children enter Kindergarten (or Reception) at around the age of five or six (Meador, 1992).

Other theorists have explored the combination of independent or seemingly incompatible factors, known as 'bisociation' according to Arthur Koestler (1964), that leads to creativity. This creativity can manifest itself as humour, scientific discovery or art. Discerned as either a collision of ideas (producing comic effects and laughter), fusion (mentally challenging effects or an intellectual fusion) or a confrontation (tragic/sobering/disturbing or an aesthetic/sensory effect) this is certainly evident in children's imaginative play and storytelling (see Chapter 4: Storytelling, imaginative and symbolic play). The non-linear nature of creative thinking is worth reiterating here. 'Creative thinking frameworks usually include specific techniques for ideation, problem-solving and evaluation, not necessarily as a linear process...' (Churchill Dower, 2020, p.98). For example, writers of children's fiction and story books have for many years used surreal humour, visual jokes and metaphors as part of the storytelling process. You only have to consider J.M. Barrie's character Wendy sewing Peter Pan's shadow back on so he doesn't lose it, or the idea of a big cat knocking at your front door in Judith Kerr's *The Tiger who came to Tea*. Young children simply embrace these ideas; however, disturbing or illogical they may seem to us as adults (see Chapter 4: Storytelling, imaginative and symbolic play).

Understanding the process

Creativity can be seen as a two-stage process. Firstly, we might have a generative or 'ideas' stage. Useful techniques to facilitate this stage might include 'brainstorming' and 'mind-mapping' (Buzan, 2009), where participants can visualise and follow different trains of thought, and importantly, all ideas are initially given equal weight. After an idea or particular theme has been prioritised, this is then followed by an exploratory or more practical problem-solving stage which provides the basis for creative actions that follow. Another way of conceiving this might be to use the familiar imagery of 'meadow thinking' and 'mountain thinking' (Claxton and Lucas, 2010). 'Meadow thinking' involves dreaming up ideas (imagine yourself lying in a meadow on a summer's day), letting your mind wander and indulging in flights of fancy. In contrast, 'mountain thinking' is more task-focused (imagine yourself climbing a steep slope on Ben Nevis) and deals with problem-solving, assessing risk and finding alternative solutions. Claxton and Lucas explore these different modes of thinking in their exploration of the concept of 'learnable intelligence' (2010). This concept combines the latest developments in neuroscience with educational philosophy and makes the case that intelligence is not fixed, but expandable, and can be developed over a person's lifetime. This has echoes in the work of American psychologist Carol Dweck and her belief that children can only really fulfil their potential by being encouraged to have a 'growth mindset' rather than a 'fixed mindset' (Dweck, 2017). Dweck's assertion is that effort activates ability and a 'growth mindset' is where a child is open to new ideas and experiences. For example, a child might respond to a new activity by saying 'Can I have a go?', rather than having a 'fixed mindset' (Dweck, 2017) where the child puts limits on themselves, gives up too quickly by saying 'I'm rubbish at this' and becomes inhibited due to a fear of failure (see also Chapter 2: Benefits of creativity).

We can equally view creativity more as a collective or group endeavour rather than an individual attribute, and a key part of economic survival, with concepts such as 'lateral thinking', an idea first developed by economist and philosopher, Edward de Bono, in 1967 (de Bono, 2015). De Bono declared creativity to be an essential part of business innovation, saying 'in any self-organising system there is an absolute mathematical necessity for creativity' (de Bono in NACCCE, 1999, p.55). De Bono believed thinking to be a skill in itself and developed tools to help improve this skill. One example of this is his 'Six Thinking Hats' method for more creative and productive decision-making in meetings and business scenarios. Team members, or even an individual, can adopt different roles and perspectives based on the brain's different modes of thinking in order to arrive at new solutions (de Bono, 2000). These ways of thinking encourage co-operation, exploration and innovation. They include 'seeking information and facts', 'weighing up the value or benefits', 'caution or potential difficulties', 'creative alternatives or new ideas', 'focus, review or keeping on track' and 'feelings, emotions and intuition'. As do Bono argued, 'there is no doubt that creativity is the most important human resource of all. Without creativity, there would be no progress, and we would be forever repeating the same patterns' (de Bono, 1992, p.69).

In the classroom

Returning to the educational environment, Ofsted in its advice to teachers in schools suggests 'thinking and acting like an artist' is key to creativity (Ofsted, 2012). What does this mean in the early years' context? I would argue this involves recognising that the creative journey is not necessarily a straightforward, logical process but involves trial and error, happy accidents, tangents and dead-ends. In his seminal work *Art as Experience* (1934), early twentieth-century educational theorist John Dewey explored this phenomenon and described it as a constant cycle, with the creator reacting to their physical and social environment. He also placed accidental discoveries or 'the unexpected turn' at the centre of the experience of being creative, rather than on the periphery,

> The painter and poet like the scientific inquirer know the delights of discovery... that of fulfilment of an experience for its own sake... they learn by their work, as they proceed, to see and feel what had not been part of their original plan and purpose. Dewey (1934, pp.144–145)

- *How can we encourage a sense of discovery in young children?*
- *What activities might allow for the 'unexpected turn' and new creative directions?*
- *How comfortable are you with the idea of flexible, open-ended projects?*

The importance of activities that are process-based and open-ended will encourage true creativity and avoid the trap of designing projects that are too prescriptive and in reality, anything but creative (e.g., 'painting by numbers'). As eminent child psychologist Jerome Bruner stated, 'the road to banality is paved with creative intentions' (Bruner, 1962, p.18). Bearing this in mind, as early childhood practitioners it is vitally important that we emphasise the importance of process over product, enjoying the energy a child has created rather than making judgements about the quality of their end 'product'. This can be challenging and create tension, especially if parental expectations are otherwise, or if colleagues do not appreciate the philosophy behind a particular approach. Despite these potential barriers, valuing child-led and unexpected outcomes has many benefits. Paying attention to a child's thought process is key to this, as Loris Malaguzzi, founder of the Reggio Emilia Approach, has highlighted, 'Creativity becomes more visible when adults try to be more attentive to the cognitive processes of children than to the results they achieve in various fields of doing and understanding' (1998, p.77).

Teaching for creativity

As mentioned earlier, yet another aspect to consider is the idea of 'teaching for creativity'. As adults working within the constraints of an educational setting, we might ask 'What should our approach be?' and 'How can we plan for this effectively?'. In terms of pedagogy, we can start by adopting certain techniques to avoid what Robert Fisher calls 'reproductive learning', that is, 'the acquisition of a fixed body of cultural knowledge, accepted skills, fixed outlooks, methods and rules for dealing with known and recurring situations' (Fisher, 2005, p.23). If the challenge for us as early childhood educators is to prepare children for an uncertain future and give them the ability to deal with rapid change on an individual and social level, then 'teaching children to think creatively becomes a clear need' (Fisher, 2005, p.24).

According to Sharp (2004, p.8), this more innovative approach to pedagogy could include such things as:

- Asking open-ended questions
- Tolerating ambiguity
- Modelling creative thinking and behaviour
- Encouraging experimentation and persistence
- Praising children who provide unexpected answers

These abilities have been defined as key 'habits of mind' (Lucas et al., 2013), attributes that can in turn lead to valuable learning dispositions within the right environment (Claxton, 2018) (see Chapter 2: Benefits of creativity). Bill Lucas, Guy Claxton and colleagues from the Centre for Real World Learning at the University of Winchester have developed these behaviours or 'habits' into more formal models for teaching and creative pedagogy. Their Five-Dimensional Model of Creativity (2013) includes characteristics such as being imaginative, inquisitive, persistent, collaborative and disciplined (see Figure 1.2). These are then broken down into subsets of skills and attitudes that can be nurtured and developed over time. I would argue there are clear connections with the 'thinking skills' of de Bono, including 'using intuition', 'daring to be different', 'playing with possibilities' and 'co-operating appropriately'.

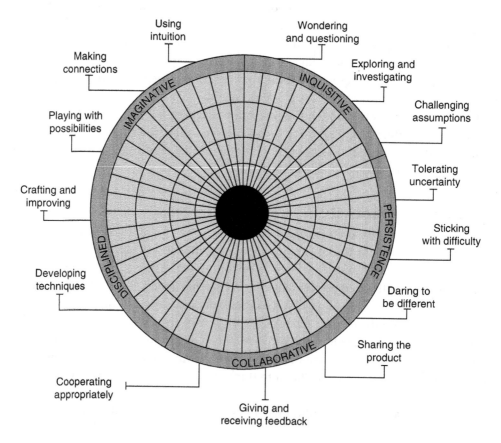

Figure 1.2 The centre for real world learning's five-dimensional model of creativity (Lucas et al., 2013)

A common misconception is to consider creative thinking as unrelated or in opposition to critical thinking, when in fact the two are closely inter-related. As Fisher (2005) notes, most problems require both types of thinking, 'Creativity is not just a question of creating new solutions to problems but of creating better solutions, and this requires critical judgement... an education that focussed on only one type of thinking would be incomplete and unbalanced' (Fisher, 2005, p.26). It is important to clarify here that 'critical thinking' does not mean 'negative thinking' but is instead the ability to look at an issue from different perspectives, analyse key ideas, weigh up the evidence and attempt to come to a balanced judgement or conclusion.

Many practitioners will be aware of scaffolding children's learning by using educational psychologist Benjamin Bloom's Taxonomy: a list of intellectual behaviours that are considered important in learning, from 'lower order' to 'higher order' thinking skills (1968). However, since the 1990s cognitive psychologists, including Loring Anderson, a student of Bloom, have revised and updated his original list to make it more relevant to the twenty-first century (Anderson and Krathwohl, 2001). These new interpretations of Bloom's ideas have an emphasis on 'creativity' replacing 'synthesis' (reaching a new conclusion based on the ideas of others) and changing places with 'evaluation' as the ultimate type of intellectual behaviour at the summit of 'higher order thinking' skills. Some might question the need to create a hierarchy in the first place, but it is interesting to see creativity is now placed as the pinnacle beyond the levels of 'application', 'analysis' and 'evaluation', possibly because it is in essence a combination of all these behaviours but also includes elements discussed previously, such as originality and divergent thinking (see Figure 1.3). Below these lie elements of 'lower order thinking' such as remembering ('knowledge') and understanding ('comprehension'), often the only levels achieved if a child is passive and subjected to the 'reproductive learning' style of the more didactic teacher (Fisher, 2005, p.23).

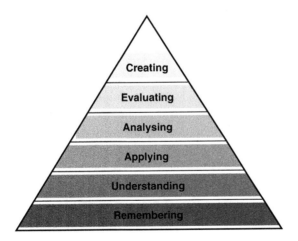

Figure 1.3 The new Taxonomy of thinking skills
Source: Adapted from Anderson and Krathwohl (2001).

Stages in the creative process

In terms of teaching for creativity and preparing for this on a more practical level, Robert Fisher (2005) advises us to conceive of five stages in the creative process:

- Stimulus
- Exploration
- Planning
- Activity
- Review

These steps may overlap, and a child may enter or leave the process at any stage, but each one has its own distinct characteristics:

Stimulus is important as creative thinking cannot exist in a vacuum. This stimulus may be prompted by a problem that needs to be solved (as discussed earlier) or by a more indistinct feeling that an idea has not yet been fully grasped or realised-possibly triggered by a challenge to their thinking by a parent or teacher. Fisher suggests, 'the task of teaching is to spark off the creative impulse within the child and to support the process of exploration' (Fisher, 2005, p.32).

The stage of **exploration** is important as children can be helped to move beyond their initial thoughts, which are often commonplace or even clichéd, investigate further, play with ideas and to consider alternatives before making a decision.

Planning involves clearly defining the problem or task to hand (something many children struggle with), gathering the necessary information, tools or materials, making thinking concrete and visible (children can be helped to be aware of this process by thinking aloud, using images, drawing or writing) (see also Chapter 5: Art and children's drawing: Making meaning and visual literacy).

Activity or active experimentation (making and doing) followed by **review** or self-reflection (stopping to evaluate) are key to creativity but also key parts of the experiential learning cycle according to David Kolb (2015). Both these stages are essential to ensure children's creative outputs are appreciated, discussed and critiqued, ideally with their peers as part of a group (see Chapter 5: Art and children's drawings: Making meaning and visual literacy).

Without the final stage of evaluation and review, the process is simply about novelty or reduced to the level of 'fun' and is unlikely to be taken seriously by either the child or the teacher, as a genuine learning opportunity. Even very young children can be trained to use their judgement to evaluate their ideas. Questions such as 'What have we done?', 'How successful was it?', 'How might it be improved?' and 'Did we achieve what we wanted to?' are all useful in this context. This is where the creative process becomes subject to critical thinking and where Piaget's second goal of education, 'to form minds which can be critical, can verify, and not accept everything they are offered' becomes so important (Fisher, 2005, p.35).

Creativity and quality

If there are clear ways to teach for creativity, a question remains about assessing quality when discussing creative approaches. How do we, or should we even attempt to, evaluate and make judgements about children's creativity or creative outputs? Again, Robert Fisher (2005) provides some useful pointers for measuring creative outcomes, which he says may be judged in terms of certain qualities;

- Fluency
- Flexibility
- Originality
- Elaboration

Fluency – the more a child is stimulated and generates ideas in play and informal settings, the more fluent they will be in generating solutions to real world problems in life. **Flexibility** – often called resilience, a child's ability to overcome barriers and alter their approach to solve a particular problem. **Originality** – an unusual or rare response, which can be assessed in terms of divergent thinking. **Elaboration** – the number of additions a child is able to make to a given starting point or stimulus. This stimulus could be their own, or the ideas of others.

━━━━━━━━ **Reflective questions** ━━━━━━━━

- *What is your personal definition of creativity?*
  Try to write it down in 50–100 words.
- *Reflect on how this definition changes and develops as you read this book and develop your experience in practice.*

Conclusion

Definitions and ideas about creativity are contested, often highly personal, context-dependent, hard to pin down and articulate. Whilst some might argue about the value of what children create, most people agree all children have an innate curiosity and creative imagination that should be encouraged and nurtured. Creativity can be seen as a range of behaviours, skills and processes which can be taught, and the stages in the creative process can be clearly identified and planned for.

Bearing all these things in mind, how do we go about creating the right conditions for creativity to flourish, and what are the particular benefits for young children of doing so? These and other questions will be explored in the next chapter.

Further reading and resources

Tims, C. (ed.) (2010) *Born Creative*. London: DEMOS.

Creativity Exchange: a space for school leaders, teachers, those working in cultural organisations, scientists, researchers and parents to share ideas about how to teach for creativity and develop young people's creativity at and beyond school:
www.creativityexchange.org.uk

2
THE VALUE AND BENEFITS OF CREATIVITY

Children's well-being and development

Nicola Watson

The child is endowed with an unknown power and this unknown power guides us towards a more luminous future. Education can no longer be the giving of knowledge only; it must take a different path. Maria Montessori (1949, p.2)

■■■■■■■■■■ **Chapter overview** ■■■■■■■■■■

Building on Chapter 1 and the idea that everyone can be creative given the right conditions, this chapter will explore the value of creativity with regard to children's holistic development and will explore pedagogy which fosters and optimises its potential to improve children's well-being by enhancing their sense of self and their relationships with others. It will argue for creativity to be placed at the heart of pedagogy in order to realise not only children's potential but also the quality of their *lived* experience, now and in the future.

How has creativity been valued in the development of policy?

In her final speech as outgoing Children's Commissioner, Anne Longfield painted a dismal picture of children's well-being over the last decade and the enormous challenges that poverty and inequality present to children's right to a good childhood. She criticised the UK government as having viewed children as 'data points' and argued strongly for children to be given opportunities to engage with theatre, music and art in order to help them in 'finding joy in finding out, with confidence and resilience by forging their own path' (Longfield, 2021). In doing so, she recognised the centrality of individual and cultural creativity to well-being.

As was explored in Chapter 1, the concept of creativity can be regarded as a social construct and as such, it is highly contestable; open to interpretation and challenge. Bruner (1996, p.28) reminds us that 'Education does not stand alone, and it cannot be designed as if it did. It exists in a culture'. Therefore, approaches to pedagogy and curricula in early childhood education and care (ECEC) will always be debatable. The premise of this book is that where creativity is overlooked, opportunities for deep learning are imperilled. There are, however, a number of obstacles to this position, including ideological, economic and historical aspects of education policy which influence and compete for credibility in the crowded priorities for ECEC. Pascal et al. (2017, p.27) reveal that a data-driven approach to education policy in early years is leading to pedagogy 'becoming more instructional, teacher-directed and narrowly focused on literacy and numeracy learning, with a loss of play and more individualised, creative approaches'. This is not good news. We need to champion the cause of creativity and illuminate its potential for improving the quality of children's lives.

It is clear that the value placed on creativity in education varies according to culture and time. Historically, creativity in Western education was framed in religious terms, unsurprisingly perhaps, given the dominance of the church well into the twentieth century and the concept of God as the divine *creator*. One of the earliest pioneers of ECEC who recognised the importance of creativity as central to learning was Friedrich Froebel (1782–1852). He used the term 'growth' in respect of learning and conceptualised it as a duality; on the one hand, *knowledge* discoverable through investigation of the external world, found 'outside' of the self (Isaacs, 1969, p.188) and on the other, *creativity* originating in the mind, 'from within', whereby each person is 'impelled to depict, to fashion and *create*' (Isaacs, 1969, p.188).

The ebb and flow of the value afforded to creativity in ECEC in England is charted in the development of policy. In 1871, The Huxley Committee promoted infant schooling on the basis that it greatly facilitated children's progress in the more advanced schools and some infant schools, influenced by Froebel's kindergarten method, implemented 'lessons of a simple character, with some exercise of the hands and eye' (Gillard, 2018), although these were not without critics. Before the Reform Act (1890), a payment by results system operated whereby schools could apply for grants if they were able to show pupil outcomes in the 'three Rs' (reading, writing and rithmetic) (Arnold, 1908, p.340). Inevitably, this resulted in a narrow focus which relied on teaching methods of drill and rote learning. The effect, according to one former school inspector was a 'system which seemed to have been devised "for the express purpose of arresting growth and strangling life"' (Holmes, 1911, p.vii cited by Gillard, 2018). Over the course of the next century, there was a gradual shift away from the traditional image of the passive and responsive child to one of the 'informationally active, socially interactive infant mind' (Bruner, 1999, cited in Glăveanu, 2011, p.3). This reflects a growing recognition of children as capable and resourceful, embodying strengths which require acknowledgement and nurturing. Further snapshots of policy reflect this change:

In 1933, the Hadow Report on Infant and Nursery Schooling recommended greater autonomy for children, proposing that 'manual and aesthetic development are better secured when the child is left to make what he likes, how he likes and, within reason, when he likes' (Chapter VI, Section 94).

Thirty-four years later, The Plowden Report (1967) recommended experiential learning; 'individual discovery, on first-hand experience and on opportunities for creative work' (Chapter 15 para. 505), and in 1978, the Warnock Report (1978) recognised the purpose of education as increasing 'a child's knowledge, experience and imaginative understanding' (Chapter 1 para. 1.4). However, Nutbrown et al. (2008, p.147) point to the introduction of the National Curriculum (1989) and the Foundation Stage (2000) as examples of 'squeezing out (or seriously limiting children's experiences of) the arts – even in the early years'. Robinson (2006) suggests that even in the twenty-first century, children are 'educated out of creativity', in an enduring deference to a public education system fashioned in the nineteenth century, predicated on meeting the needs of industrialisation.

In her 2011 review of ECEC, Tickell (2011, p.20) reiterated the importance of play as a vehicle for creativity as 'through play, children learn to see problems from different viewpoints, helping them to develop a generally positive and creative attitude to learning'. Her report informed the revised Early Years Foundation Stage (EYFS) of 2012, the first iteration of the current policy in England, (EYFS, DfE, 2021a). The 2021 revisions of the Early Learning Goals (EYFS, DfE, 2021a) place greater emphasis on children's articulation of their own ideas and experiences, and the new ELGs for Expressive Art and Design provide for the development of aesthetic appreciation. In addition to being imaginative, children's expression is given equal weight.

▬▬▬▬▬ Reflective questions ▬▬▬▬▬

The Characteristics of Effective Learning (EYFS, DfE, 2021a, p.16) represents policy in England today regarding what children's learning looks like. The three characteristics are:

- Playing and exploring - children investigate and experience things, and 'have a go'.
- Active learning - children concentrate and keep on trying if they encounter difficulties and enjoy achievements.
- Creating and thinking critically - children have and develop their own ideas, make links between ideas and develop strategies for doing things.

How clearly can these characteristics be aligned with creativity?
How might practitioners ensure that the learning environment supports these characteristics?

Well-being
Defining well-being

Although the concept of well-being is debatable, it is universally accepted as an ideal across health, education and social services (Ereaut and Whiting, 2008; Sprat, 2016). A focus on children's well-being is not just desirable; it is a matter of urgency. The Children's Society (2020) report that one in six children aged 5–16 is likely to have mental health issues. Educators have a professional and moral responsibility to promote the well-being of children in their care.

At its simplest, well-being can be defined as having a good quality of life. Statham and Chase (2010, p.2) recognise well-being as 'a dynamic state that is enhanced when people can fulfil their personal and social goals'. This definition is helpful in that it distinguishes between the personal and the social aspects of well-being, resonating with Froebel's recognition centuries earlier of the distinction between our internal minds and the external social world. The National Institute for Clinical Excellence (NICE, 2012) separates these elements further, conceptualising well-being as comprising:

- Emotional well-being – this includes being happy and confident.
- Psychological well-being – this includes the ability to be autonomous, problem-solve, manage emotions, experience empathy, be resilient and attentive.
- Social well-being – having good relationships with others.

Holistic well-being

Emotional, psychological and social well-being provide firm foundations for learning and development and influence every aspect of the individual, including physical, as well as mental health. The relationship between health and well-being is generally accepted across disciplines and indeed, according to Sprat (2016, p.224) 'health is conceived as a state of well-being'. The World Health Organisation (WHO, 1986, online) defines health as 'a positive concept emphasising social and personal resources, as well as physical capacities'. The roots of holistic practice; that is practice based on the recognition that each aspect of a person is connected and inter-dependent, can be traced all the way back to Pestalozzi (1746–1827), who is credited with developing the idea of a holistic approach, conceptualising education as developing 'head, hands and heart'. He asserted that children's 'faculties should be developed equally, [and that] through the cultivation of one all the others will be strengthened' (Silber, 1960, p.174). Indeed, in modern medicine, the value of creativity to holistic well-being and health been recognised. Bloem et al. (2018, p.1) suggest that medicine and art are 'closely intertwined, perhaps even inseparable'. This view encapsulates the idea that creativity is essential to human health and well-being.

Creativity and emotional and psychological well-being
Honouring the uniqueness of children

Pedagogy which places creativity at its heart, necessarily seeks to provide conditions which support children's emotional and psychological well-being. It requires recognition of the intrinsic value of the individual; the 'unique child' (EYFS, DfE, 2021a). The way in which each of us experiences and interprets the world is subjective and non-replicable. Robinson (2006) reminds us that creativity is dynamic, meaning that it's changeable, sometimes fleeting, interpretive and responsive to stimuli. It may be purposeful but without goals or outcomes. In this way, it is related to play; a highly subjective enterprise which often provides a vehicle for creativity. Piaget suggested that children's cognitive development takes the form of mental constructions of the external world based upon experiences, interactions and manipulations of stimuli in their surroundings (Craft, 2006, pp.32–33). As they begin to be aware of their own potential to effect change and develop mastery and control in their surroundings, children are empowered to represent their own image rather than someone else's (Duffy, 1998, p.8).

Making opportunities for children to construct their own ideas about and respond to their experiences involves providing resources which are various and open-ended so that their possibilities can be chosen and shaped in a way which corresponds to the child's expression of the meaning they are making in the moment. The ways in which humans are able to communicate their lived experience is unlimited. Duffy (1998, p.6) points out that, 'When only the rational aspects of learning and development are stressed, we deprive ourselves of the full range of the human ability to think'.

The Reggio Emilia approach to ECEC is perhaps *the* outstanding exemplar of child-centred pedagogy. Responding to the devastation wreaked by the Second World War, the founders of this approach wanted to reimagine education in the hope of realising a world which avoided war, strife and suffering but instead focused upon the potential of humanity to achieve equality and justice. Malaguzzi (1920–1994), one of the founders of the Reggio approach, was influenced by John Dewey, the American educationalist and philosopher who regarded children as 'an oppressed group, lacking a voice and always subject to the control of adults' (Smidt, 2013, p.14). In Reggio Emilia, the focus is not on teaching, but on children's learning and 'Reggio teachers emphasise achievement in personal expression and reflection on one's own patterns of thinking' (Edwards et al., 2011, p.7).

Aesthetic appreciation

As well as supporting children in finding their voice and giving expression to their thoughts and feelings in multi-modal ways, creativity supports the development of a distinct and particular pleasure: the recognition of and appreciation of beauty. Dewey (1900, p.118) recognised the importance of aesthetic experience in education when he suggested that an appropriate education for young children should include 'added insight into reality and beauty'. The EYFS (DfE, 2021a, p.10) provides for the first time in early years policy, the recognition that children should be able to appreciate and develop awareness of artistic and cultural aspects of experiences. In an outcome-focused approach to learning and development, the sheer pleasure and appreciation of colour, shape, form, movement and sound are easily overlooked or dismissed as peripheral, but pleasure and appreciation of beauty are important to emotional well-being and a sense of what it is to be alive and to undergo experience.

Supporting children's aesthetic appreciation can help to promote inclusion. Acer and Ömeroðlu (2007, p.336), suggest that 'The objective of aesthetic education is not to raise children as artists, but to create individuals who know how to look and see'. In our twenty-first century consumerist society, children are bombarded with tropes of what constitutes 'beauty' often superficial and idealised stereotypes. This can be inimical to children's self-esteem in that they may convey powerful and exclusive messages regarding race, gender, disability and size. Therefore, it is important to counter this and raise awareness of our perceptions; how we interpret and give meaning to our environment. Acer and Ömeroðlu (2007, p.336) point out that 'Aesthetic development in children requires an awareness of their own responses to the qualities of things they observe'. Talking with children about the qualities of abstract phenomena including colour, form, shape and texture and the sensations and emotions they evoke, can support children in developing an aesthetic sensibility by recognising and processing their lived experiences of things in the world. Thus, children's developing self-awareness is supported and if their expressions are given due value, their self-esteem and developing confidence are nurtured.

Learning to recognise and appreciate the unique features that make us individuals, as well as the aspects we share, helps encourage children to understand that they themselves need to be inclusive as active participants in the setting. The following case study demonstrates how looking and seeing brought a new perspective to understanding similarities and differences between the children in one setting.

Case study - Not just looking but seeing

The following case study is based on an actual event although the names of the participants have been changed.

Kenny and Abu were playing outside with a group of other three- and four-year-olds. Kenny approached Olivia, the practitioner and pointed at Abu, asking, 'Why is he black?' Olivia fetched some mirrors and encouraged Kenny to look at his own face and describe what he could see. Other children began to gather and examine their faces. They noticed their eyes, their hair, their skins were all different in colour, texture and appearance. They talked about variation between and within themselves. Many of the group became absorbed in looking, describing, using metaphor and similes, analysing and representing themselves and others using the Art resources available to them. By supporting the children's own curiosity and engagement, Olivia did not need to control the (potentially sensitive) narrative. The children were able to explore their similarities with appreciation and wonder. The focus on analysing and interpreting what they saw enabled them to explore more deeply and without judgement.

Reflective questions

- Why do you think the practitioner responded in the way that she did to Kenny's question?
- What were the potential consequences of her approach:
  - in the immediate term?
  - in the longer term?

Expressing the ineffable

Bruce (2011, p.4) recognises the pleasure that creativity can bring and that the fulfilment in creativity 'is deeper than happiness or enjoyment – it helps us through the difficult times as well as the easier side of our lives'. Where children have opportunities to choose *how* to communicate their feelings, they are more able to tell a story which might otherwise remain unsaid. The story may be of trauma, working through confusion and sadness. It may be that the child telling her story is pre-verbal or has a social, emotional or learning disability. Bruce (2011, p.9) points out that children with behavioural and emotional difficulties can engage in 'imaginative and creative play, in the same way as most other children', thereby widening the avenue towards inclusion.

How children are able to represent their worlds will depend upon their stage of development and Bruner's modes of representation will be explored in detail further in Chapter 3. However, it is important to bear in mind that the multi-modality of children's expression is not exhaustive. It is more than using resources, paint, clay, music, role-play or dance. Creative expression may have no outcome or product and may not be visible to the observer. Using imagination and giving their thoughts expression can support children in processing painful or confusing events and situations. Children can use simile, metaphor, ideas and imagery within any form of activity. This is illustrated in the case study below (Case study: Using imagination to make sense of experience).

Autonomy

Imagine if you were told that you had to read a particular newspaper. If you were to choose your own, you might have a number of criteria: the political stance of the editor; availability online; the front-page headline; the presentation, font and photographs. If the selection were made for you, those choices would be taken away. Autonomy is the ability and opportunity to exercise choice. Laevers (2015) suggests that 'The more children can choose their activities, the higher will be the level of their involvement'. This is significant as, as we saw earlier, concentrating and perseverance 'keep[ing] on trying' is key to active learning, one of the Characteristics of Effective learning (EYFS, DfE, 2021a).

In their report regarding social and emotional well-being, Weare and Gray (2003, p.61) recognise that independence and autonomy are key to well-being and that 'learning to be autonomous is particularly important for those who come from homes where it is not so encouraged. We need to start this from an early age and build gradually towards independence'.

Deci and Ryan's self-determination theory (SDT) identifies three universal psychological conditions for intrinsic motivation (motivation from within): autonomy, relatedness and competence. They define autonomy as acting 'volitionally, with a sense of choice' (2008, p.15) and distinguish this from independence which can be understood as acting alone. Creativity is predicated on exercising choices, selecting resources, making judgements, evaluating, adapting and shaping an expression to create something new. According to SDT where the inter-personal context is 'informational and supportive' as opposed to 'administered in a controlling context' intrinsic motivation is increased (Deci and Ryan, 2008, p.15). Open-ended creative opportunities offer a safe space where children can rehearse and reify autonomy. Pedagogies which centre around play support the optimising of children's autonomy. Play provides a fertile arena in which the seeds of creativity can potentially flourish. The act of playing affords the conditions (intrinsic reward, autonomy, agency, engagement, curiosity, imagination, exploratory, problem-solving and experimentation) for creativity, an expression of something unique which has value.

Agency

The ability and opportunity to act upon intentions, which is to say, exercise agency, is intrinsic to creativity. Making choices and acting upon them are always present in the creative process. Bandura (2001, p.3) describes human beings as 'agents of experiences rather than simply undergoers of experiences'. This means that they are hard-wired to be active participants in, rather than merely reactive to, their environments. For young children, the discovery that they can intentionally make things happen and bring about change through their actions can be a source of satisfaction and fulfilment. Pedagogy which optimises children's agency helps support their curiosity and desire to generate and create as the human mind has evolved to do (Bandura, 2001, p.4). In this active participation with their environments, children begin 'hatching out their theories' (Bruce, 2011, p.12), locating their own, unique perspectives and thereby making sense of the world. Bandura (2001, p.4), explains that rather than exposure to stimulation in the environment (as a passive recipient), it is the agentic element in exploring, manipulating and influencing the environment that counts in shaping and forming the neuronal function of the brain. Unsurprising then, that the unfortunate children who were taught by drill and learnt by rote in the early twentieth century, as described earlier, had such a dispiriting experience.

Creativity and social well-being

So far, we have explored creativity in terms of the individual child and its value in respect of emotional and psychological well-being. However, pedagogy which promotes children's creativity can make a significant contribution to social well-being, defined as relationships with others which are mutually satisfying (Katz and McClellan, 1997). In developing social competence, children need to learn specific skills such as emotion regulation (being able to manage their feelings) and theory of mind (the understanding that others experience the world differently to them). Additionally, the involvement of adults and other children can sometimes present obstacles to children's exercising agency and autonomy which can result in social challenges and conflicts.

Whereas Piaget identified constructivist theories of the nature of individual learning, Vygotsky (1978) emphasised the social elements of learning and the importance of the culture in which learning is situated. Social constructivist theory has been very influential in education over many decades and can offer insights into the opportunities that collaborative, creative enterprises present.

The need to feel a sense of relatedness (belonging and connection with others) is one of the universal conditions identified by Deci and Ryan (2000), as essential to motivation. In thinking about well-being, we are concerned with intrinsic, or motivation 'from within'. A growing awareness by children, of their being recognised as members of families, communities and cultures who can make contributions to their social groups can be emotionally rewarding and thereby enhance well-being. The ECEC statutory framework of New Zealand, Te Whāriki (Ministry of Education, 2017) exemplifies a recognition of that awareness. The framework was developed to reflect the cultural diversity of New Zealand society and inclusion is placed at the heart of the curriculum. It states that 'Learner identity is enhanced when children's home languages and cultures are valued in educational settings and when Kaiako (Maori for 'feeders of knowledge' or teachers) are responsive to their cultural ways of knowing and being' (Ministry of Education, 2017, p.12). The framework embodies a strength-based approach to children in that it recognises as 'funds of knowledge' (Moll et al., 1992, p.134), the cultural knowledge, understandings and identities developed and developing which children have and bring with them to the setting. Hedges (2020, p.3) emphasises the role of culture in the idea that 'all families, whatever their social and material circumstances, have historical and sociocultural knowledge, skills, resources, and ways of learning *specific to their particular* experience in their communities and culture'. The Te Whāriki framework provides for children's developing 'their imaginations to explore their own and others' cultures and identities' (Ministry of Education, 2017, p.15) and includes creativity as a 'learning disposition', valuable to supporting life-long learning.

The role of the adult

The education environment is crucial to determining if and how children recognise and respond to learning opportunities. Claxton and Carr (2004, p.88) call these learning pro-pensities, 'learning dispositions'; the 'default responses in the presence of uncertain learning opportunities and circumstances' and they recognise that adults have a significant impact on children's learning dispositions. The environment which optimises learning potential is one involving frequently shared activity, but where children, as well as adults, take responsibility for directing the activity (Claxton and Carr, 2004, p.92). This, they call a potentiating environment; one which 'stretches' children's potential. As anyone who has worked with young children will recognise, it is very tempting to impose one's own ideas, interests and enthusiasms onto chil-dren and although they may resist, children are largely powerless to override adult interference. A potentiating environment is one in which power imbalances are minimised and where adults share power with children (Claxton and Carr, 2004, p.92). Jeffrey and Craft (2004, p.81) point out that having control presents children with opportunities to be innovative and creative. In collaborative activity, the minimisation of power imbalances is evidenced when children's influence and effect are apparent during interactions between adults and children (James, 2009, p.34). Being aware of who is holding the balance of power and why is a helpful strategy in pedagogy which seeks to nurture children's agency in collaboration with one another and with adults. Agency is fundamental to children's identity development (Hedges, 2020, p.1), and fostering their agency within an environment which celebrates diversity and difference, while also promoting belonging and community, supports children in developing a positive sense of self and others.

Working creatively in collaboration enables children to learn from one another through the sharing of ideas and perspectives, thereby enlarging the scope for possibility thinking. Collaboration also offers great potential for developing the social skills involved in negotiating, explaining, sharing and recounting, as well as for forming and reinforcing social bonds, including friendships and attachments. A strategy useful in supporting these skills is that of sustained shared thinking. This was one of the recommendations made by Sylva et al. (2004) in their longitudinal study of effective provision of pre-school education (the EPPE project). They identified the elements of sustained shared thinking as where individuals, adults or children, worked together, 'in an intellectual way to solve a problem, clarify a concept, evaluate an activity, extend a narrative, etc.' and where all parties contributed to and developed the thinking. This pooling of ideas offers the potential for extending imagination, problem-solving and possibility thinking and adds to the child's personal repertoire of creative potential. Adults can support this by asking open questions, modelling their own thinking and providing feedback (Sylva et al., 2004, p.6). This situates sustained shared thinking firmly in the social constructivist tradition. Back in the 1930s, Vygotsky recognised that development requires social interaction within a shared cultural context, and Dewey (1938, p.67) argued for the 'the importance of the participation of the learner in the formation of the purposes which direct his activities in the learning process'.

The power of imagination extends to every area of life. In her work on the contribution of agency and imagination to the development of identity, Hedges (2020, p.5) suggests that 'Imagination draws on life experience but creates new combinations of ideas, emotions, thoughts and meanings'. Bruner (1997) recognised that narratives offer a powerful vehicle for identity formation and the following case study illustrates how, through constructing a shared narrative and by applying imagination, children are able to make sense of experience, build empathy and strengthen social bonds. By recognising and valuing what the children were doing, the practitioners were given privileged insights into the children's inner lives.

Case study – Using imagination to make sense of experience

The following case study is based on actual events although the names of the participants have been changed.

Mia and Zainab aged four were constant companions in their nursery setting. Mia had a speech impediment which made her difficult to understand. A year before, Mia's father had died of cancer and although she had memories of him and experienced her mother's sadness at home, Mia did not talk about her daddy to the staff at the setting. She and Zainab gravitated towards the role-play area most days and chose to play with baby dolls. Over weeks and months, they collaborated in building

(Continued)

scenarios about illness and hospitals, ministering to the needs of their patients and constructing elaborate stories around issues of medicine to cure their babies or sometimes, being unable to save them. Mia would guide the action and Zainab would maintain a verbal narrative. It was clear to the practitioners that she was interpreting and articulating her friend's making sense of her own lived experience and using imagination to explore questions of life and death. In their collaboration they were co-constructing an understanding of what had happened to Mia.

Reflective questions

Think of the role that creativity plays in your own life which is:

- For personal satisfaction, not shared or intended to be shared with others
- Expressed, shared with and potentially evaluated by others
- Born in collaboration with others

How are they distinguishable from one another? What elements of creativity, if any, do they share? How do these activities potentially enhance your emotional, psychological and social well-being?

Conclusion

This chapter began with an inspirational quote from the last century. Writing in the aftermath of the Second World War, Maria Montessori implored educators to discover and develop the 'unknown powers' of children in order to change the world. In the twenty-first century that call has become urgent. In this age of anxiety where more and more children are suffering from poor mental health and low self-esteem, we need to show them that through agency and imagination, they have the capacity to bring about positive change. In this era of climate change and ecological destruction, we need to nurture children's appreciation of the beauty of the Earth, our only home. By placing creativity at the heart of education where head, hands and heart work in synergy, we can help build a better future where individuals can flourish and find the joy Anne Longfield (2021) alluded to in her outgoing speech as Children's Commissioner and where families, communities, societies can work together to build and sustain well-being.

The concept of creativity and its place in education will always be vulnerable to policy directives fuelled by the prevailing political agenda. However, this chapter has sought to adduce evidence to support the contention that creativity is not just a useful concept but is essential to understanding how children learn and develop holistically and how creativity feeds emotional and social well-being. Children need, those who work with and care for them to provide environments which value and foster creativity as much as, and perhaps more than ever.

Further reading and resources

Longfield, A. (2021) *Building Back Better; Reaching England's Left behind Children*. 17 February. Available at: https://www.childrenscommissioner.gov.uk/2021/02/17/building-back-better-reaching-englands-left-behind-children/

Maria Montessori Institute – https://www.mariamontessori.org/

The Reggio Emilia Approach® – https://www.reggiochildren.it/en/reggio-emilia-approach/

3

THE MODES OF
CREATIVITY

Creativity becomes more visible when adults try to be more attentive to the cognitive processes of children than to the results they achieve in various fields of doing and understanding. Loris Malaguzzi (1998, p.77)

■■■■■■■■■■■■■■■ **Chapter overview** ■■■■■■■■■■■■■■■

Whilst continuing to explore the benefits of creativity in terms of children's well-being, this chapter examines the ways in which children construct their understanding of the world and make sense of experience. It will argue that to fully understand children's creativity it is important to look at the different stages of their learning and development and explore psychological theories about how children are able to re-organise previously known ideas. Potential barriers to creative development will be examined, alongside the different 'modes' of children's thinking, essentially the different ways in which they understand the world, alongside examples of 'multi-modal' learning and creativity.

Theoretical perspectives

Theories of childhood development are evolving constantly and are informed by the latest developments in areas as diverse as psychology, neuroscience, education and sociology. However, when considering creativity, practitioners must examine their own position and epistemology (conception of knowledge or 'how we know what we know') and consider those elements that best support their personal approach.

For early childhood practitioners interested in creativity, the nursery setting can be seen as part of a wider culture where 'learning, remembering, talking and imagining' are only made possible by the children's participation in that culture (Bruner, 1996, p.xi). This participation might take the form of simple family traditions or annual festivals, through the influence of extended family members or links with local religious and community groups. I am sure we all remember certain traditions that seemed special to our own families, but often with hindsight, we realise these traditions were part of a wider pattern of cultural codes of behaviour that were common in our particular community. Examples might include communal meals, birthdays/gifts for special occasions, marriage ceremonies, songs, music or particular narratives in the form of children's stories, familiar nursery rhymes, fairy tales, myths and legends. Indeed, many would argue that the act of storytelling is a natural part of human evolution and is how we make sense of experience (see Chapter 4: Storytelling, imaginative and symbolic play). As mentioned in the opening chapter, American child psychologist Jerome Bruner (1915–2016) was concerned that we see both education and learning in their situated, cultural context rather than simply an internal process that goes on in the mind (1996). Bruner was particularly interested in developing the idea of a new 'cultural psychology' where he could explore 'the making and negotiating of meanings, about the constructing of self and a sense of agency, about the acquisition of symbolic skills, and especially about the cultural "situatedness" of all mental activity' (1996, p.x).

Socio-cultural theories, by contrast, provide another perspective by looking at the social environment and the influence of different social relationships on a child's development. One such theory is Bronfenbrenner's model (1979), which looks at the wider ecology or social context surrounding a child. His model divided an individual's environment into a set of interrelated systems, 'a set of nested structures, each inside the next, like a set of Russian dolls' (Bronfenbrenner, 1979, p.3): the microsystem, mesosystem, exosystem and macrosystem (see Figure 3.1).

The inner circle or 'microsystem' is the immediate environment in which a child lives and might include family, peer group or school setting. The 'mesosystem' describes different interrelationships between microsystems, for example, parental attitudes and involvement in the child's nursery or schooling, which might be evidenced by a child learning to read at home. Bronfenbrenner conceived the 'exosystem' as the settings and contexts in which children are not actively taking part in, for example, a parent's or carer's workplace, but which might have a significant impact on their lives. Changes in the workplace, such as working weekends or redundancy, can affect a child's development. The final level is the 'macrosystem' which describes the wider society and includes cultural values and the economic conditions under which families may live, their material resources and the structures that afford them opportunities. Patterns of interactions within and between these systems influence each other and affect an individual child's developmental outcomes (Bronfenbrenner, 1979). Bronfenbrenner later updated his ecological theory, based on extensive research, and conceived of a 'bioecological model' which acknowledged the impact of 'proximal processes' (parent–child interactions) and the concept of time as it relates to human development (Bronfenbrenner, 1999, in Ashiabi and O'Neal, 2015). As practitioners, it is essential we take time to consider the different environmental conditions that each child might be experiencing and the factors that might be impacting their lives at any particular moment.

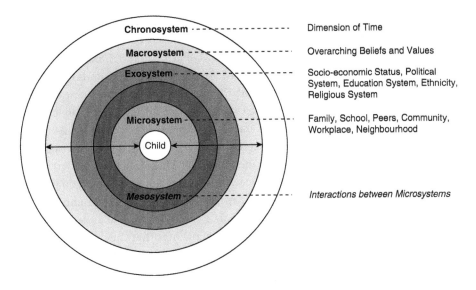

Figure 3.1 Bronfenbrenner's Ecological Systems Theory

Thinking about the children in your setting:

- Do you know the home context for each child?
- How supportive is the home environment to their learning and development?
- What social and cultural influences might be affecting them?
- How are they already taking part in culture? and what does that culture look like?

Social constructivism

Bruner and Bronfenbrenner's ideas could be seen as part of the wider psychological paradigm (model or set of ideas) known as 'social constructivism' which focuses on the social nature of learning, that is to say, learning is formed socially through interaction with others (Pritchard and Woollard, 2010, p.16).

As mentioned in the previous chapter, this approach promotes the idea that children are active agents in their own learning and have autonomy (control) over the process of 'constructing' their knowledge of the world. Indeed, it even asserts that knowledge is constructed by, and reflective of, a world understood through the lens of culture (Hoy et al., 2013).

One of the most influential theorists in this area of child development, Jean Piaget (1896–1980), believed children learn by experience and have an innate ability to construct their own understandings of the world through active participation and problem-solving.

He conducted a series of experiments and developed a progressive, age-related model in which children move in distinct stages from simple to complex concepts and from concrete to more abstract modes of thinking (Piaget, 1952). Piaget highlighted the concepts of 'assimilation' where the learner attempts to fit new information into existing schemas (structures of thought) and 'accommodation' where the learner creates new schemas for information that cannot be incorporated into existing concepts. Piaget's theory of cognitive development emphasises four distinct stages: sensorimotor (birth to 24 months), pre-operational (two to seven years), concrete operational (seven to eleven years old) and formal operational. In the early years of their life, the child is constantly creating new schemas when they encounter new experiences, such as the idea of 'object permanence' (the fact that an object still exists, even if you can no longer see it) (Boyd and Bee, 2014). According to Piaget, the child reaches the 'formal operational' stage at around 12 years old when they are able to imagine or think about abstract things that they have never seen, or which will occur in the future. They can organise their schemas 'systematically' and think 'deductively' (Boyd and Bee, 2014, p.138).

However, critiques of Piaget's ideas have cast doubt about these stages in a child's cognitive development and his concept of age-related 'readiness' preferring a more fluid and open approach that is responsive to the individual needs of the child (Wood and Attfield, 2005). Bruner's own ideas placed more importance on recognising a child's present and potential stage of development. 'As a teacher, you do not wait for readiness to happen; you foster or scaffold it by deepening the child's powers at the stage where you find him or her now' (Bruner, 1996, p.120). Early Years practitioners can be active in this regard, creating the right environment that is supportive and meaningful for the learner, providing the right structures or 'scaffolding', not through directions that are too prescriptive, but instead through questions that are open-ended enough to encourage creative thinking.

The key role that language and communication play in children's learning was highlighted by Vygotsky who believed that full cognitive development requires social interaction, and that language was an essential psychological tool for thinking and learning (1978). Language allows us to express ourselves, be sociable, be understood and to understand other people's point of view. He believed that the significant people around an individual child have a central role in regard to this social interaction. Vygotsky developed the idea of 'the more knowledgeable other' – often an adult, but potentially also a peer, who can support or 'scaffold' our learning and influence the way we see the world (1978). A key component of Vygotsky's theory is the Zone of Proximal Development (ZPD) – a range or new area of development characterised by what the learner can achieve with assistance (or 'scaffolding'). This area or 'zone' sits between what the learner can currently achieve independently, and what the learner will be able to achieve in the future, but which sits just beyond their current capabilities. Over time, the level of challenge can increase as the learner's level of competence gradually increases (see Figure 3.2). The role of the more knowing or 'more knowledgeable other' within the ZPD is to support or 'scaffold' this process.

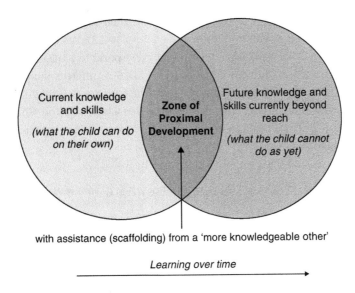

Figure 3.2 Vygotsky's 'Zone of Proximal Development' and its significance for learning

A useful link could be made here with Csikszentmihalyi's concept of 'flow' (1997). Csikszentmihalyi claimed one of the key components of flow is that there is a balance between the level of challenge and the level of skill. If the task is too difficult for us, then anxiety starts to creep in. If it is too easy, then we can easily become bored or distracted. Flow stops as soon as we are interrupted, so it is important to find the right conditions for creativity and flow in your own setting:

- Give children choice and autonomy within the activity
- Ensure a balance between the challenge and the child's skills (ZPD)
- choose something intrinsically motivating and enjoyable, without the need for an external reward
- Make sure there are no external interruptions (as much as possible!)
- Take part in the activity along with them (as a 'more knowledgeable other')

(Afzal, 2018, p.131)

Potential barriers

An important point to consider as an Early Years practitioner is the wide range of language competence and even other language backgrounds which we might encounter in our day-to-day roles. This might pose a challenge when facilitating children to think and communicate through describing, questioning, instructing and reading and writing in all its forms. Anitra Vickery points out that many four- and five-year-olds are still novice learners of language, as well as users of language for learning. When children are more physically active in their learning, they are less reliant on language to represent their understanding, for example by enacting, drawing, making or building (Vickery, 2014, pp.24–25). We can go even further and think about children's other 'languages' that might correspond to Malaguzzi's concept of the 'One Hundred Languages of Children' (Cagliari et al., 2016) – different modes of communication and expression that are all important and form the basis for the child-led pedagogy that underpins the Reggio Emilia Approach, as we discovered in Chapter 2. The following case study illustrates how language barriers might be overcome to create a setting that is as inclusive and as welcoming to families as possible.

Case study – Here and elsewhere

Tarik has just started attending the local nursery school and is keen to make friends with the other children. He does not yet speak English as his first language is Kurdish, but like the other children, he loves playing, exploring... and eating food! Mandy, a local children's author, is visiting each week and has asked parents to bring in recipes from home to share their favourite meals and talk about their family traditions. As Tarik's family are newly arrived in the UK, his father and he have made Yaprakh, a dish from Kurdistan. They explain, 'it is traditionally cooked at the weekend or on a day off and families take it for a picnic when they make a day out in the mountains or beside a river'. The collection of recipes and dishes will be shared in the form of a recipe book for all the children to try out at home with their families. The book is illustrated with photos, drawings and collages by the children to encourage a sense of ownership. The process is inclusive, interactive and enables everyone to experience the rich cultural heritage of all the children at the nursery and their wider communities.

Reflective questions

- How many different languages are spoken in your setting?
- Consider the different ways in which you can encourage every child to interact, take part or contribute.
- If communication is an issue – how can children express themselves in ways that are less reliant on language?

Alternative perspectives

These understandings of how children learn are in sharp contrast to other perspectives that come from behavioural psychologists such as Pavlov, Skinner and Watson. These influential thinkers from the nineteenth and twentieth centuries based their observations on experimental science and viewed the child as a tabula rasa ('blank slate'). According to this paradigm, the child is simply responding to external stimuli and changing their behaviour or acquiring new behaviours accordingly. Behaviourism sees children as passive recipients of environmental influences that shape their behaviour, and that learning takes place as the result of conditioning (learning by association or learning by consequence), rather than through changes to our cognitive or internal mental state. Positive and negative reinforcement is a key idea from behaviourism that is often used very effectively in behaviour management strategies in schools and contemporary educational settings. Examples might include reward charts, a token economy (trading points for desirable outcomes/prizes) or target boards. Woollard comments that these theories are sometimes linked to punishment in people's minds, but punishment alone does not reinforce learning. 'Many behaviourists believe that punishment is less of an influence upon behaviour than reward and that reward alone will be just as effective' (Woollard, 2010, p.2).

Despite their basis in experimental science and observation, behaviourist theories of child development often ignore the significant contribution of a child's social contacts and the language and culture that surrounds them, ideas that were so important to Piaget, Vygotsky and Bruner, as highlighted earlier in this chapter. It is Bruner's ideas that we will explore in more depth in this next section.

Bruner's modes

One of Bruner's most powerful ideas was that newly acquired knowledge was most useful to the learner or child when it is 'discovered' through the learner's own cognitive efforts (1996, p.xii). As early years practitioners it is our role to support and encourage these acts of discovery, known as 'discovery learning'. Bruner's concept promotes the pedagogical idea of the 'teacher as guide', someone who is 'a guide to understanding, someone who helps you discover on your own' (1996, p.xii). If we take a more detailed look, we can see that Bruner's model of learning and child development has three distinct 'modes' or ways that a child builds on current and past knowledge in a developmental way (Figure 3.3):

- **Enactive mode**
  Beginning with the very early manipulation of materials and objects, the enactive mode describes how children develop their understanding of the world and represent experience through actions. For example, a baby might grasp their cup and shake it when it is empty or place it in their mouth to indicate they are thirsty.
- **Iconic mode**
  Moving towards visual representations, the iconic mode allows the child to recognise and understand that pictures and images represent a real object, even if they do not yet know the object's name. A picture book might show an image of a plastic cup, or a child might make a drawing of their favourite beaker. The child makes the connection between the flat image and the real three-dimensional object.

- **Symbolic mode**

  And finally, moving towards increasing levels of abstract thought, the symbolic mode is how a child represents their world through symbols, particularly through the use of language, both written and spoken. For example, a reading book might contain words for items used in a meal, including the word 'cup', which the child reads, understands its meaning and can say out loud in order to communicate with others.

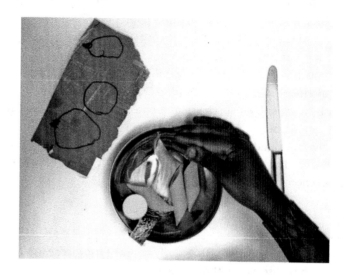

Figure 3.3 Bruner's modes in action
Source: Image courtesy: Lillian de Lissa Nursery School.

Young learners in early childhood settings might use all three modes to demonstrate their understanding, but those children who are less fluent or whose vocabulary is more limited will rely more on the enactive mode to recall and represent experience. They may need to be more physically active than other children in their cohort to fully engage with learning (Vickery, 2014, p.24). The following section demonstrates how practical creative projects can allow children to communicate about their cultural experiences using different modes other than just language.

Children's creative modes in action

As mentioned in Chapter 2, the pre-schools of Reggio Emilia in Northern Italy have developed a socially constructed and culturally specific early years curriculum that has proved hugely influential. Their use of a range of themed spaces or 'ateliers' is of particular note for practitioners – these places for play and exploration are open to schools, families and children of all ages. These 'ateliers' or spaces are developed using the model of the artist's studio and are staffed by specialist artist-teachers ('atelieristas') whose approach is based on a creative, experimental and holistic approach to education and pedagogy inspired by Educational Psychologist Loris Malaguzzi (Cagliari et al., 2016). What is remarkable about these ateliers or creative spaces is the combination of technology with traditional materials and themes that very young children can explore, for example:

- Digital Landscapes
- Ray of Light
- Secrets of Paper
- In the Shape of Clay (Figure 3.4)
- Ateliers on the Body
- Ateliers on Food

Figure 3.4 'In the shape of clay' Atelier
Source: Image courtesy: www.reggiochildren.it

> Our hands listen, they observe and manipulate, they enter clay and fragment it with fine gestures, digging into the material with pressure and pleasure. They work the clay with fist, palm, and fingertips, experimenting with verticality and balancing different volumes. Smaller children, older children, and adults, all discover the force of contact with *terra*, the earth, shaping it in different ways, with alphabets of plasticity, layers and strata, structures rich in solids and voids, creating complex compositions and forms in different colours. Reggio Children (n.d.)

Visual documentation (photographs or videos) of the children's participation and progress is key and this approach means that through the visual and plastic arts, children can make their thinking visible (Cagliari et al., 2016). Not only does this link to Bruner's ideas about child development and his three 'modes' but also to the idea of 'potentiating environments' and all the benefits that this can bring (Claxton and Carr, 2004) (see Chapter 2: Benefits of creativity).

Theory in practice

Lillian de Lissa Nursery School in Birmingham, UK, is named after Lillian Daphne de Lissa (1885–1967), an early childhood educator and educational theorist who lived and worked in

Australia and the UK in the twentieth century. She instigated a child-centred programme of teaching and learning which included learning in the outside environment as much as possible.

At Lillian de Lissa Nursery School today, professional artist, staff team member and artist in residence, Lorna Rose, uses creativity to engage pre-school children in activities, experimental ideas and community-facing partnership projects. This is an ethnically mixed and multi-faith setting, within a priority ward of one of the most culturally diverse cities in Europe. Children attending the nursery live in local social housing, there are newly arrived families, some of whom are refugees and asylum seekers, second- and third-generation immigrants and parents who rely on benefits. It is common for the children to have English as an additional language (EAL) and for up to 28 different languages to be spoken at the setting at any one time.

However, these challenges could equally be viewed as opportunities. Executive Head Teacher, Mandy Cryan, says that 'creativity flows freely' at the centre, describing it as 'a setting for all children'. She goes on to say, 'we welcome many different styles of teaching and learning to provide a broad and balanced curriculum' (Source: https://lilliandelissa.sch.life/ [accessed 25 February 2021]). Having a permanent 'artist in residence' on the staff team certainly makes this setting unusual in the UK, but not unique, and the model is inspired by the municipal pre-schools and nurseries of Reggio Emilia with their in-house 'atelieristas'. Importantly for this context, the creativity at the heart of the centre allows for an inclusive approach that reflects the multi-cultural nature of the school and the staff who are committed to promoting community cohesion. Within their 'Statement of Values' the nursery declares, 'Creativity is at the heart of our school and is used everyday to provide purposeful learning opportunities taking into consideration the rhythm, space and time needed for every type of learner. We want our children to be: Valued, Confident, Curious, Communicative, Independent and Secure' (Source: https://lilliandelissa.sch.life/ [accessed 25 February 2021]) (see also Chapter 14: Conclusions and next steps, for more advice on developing a set of core principles and values for your setting).

Rose, in her own words, describes her artist-in-residence role as 'a provider of, not entertainment, but possibility and creative facilitating'. She does this by setting up 'situations, provocations, activities for children to be interested in, to explore and to discover...'. Importantly, she also takes this approach with teachers and practitioners if they are trying to address a particular question or issue within their own teaching or practice. Parents of children attending the nursery are also looking for help with finding employment, healthcare, childcare, guidance from agencies and the social care system and staff need to be sensitive and responsive to this need. Rose goes on to say, 'creativity is a way we can communicate and observe our children working and we feel that it answers a lot of the questions we need to ask'.

'We want our children to be curious, to develop holistically and with life skills. It's not all based on the curriculum... we want them to have independence and autonomy to go and face challenges and solve them creatively'. Rose gives the children the tools to do just that, not only through the provocations and environments she sets up, but by encouraging curiosity where they can 'explore things and find answers, find more interests or design their own learning in a different direction'. Rose acknowledges that the greatest challenge is trying to meet the needs of all the children, 'to extend their learning and give them a fuller experience', but she advises 'flexibility which is embedded'. The end goal is not an outcome which is physical, but something more intangible, 'if they are interactive and working well together... if they have got a quality experience in anything they wouldn't have had normally, I am happy with that'. 'The child-centred ethos within school helps me support practitioners, support children in the way that it's needed...' (Penfold, 2016)

Multi-modal learning

For children, communication occurs in many forms simultaneously. As we saw earlier in this chapter's case study, children move between these forms easily and unselfconsciously. Gunther Kress calls these 'different but synchronous modes: language, print, images, graphics, movement, gesture, texture, music and sound' (Kress, 2003, p.51). This provides us with a good definition of 'multi-modality', that is to say, an approach 'that looks beyond language to all forms of communication' (Jewitt et al., 2009, p.11). How can we support this and develop a multi-modal teaching strategy for developing communication skills in young children? It could be argued a good place to start is the Reggio Approach and the model of ateliers (studios) that encourage children's learning through discovery and allow them to make their thinking visible (See also Chapter 5: Art and children's drawings: Making meaning and visual literacy).

Following on from the idea of multi-modality is the concept of 'multi-literacies' in developing young communicators (Charles and Boyle, 2014); the ability of children to not only use physical and verbal language creatively but to also develop their own visual metaphors and visual grammar (Kress, 2010) (see also Chapter 5 for an exploration of visual literacy and Chapter 11 for a discussion of multi-modal learning in museum environments). These 'multi-literacies' could be explored through storytelling, sharing picture books, drawing and painting characters, modelmaking, and with children dressing up and acting out a particular narrative. Fiona Maine, a lecturer in literacy education at the University of Cambridge, has taken this idea one step further. In her book *Dialogic Readers: Children Talking and Thinking Together about Visual Texts* (Maine, 2015), she celebrates the sophisticated and dynamic discussions that young children can have as they talk together to co-create meaning from a variety of texts, including 'wordless films'. Maine highlights the potential for talk between children as a tool for critical and creative thinking. Her DIALLS Project (Dialogue and Argumentation for Cultural Literacy Learning in Schools, 2021) is discussed in more detail in Chapter 10 and encourages cultural literacy as a social practice through understanding texts in a multi-modal way. The inspiration for classroom-based discussions is a set of 'wordless films' and 'wordless picture books' that explore themes of tolerance, empathy, identity, diversity and inclusion in an accessible way.

Accompanying 'lesson prompts' are designed to help teachers and practitioners by providing useful questions and points for discussion. Originally aimed at Primary and Secondary pupils (KS1-3), the themes and values explored in the project could easily be linked to the new EYFS Early Learning Goals (DfE, 2021a), in particular:

- Community – the importance of collective ideas and actions, and working together
- Strength of one's own argument – justifying and reasoning
- Relating to others – empathy, considering other's ideas, prioritising dialogue and connection
- Dealing with multiple perspectives – accepting different points of view (plurality)

(DIALLS, 2021)

Wider cultural themes can be explored beyond the films and books, taking the discussions to a new level and moving into more philosophical and value-driven debates, akin to the 'philosophy for children' approach (Lucas and Spencer, 2017, pp.54–56), exploring subjects as diverse as living together, social responsibility and belonging. Sub-themes that can also be explored include progressively more complex ideas such as democracy, citizenship, globalisation, co-operation and cultural identity. It is acknowledged that these might pose challenges to the children as they listen to and engage with each other's ideas; however, there are practical suggestions for creative 'cultural expression' beyond the initial discussion, often using art and drama. These could include:

- Drawing storyboards or pictures
- Designing posters
- Acting out key roles or characters from the stories
- Making three-dimensional models of the scenes

━━━━━━━━ **Reflective questions** ━━━━━━━━

- How could you support children's communication in a multi-modal way?
- What strategies might encourage 'dynamic discussions' between the children in your setting?
- How could 'discovery learning' be designed to your resources and spaces for learning?

'Learning styles' and other issues

Whilst a basic understanding of psychology is useful for early childhood practitioners, it is worth stating here that there are also certain theories that are widespread and still widely accepted within the education sector that have no substantial evidence to support them. Statements such as 'we only use 10% of our brain' or that 'we are born with all the brain cells we will ever have' could be described as 'neuromyths'. These neuromyths include the idea that every child has a preferred 'learning style' to which teachers should match their delivery, commonly described as either Visual, Auditory, Read/write or Kinaesthetic modalities (also known as 'VARK'). Despite the lack of empirical evidence, a whole industry has grown up around these ideas, including a range of training programmes, online products, diagnostic questionnaires and associated literature. A number of studies suggest that many educators (nearly 90% surveyed from 2009 to 2020) believe that matching instruction to learning style(s) is effective (Newton and Salvi, 2020). There is some concern that belief in learning styles might actually be harmful to learners if they are pigeonholed or demotivated by being allocated to a particular learning style. Another concern is that practitioners might waste resources and effort trying to match their teaching to a particular 'style'. Educators are without doubt motivated to do the best for their learners, but the logical extension of this idea is that they would need to try and generate four or more versions of their teaching materials and activities to match the different perceived styles (Newton and Salvi, 2020). Early years practitioners are urged to use caution when adopting learning theories and approaches that do not have a sound basis or foundation in empirical evidence, no matter how popular they may appear.

Positive psychology

As discussed in Chapter 2, creativity can play an important role in a holistic approach to children's emotional, psychological and social well-being. Practitioners can take this one step further by adopting an approach of mindfulness, that is 'the act of paying attention to our direct experience as it unfolds in the present moment and without judgement' (Afzal, 2018, p.12). This approach could be seen as part of the new field of 'positive psychology', inspired in part by the work of Martin Seligman, based on years of clinical research with children and young adults. His PERMA model (2018) encourages children to have more positive interior dialogue, what he terms 'learned optimism', and consists of:

- **P**ositive emotions
- **E**ngagement and flow – activities which match our abilities, which we enjoy and can 'loose ourselves' in
- **R**elationships with others
- **M**eaning – having a purpose that amounts to more than ourselves
- **A**chievement – recognising what we can do, using and celebrating such achievements

(Seligman, 2018)

The alignment with Csikszentmihalyi's ideas (Seligman and Csikszentmihalyi, 2014) is clear and this approach could be considered more important than ever in the wake of the coronavirus disease 2019 (COVID-19) pandemic and the potentially devastating impact on young children's education, health and well-being. Positive psychology is increasingly being adopted in schools and could be a key part of any 'recovery curriculum'. Dr Rachel Payne, Principal Lecturer in Student Experience at Oxford Brookes University and past President of The National Society for Education in Art and Design has articulated this very clearly, saying:

There has never been a more important time to give voice to children's cultural experiences. To make something is a means to understand something, and children make things to generate new meanings, to make sense of feelings and experiences, just like adults do. Rainbows and artworks displayed by children in their front windows during the COVID-19 pandemic serve to remind us of the importance of children as cultural creators... I challenge you to consider how you can establish opportunities to make art, craft and design in your school which support children to articulate their experiences of the pandemic. (Payne, 2021)

Conclusion

This chapter has explored a range of models for child development and learning in the early years, and the way children appear to construct their own understanding of the world through social interaction is of particular interest in terms of developing creativity. Different modes of representation (enactive, iconic and symbolic) can manifest themselves through children's creative expression, and practitioners should encourage children to develop their own modes of communication and visual language (multi-modalities). Dedicated creative spaces and creative practitioners can enable children to make their thinking visible and encourage a sense of flow. This has potential benefits far beyond the classroom in terms of positive well-being and a sense of optimism within the child.

Further reading and resources

Afzal, U. (2018) *Mindfulness for Children: Help Your Child to Be Calm and Content from Breakfast to Bedtime.* London: Kyle

The Thrive Approach: Public Health England endorsed training for staff to support children's social and emotional well-being: https://www.thriveapproach.com/

SECTION II
CREATIVITY IN PRACTICE

4

STORYTELLING, IMAGINATIVE AND SYMBOLIC PLAY

...It is particularly important in the early years to encourage imaginative play and discovery learning as essential processes of intellectual, social and emotional development. NACCCE (1999)

================= **Chapter overview** =================

This chapter will look at the positive impact of holistic, play-based curricula that use creative story-telling to develop children's social, language and narrative development. Taking inspiration from Vivian Gussin Paley's 'storytelling curriculum', this chapter will provide an analysis of what happens when children dictate and dramatise original stories in the early years' classroom. It will look at the opportunities for an inclusive outlook within literacy learning as well as the adult's role in the process. This approach is highlighted as offering an important balance to an increasingly narrow curriculum that focuses on specific sub-skills of the reading and writing process and a perceived need for 'school-readiness'. This chapter will also look at the different stages in a child's imaginative, socio-dramatic and symbolic play and the importance this has in terms of emotional and psychological well-being, language skills and literacy development.

Let's play pretend...

As we have explored in previous chapters, engagement with the arts and creativity can aid physical, cognitive, social and emotional development, but it can also play a key role in language development. Pretend play seems a completely natural way in which children use their creative imagination and interact with each other, but it is also known as 'symbolic play' because it involves the use of symbols. When we use symbols, we use something to stand for something else. In the case of pretend play, children may use one object to stand for another, such as pretending a stick is a magic wand, or a tablecloth is a cape. This type of symbolic thought is also needed for language, as our words are also symbols. Our words stand for our thoughts and ideas, therefore pretend play and language both involve the same underlying ability to represent things symbolically (Weitzman and Greenberg, 2002).

How pretend play develops:

- **Self-pretend (12–18 months)**
  During this stage, children perform one pretend action at a time on themselves, such as pretending to eat, drink or sleep.
  Children tend to use toys that look quite realistic (e.g., a plastic toy spoon) or real-life objects (e.g., a real spoon).
- **Simple pretend (18-24 months)**
  Children at this stage perform simple pretend actions on toys or people.
  They continue to use realistic-looking toys at this stage, e.g., feeding a doll with a toy fork or making a toy aeroplane 'fly'.
  Children also imitate familiar adult actions at this stage, such as pretending to talk on a toy mobile phone.
- **Series of familiar actions (24–30 months)**
  Just as children this age are learning to combine words to make little sentences, they are also learning to combine pretend actions together.
  At this stage, children can act out a series of pretend actions related to a familiar routine, such as the steps involved in eating or going to bed.
  Children can use less realistic objects, as long as they are similar in shape to the real object. For example, a toy ball could be used as an apple to feed a doll.
- **Series of less familiar actions (30–36 months)**
  Less familiar themes enter children's play at this stage. They may pretend to go to the doctor or be a waiter at a restaurant.
  Children can pretend without an object (they can pretend their hand is a cup and drink out of it).
  Children can also substitute objects that do not resemble the 'real thing'. For example, a child can pretend a wooden block is a truck on its way to the rubbish dump.
- **Role-play with other children (3–5 years)**
  Children pretend about imaginary themes now (things which do not really exist or that the child hasn't experienced yet in real-life), such as pirates, castles and superheroes.
  Children start to pretend with other children at this stage, each taking on different roles during the play. Realistic objects and toys are not needed as children can now pretend using gestures, mime, or unrealistic objects.

Language often drives the play at this stage. Children explain their roles and use language to act out their role, e.g., a child pretending to be a doctor might say to another child *'I'm the doctor, you be the patient, ok? Where does it hurt?'*

Dramatic play/socio-dramatic play

As children's interactions and linguistic abilities become more sophisticated, they start to explore what is known as dramatic play or socio-dramatic play. The main characteristics of dramatic play are pretending to be someone else, role-taking, imitating another person's speech patterns, using real and imagined props, using first- or second-hand experience and knowledge of characters in a certain way. According to Wood (2013), socio-dramatic play is the cooperation between at least two children; the play develops on the basis of interaction between players acting out their roles, both verbally and in terms of the acts performed (Wood, 2013, p.27). There are six distinct elements of dramatic or socio-dramatic play that have been identified:

- Role-play by imitation
- Make-believe with objects
- Make-believe with actions and situations
- Persistence in the role-play
- Interaction
- Verbal communication

As practitioners it is important to consider how we can support and encourage this type of development within the children in our care, asking for instance; what spaces and resources do they need? how can we facilitate this type of interaction? what might the effects be on the children themselves? Considering this last question in particular, the next section will explore the wider psychological and therapeutic benefits of play and developing spaces for play.

The power of play

> Play is creativity, it is abandon. It is risk, collaboration, interpretation and re-interpretation. Its meaning is infinite, and its importance cannot and must not be ignored. (Bottrill, 2018, p.26)

The unplanned and spontaneous nature of play is what gives it a unique space in terms of creativity in the early years. The fact that it can't be confined and has a reactive element, combined with choice, means that it can also provide an important psychological function and even healing and therapeutic possibilities according to some.

Sturrock and Else (1998), two American academics, developed this idea into a theory they called 'Psycholudics' (from the Latin 'ludus' meaning 'play'). They first presented their thinking at a conference in Colorado: *The Playground as Therapeutic Space: Playwork as Healing* (known as the Colorado paper) and within it Sturrock and Else claim that play is definable. They suggest that the act of play is to act as a prefiguring element to creativity, which might be seen as the source of all mental health. Therein lies a means of healing trauma, neurosis and psychic ill... (Brown, 2019, p.279).

Understanding 'psycholudics' and the play cycle

For the play cycle to occur, Sturrock and Else suggest that it all starts with the *Metalude* (internal) – this is the thought, daydreaming within the child's mind before they start to play. This then results in the *Play Cue* (external). This can be verbal or non-verbal but is an invitation from a child to either another child, adult or object to play.

Once a *play cue* has been issued it is expected that there will be a response to this and if this is positive a *play return* is issued – this could be the ball bouncing off the ground or it could be that the cue is returned by another child. Once a return has been issued there is the establishment of the *play frame*.

Within the final stage, once the *play cycle* has been established the players will become engrossed in the content, but there will come a time when the players bring the cycle to an end this is known as *Play annihilation*. This is often misunderstood by practitioners as destructive and they might feel that they need to intervene and maintain the frame. This can have value but only if the players desire this to be so. For example, you might see that the children need more artefacts to continue the play – an example here might be that they have run out of balls to play with. A sensitive interaction here would be – 'Do you need some more?'

There is, however, potential for conflict here within the therapeutic approach and practitioners may feel there are certain expectations placed upon them. As adults working in Early Years, we may have been exposed to a culture that expects us to be doing 'Playing' with the children. However, this can result in what Sturrock and Else term the *Adulteration* of a child's play. This means we take something that is not ours and try to make it ours – this could be in our shaping of play to a certain outcome. If we accept the healing power of play as suggested by Sturrock and Else, then we must challenge this notion in practice. Here are some suggestions:

- Stand back and watch the play unfold. This can lead to a new understanding of what is happening.
- Remind yourself that play has therapeutic and healing powers for the child. We have been conditioned to think as play as a means for children to learn, but it is so much more than this.

Bearing these things in mind, can we talk about re-defining play in terms of mental health and well-being within our settings? The next section explores open-ended approaches to creative play and considers some important issues that might affect children's ability to experience these wider benefits.

Free play and the value of discovery

Ever since British Architect Simon Nicholson published his seminal article in the early 1970s on creativity and the nature of children's play: *'How NOT to cheat children: the Theory of Loose Parts'* (1971), many writers have commented on the reduction in the number of spaces for free play and children's freedom to experiment, invent and explore over recent decades. It could be argued that the phenomenon of reduced opportunities for free play has been accelerated recently by the impact of coronavirus disease 2019 (COVID-19) and national lockdowns during 2020–2021. It is interesting to consider for a moment what research is saying about play as a way out of the pandemic:

> During the present crisis, measures have been applied which severely restrict the freedom of children and adolescents. Little consideration appears to have been given to children's welfare outside of the impact on education. Play, as has often been the case, has been forgotten or side-lined, yet there is copious scientific evidence of its importance for development. In contrast, there is little evidence that permitting children to play outside will increase risk in any significant way providing common sense measures are maintained. (Ball et al., 2020)

Nicholson himself had a rather unorthodox childhood, being one of triplets and the son of renowned artists, sculptor Barbara Hepworth and painter Ben Nicholson. This extraordinary home environment no doubt influenced his thinking. His original theory explored environmental design and his assertion that everyone was creative, not just the 'gifted few' (see also Chapter 1). He was particularly concerned with the variety and level of choice within children's play. 'In any environment, both the degree of inventiveness and creativity, and the possibility of discovery, are directly proportional to the number and kind of variables in it', Simon Nicholson (1971, p.30).

These variables, or 'loose parts' are typically low-cost and recycled items or elements within the environment around us, such as (the classic) cardboard boxes, packaging materials, tubes, old tyres, rope, trees, plastic chairs, tablecloths, old clothes, sand, mud, water, wooden objects, etc. They are important because these objects or aspects of the environment invite us to use them in multiple ways (see Figure 4.1).

There may be many uses or 'affordances' in an object – it's proper use and potential variants. The term 'affordances' was coined by Gibson who stated 'the affordances of the environment are what it offers (a person), what it provides or furnishes for good or ill' (Gibson, 1979, p.127). The quality of these play objects can affect dramatic and symbolic play and the more open-ended and ambiguous those objects are, the better they function. It is important to note, however, that Nicholson's own definition was complex and goes beyond open-ended materials to include phenomena such as music, gravity, and playing with words, concepts, ideas and much more. This is considerably broader than natural, junk and recycled materials. We need to

Figure 4.1   Loose Parts in action
Source: Lillian de Lissa Nursery and Pre-School.

be mindful of the breadth of possibilities according to outdoor education specialist, Juliet Robertson (2021).

The value of 'Loose Parts'

- **Promote active learning** – Piaget's developmental theory emphasised the need for children to actively manipulate their environment
- **Deepen critical thinking** – encourages investigation, analysis and questioning
- Promote **divergent and creative thinking**
- Loose parts **support all the developmental domains** – physical development (fine and gross motor skills), social-emotional development and cognitive development
- **Developmentally inclusive** – equally valuable for children with special needs and disabilities
- **Supports a wide range of play** – functional, constructive dramatic and symbolic play

Exploring these points in more detail, we see that this approach can **promote active learning** – loose parts can be used any way that the child chooses. Piaget believed children were like researchers constantly exploring their environments (see also Chapter 11: Children as researchers). Whilst Piaget did not address loose parts, he believed that children create their own understanding when they are actively engaged in working with people and objects (1952).

Loose parts can introduce novelty to settings and support high levels of stimulating play because they stimulate children to **deepen their critical thinking** and consider a wide range of possible uses and meanings for the parts. Once the children have exhausted the possibilities of one arrangement, they can rearrange the materials for another game or purpose. By continually re-arranging the loose parts they are showing evidence of **divergent and creative thinking** – children will create settings that match their own skills and when they have plenty of objects to manipulate, they seldom get bored. In his book *Creative Schools* (2016), Ken Robinson makes the point that young children, when they grow up, will work in careers that have not been invented yet. To meet the challenges and opportunities of the future today's children must become critical and creative thinkers, intelligent problem solvers and good communicators.

Children build on their existing knowledge and to do so they must interact with their environments. Robinson observed that very young children have 'a natural predisposition to immerse themselves in role-play and highly experiential learning' (2016, p.40). Loose parts provide many opportunities for these 'dynamic forms of learning' (Robinson, 2016, p.40); to handle, build, re-build and re-create ideas and experiences, allowing children to grow across **all the developmental domains**. This type of cognitive development is concerned with *how* children learn rather than *what* they learn. It includes critical thinking, language, concepts of numbers, classifications, spatial awareness, representations of experiences and ideas and solving problems. The latter could also include developing resilience in children and encouraging them to embrace failure, for example, a child building a tower out of carefully balanced parts – when one arrangement of objects collapses or falls over a different idea or system is called for to solve this particular problem.

Children of all ages, physical abilities, neurodiversity and genders can use loose parts successfully and in this way, it is **developmentally inclusive.** Because there are no right or wrong answers all children can achieve competence, build on existing strengths and feel successful and independent. By their very nature, these objects and environments are open-ended so they can support play for every culture, background, class, ability and gender, but only if we choose them wisely (perhaps by avoiding 'branded' items or those with questionable origins e.g., plastic toy guns, Barbie dolls etc.).

This approach **supports a wide range of play**, from 'functional play' that explores what objects are like and what can be done with them, to 'constructive play' – using materials to create something new, for example, a tower, robot or house, and finally socio-dramatic and symbolic play which, as we have explored earlier, is particularly important for children's social and emotional development.

However, one criticism of a play-based approach is that it does not scaffold the child sufficiently to achieve the sub-skills of literacy that are now perceived as needed for 'school-readiness'. Recent research by Bakapuolou et al. (2021) has shown that COVID-19-related restrictions have increased the proportion of children that are reported by their teachers to have difficulty in adjusting to formal schooling (this was already around half of all children pre-pandemic). This period of transition from pre-school to primary settings is a critical period for children and their families and during this time children experience a new and different environment with increased demands and expectations. This can lead to higher levels of anxiety and stress. The closure or disruption to pre-school provision during the pandemic in 2020–2021 was reported as having an impact on children's language development and communication, social development, emotional well-being, risk-taking and resilience, independence skills, physical development (especially fine and gross motor skills) and early learning skills (Bakapuolou et al., 2021). For those children in their first year of schooling, there was a noticeable 'regression' of skills. Data also showed that the negative impact of the pandemic on children from disadvantaged backgrounds and children with SEND has been much greater (Bakapuolou et al., 2021). It is worth noting the strategies this research highlights that were most effective in enabling successful transition – an experience that can predict later school achievement, socio-economic outcomes and well-being in the long-term. The most common of these transition activities related to achieving positive relationships with families and parental engagement in particular. The use of online/digital communication, although seen as less desirable than face-to-face interactions, was very effective in achieving engagement, sometimes more effective for families who have English as an Additional Language (EAL) (Bakapuolou et al., 2021).

In an attempt to answer the criticisms about the potential limitations of learning through play and 'school-readiness', the next section will explore creative approaches to literacy learning and how these specific skills and the curriculum itself can be accessed through stories and play.

A storytelling curriculum

Vivian Gussin Paley (1929–2019) was an American nursery (kindergarten) teacher for 37 years and started to write books about her experiences of helping children learn. *The Boy Who Would Be a Helicopter: The Uses of Storytelling in the Classroom* (1990) is one of her best-known works and in it she describes ways in which an early-childhood curriculum can be accessed through stories and play. In particular, she outlines a technique whereby stories are scribed by adults but also observed for clues regarding children's understanding. Paley promotes the value of paying attention to the individual child and valuing their ideas: 'In this way, a story often contributes lessons worthy of the best kindergarten curriculum' (Paley, 1981, p.167).

Paley's pedagogy is based on the idea that the education of children must include intellectual and academic rigour, avoiding the temptation to patronise. Pretend play is essential according to Paley, both for achieving Early Learning Goals and learning to live and understand others. She promotes the importance of inclusive classrooms (more on this later) and providing support to enable young children to become morally responsible future citizens (1990). Paley also recognised some elements that she believed to be universal characteristics of children's play:

- Fairness
- Fantasy
- Friendship
- Fear of losing one's special place

In her book *A Child's Work: The Importance of Fantasy Play* (2004), Paley reminds us that play, including the stories children invent and perform, is essential to all early academic learning. Paley argues that 'fantasy play, rather than being a distraction, helps children achieve the goals of having an open mind, whether in the service of further storytelling or formal lessons' (Paley, 2004, p.26). Vygotsky (1978) makes a similar argument for play as a means by which children can stretch themselves cognitively, taking place in their 'zone of proximal development' (see Chapter 3: Modes of Creativity) where children act not as they are, but as they might be. Play also requires children to regulate their behaviour, in the presence of their peers, to fit in with the 'rules of the game' or fantasy. Cooper argues that this is an essential, if underrated characteristic of the successful learner (Cooper, 2005, p.237).

However, this model of a play-based storytelling curriculum is a type of integrated developmental learning more usually associated with historical early-childhood education in America and other Western countries (Williams, 1992). In more recent years, we have seen a push in policy and legislation, both in the United States and the UK, towards a narrowing of the early-childhood literacy curriculum to direct instruction or teacher-led activities based on very particular academic sub-skills or areas of reading (Cooper, 2005). These areas include awareness of phonemes, phonics, fluency, vocabulary and comprehension. Cooper highlights that supporters of this move claim that 'the traditional developmentally comprehensive and play-based curriculum does not provide sufficient preparation for young children's literacy development in these areas' (Cooper, 2005, p.230). Any play-based curriculum is certainly vulnerable to accusations that it is not rigorous enough, especially with the increasing pressure to ensure 'school-readiness'. With this in mind, how can early-childhood practitioners ensure that pre-school children develop these academic sub-skills whilst retaining the central premise of learning through play and encouraging embedded learning opportunities?

Theory in practice: 'Helicopter stories – Letting imagination fly'

Paley's step-by-step process of creating a 'storytelling curriculum' is encapsulated in the concept of 'helicopter stories' – a process characterised by its immediacy, responsiveness and non-judgemental nature (1990). The important role of the adult is highlighted in recording each child's ideas, via dictation, and then involving the whole group in acting their stories out through dramatisation. Children dictate their story, which is recorded verbatim (word for word) by the adult who acts as a scribe. The adult can ask for clarification on any points that might be confusing, and children are permitted to make changes to their narrative. All topics are welcome, real or imagined, but to ensure everyone is included it is sensible to limit the story to one page. The adult then re-reads what the child has created to offer the opportunity for revision.

Each story is then read out loud to the group to familiarise them with the plot or narrative. It is then re-read and acted out by the group in a 'performance space' where children are invited to choose how they would like to re-create the various characters, sounds and actions. This is a once-off, no-rehearsal event and expectations of the level of dramatic performance may be low.

However, by doing so the adults present are not dictating how the story should be interpreted or dramatised but are encouraging the children to use their own creative imaginations. The process also encourages teamwork, collaboration and a sense of collective achievement, alongside individual performance.

It is recommended that stories are performed on the same day that they are dictated to maintain their immediacy, as 'the stories children tell and act out are synonymous with the lives they lead, and life cannot be regulated to special occasions' (Cooper, 2005, p.233). However, no child should be forced to take part, and it is also worth noting that some children may need the support of their peers, working in pairs, for example, to perform a particular character or action if they are less confident. Alternatively, they may benefit from receiving private one-to-one dictation processes, especially individuals who may find group work difficult.

Here is an outline of the process and key considerations:

Part 1: Dictation

1 The practitioner invites each child to dictate their story (this can be privately one-to-one)
2 Stories are recorded word for word (as short as the child likes, but a maximum of one page!)
3 Ask for clarification or more details for any points that lack clarity
4 Re-read the story back. Children are permitted to change their narrative and edit their ideas

Part 2: Dramatisation

1 A performance space is marked out on the floor (e.g., using masking tape)
2 Practitioner reads the story to familiarise the group with the narrative
3 Select children to act out various characters, sounds and actions
4 Children use their own imaginations to interpret how these are performed and dramatised
5 Responses are immediate, spontaneous and 'in the moment'
6 Performances must happen on the same day as the stories are dictated
7 No child should be forced to take part
8 Children can work together to support each other

Following Paley's formula gives children agency and the chance to talk about things *they* want to talk about. A critical aspect of the dictation process is its use of open-ended conversation and questions between teacher and child. Practitioners can use the experience to help children expand their language and vocabulary by asking for more details or to expand on an idea, for example, saying, 'How does your story begin?' and 'Tell me more'. By doing so, we are suggesting that stories are a different phenomenon than oral speech or conversation. It may have a stylised beginning, such as 'One day...' or 'Once upon a time...', but these conventions are useful and indicate that the narrative is beginning. Young children can grasp the overall concept of narrative, but with enough regular experience and feedback from the audience (their peers) when the story is dramatised, they develop a strong sense of what makes a good plot, how to give characters depth and the fundamentals of creative writing. These are learnt best through demonstration and action (Cooper, 2005, pp.241–242). Hardy suggests the act of storytelling is natural and this is how we make sense of our experiences, describing narrative as 'a primary act of mind' (cited in Gamble and Yates 2002, p.20). Fox develops this further, stating that stories are 'powerful fundamental forms for the mental organisation of experience' that arise with the 'onset of language, memory and mental imaging' (Fox, 1993, p.193).

Case study – Permission to explore feelings

It is Charlotte's turn to dictate her story so it can be acted out by the group of children who are sitting expectantly in a circle around the teacher. She begins, 'Once there were two friendly lions...'. 'Once there were two friendly lions', repeats the teacher as she scribes the words into her notebook. 'They were best friends and always played together', continues Charlotte. 'What did they play?', asks the teacher. 'They played like this!', answers Charlotte, making pawing actions with her hands and smiling. She continues, 'Then one yesterday they were not friends any more...'. 'What happened then?', asks the teacher. 'The wind blew them away...', says Charlotte looking down at the carpet and pausing for a second. The teacher waits for the next part of her story, but Charlotte just looks around at the children sitting around her and then smiles. 'Then they come friends again!', she exclaims and claps her hands together as if applauding her own ability to bounce back from a difficult moment.

Reflective questions

- How does Charlotte's story provide an insight into her understanding of the world?
- What issues do you think she is grappling with?
- How would you follow this activity up? What might you do to support Charlotte?

An essential part of Paley's storytelling curriculum is the element of choice, autonomy and permission to experiment with content and language – both essential to the development of narrative skills. Cooper (2005) makes the point that children want to write down their own stories as soon as they are able, but the fact is that 'very few young children have the physical or mental stamina, writing vocabulary, and basic skills to encode the long and complex stories they have in their heads' (Cooper, 2005, p.242). Dictation can spur independent creative writing, but it delivers the whole experience of creative storytelling well in advance of the child's ability to produce it on paper. Indeed, Charles and Boyle (2014) state that 'writing is a complex problem-solving activity' and that complexity requires socio-dramatic play to provide a framework that helps to structure the child's development (2014, p.9). Indeed, when the child enters formal schooling there is a growing concern that writing is no longer based on the needs and interests of the child as they naturally develop. Research evidence has even led some to conclude that in school 'learning to write is reduced to conquering a code, the exercise becomes a surface imitation of genres and text-types without being rooted in what is the core of language' (Nilsson, 20210, p.2). Nilsson goes on to claim that 'literacy in educational contexts is most often approached as a motor skill and not as a complex social, cultural and creative activity' (Nilsson, 2010, p.2).

Interestingly, the new Statutory Framework for the Early Years Foundation Stage from England's Department for Education (2021a) recognises the central importance of language and storytelling:

> The development of children's spoken language underpins all seven areas of learning and development. Children's back-and-forth interactions from an early age form the foundations for language and cognitive development. (DfE, 2021a, p.8)

The 'seven areas of learning and development' mentioned here are separated into the 'prime areas' of communication and language, physical development and personal, social and emotional development. These are to be supported by four more 'specific areas' of literacy, mathematics, understanding the world and expressive arts and design (DfE, 2021a, p.8). The word 'creativity' is notable for its absence and further analysis reveals more of an emphasis on baseline assessments, measurable 'Early Learning Goals' and frameworks for data collection for the Early Years Foundation Stage Profile (EYFSP) at the end of the child's time at pre-school (a more detailed critique of this and other policy documents can be found in Chapter 7: Creativity and the policy context).

Storytelling for inclusion

It could be argued that experiencing the structure of stories and storytelling makes it a perfect opportunity for children to learn many things directly or indirectly about language, print and narrative – three critical components of early literacy development (Morrow, 2002).

However, as early years practitioners it is quite easy for us to make assumptions about a child's home environment, especially when it comes to reading and the access they may or may not have to books within the home. There is growing evidence that demonstrates a direct link between reading aloud to children and greater literacy and comprehension. Recent research has found that 20,000 fewer words per day are addressed to children from poorer socio-economic backgrounds than their wealthier counterparts, which could compromise their linguistic development (APPGAHW, 2017, p.86). However, the relationship between family income and early-childhood development is not fixed and so it is also important not to generalise and make assumptions based on perceived social class or economic status.

An important factor in the development of young children's literacy is the role of public libraries. 'Storytime' sessions for pre-school children take place weekly in many public spaces up and down the country. These inclusive sessions are usually free of charge, with stories aimed at 0- to 5-year-olds read aloud, often with families seated within colourful and stimulating environments. Basingstoke Library is a case in point – one of many rebranded by Hampshire County Council as a 'Discovery Centre' in the 2010s. It boasts a children's section with an impressive mural entitled *'My Life is a Story'*, designed by author Lauren Child and children from the local Primary School. The mural has text and illustrations in the style of her popular 'Charlie and Lola' series of books and features quotes from the school children themselves, talking about their likes and dislikes, passions and interests: *'At the moment I am very happy'*, *'I love art because I love drawing and doodling...'*

On the subject of creativity, former Children's Laureate Lauren Child is quoted as saying,

> It is now widely recognised that creativity is as important as literacy or numeracy, and that allowing ourselves the time, space and freedom to be creative is essential for good mental health... Sometimes we need to stare into space.
> (Lauren Child, The Book Trust, 2019)

This idea about the value of 'staring into space' and letting children daydream has been developed by Child further. In partnership with The Book Trust and together with teacher Josey Scullard she has developed a series of resources inspired by her favourite children's books from around the world. These activities are designed as 'inspiring ways to get children to think creatively' (2019) and include:

- Toast sculptures
- Charcoal journey drawings
- Warli (Indian) style stories
- Making your own book
- Creating a 3D space
- Making your own miniature world

(see Further Reading for details)

When considering the power of storytelling it is also important to highlight the wider opportunities for inclusive practice offered by story picture books and contemporary children's literature, in particular the wealth of reading resources currently available that explore relationships and link to the new RSE (Relationships and Sex Education) curriculum for England (DfE, 2020). Richard Woolley, former Professor of Education and Inclusion at The University of Worcester, determined that these should include representations of 'non-traditional' families and diversity within the family unit, including issues that may affect any child, such as separation, divorce, bereavement and adoption. He believes these books are potentially more representative of children's everyday lived experience.

> picture books ...can provide a means of discussing sensitive topics with children without needing to speak directly about issues personal to them or their family.

This distancing technique helps to explore matters "one step removed" looking at the experience of others and questioning how they might feel or what decisions they might make. (Woolley, 2021)

Dealing with difficult conversations

Anyone who has spent any time in an educational setting will know that classrooms include children with diverse experiences of family life. According to Morris and Woolley (2017), sometimes these circumstances change dramatically and unexpectedly and this can raise many questions in a child's mind. The level of security and care experienced by children can also vary over time. It is in this context that teachers and other childcare professionals seek to nurture individual development and promote learning. As practitioners in early years, it is important to appreciate the backgrounds and life experiences of the children in our care so we can maximise opportunities for learning (Morris and Woolley, 2017).

■ Case study – Heather has two mummies ■

Heather feels loved and is happy to have two mums until she starts attending pre-school and hears other children talking about their families. At this point, Heather realises that she does not have a dad. Her teacher and the other children talk about their families, and it becomes clear that all parents, including single parents, two mummies or two daddies as parents, and step-parents are represented in the class and are special; the important thing is that these families love each other. The staff decide to create a display board at the entrance to the nursery showing drawings by the children representing a range of family models in a positive manner.

■ Reflective questions ■

- Do you know what different home situations and family structures the children are from in your early years' setting?
- How could you use drama and storytelling in a creative way to explore and share these diverse family histories and backgrounds of the children?
- What changes could you make to turn your setting into an inclusive 'centre of discovery' with creativity and storytelling at its heart?

Conclusion

This chapter has explored creativity through different types of play, including imaginative, socio-dramatic and symbolic play; the ways in which they are all beneficial and the reasons why they should be encouraged. We have examined how a 'storytelling curriculum' might offer a creative and holistic approach to developing children's literacy. This chapter has also considered ways in which practitioners can increase the amount of free play through 'loose parts' and the number of 'affordances' within the environment of their setting. Inclusive approaches have been highlighted through the use of story picture books and contemporary children's literature which offer many opportunities to explore different cultural experiences, diverse families and backgrounds in a creative and imaginative way.

Further reading and resources

The Book Trust – *Staring into Space* Resources by Lauren Child and Josey Scullard includes six creative activities for children inspired by books and storytelling: https://cdn.booktrust.org.uk/globalassets/resources/childrens-laureate/lauren-child/staring-into-space/staring-into-space-all-six-resources

The Family Diversities Reading Resource (2nd edition) can be downloaded via this link and includes over 150 high-quality picture books suitable for children. These books include families with one or two parents, carers, families experiencing separation through divorce, bereavement or distance, children living in public care and adoptive families, to name a few: https://libguides.bishopg.ac.uk/ld.php?content_id=31126500

5
ART AND CHILDREN'S DRAWINGS
Making meaning and visual literacy

To draw, you must close your eyes and sing. Pablo Picasso

━━━━━━━━━━ **Chapter overview** ━━━━━━━━━━

Drawing and mark-making can be described as 'thinking in process', which provide clues as to how a child understands the world, how they go about the co-construction of learning and the making of meaning. This chapter will explore how the visual arts, especially drawing, mark-making and 3D, can encourage self-expression and the skills of interpretation, dialogue and discussion based on a child's lived experience. The chapter will include an in-depth exploration of theory in practice along with case studies and some inspiring exemplars of best practice for using drawing and mark-making within early childhood settings. The argument of the chapter is that 'drawing makes children powerful', (Bob and Roberta Smith, 2023). It opens up imaginative possibilities and precedes but is not necessarily a precursor to writing. It not only makes a child's learning visible but also has a value in its own right. Drawing facilitates cognition, understanding and language production, but as adults, we often fail to acknowledge the everyday uses of drawing and mark-making. So, its importance as a vehicle for communication is often-undervalued.

The making of meaning

Anyone who has ever been around very young children for any length of time will have observed the natural ease and delight with which they will take up a pencil, crayon, pen or any other tool, whatever is at hand that can make a mark, and go to work. In my experience, this can include objects and materials as surprising and unexpected as a stick in a patch of mud, a puddle of water on a patio, a finger dragged through flour or icing sugar on the kitchen worktop or a spade on a sandy beach. . . it is worth stopping for a moment to consider what is going on here. Are children just satisfying their curiosity and exploring the world, or are they trying to communicate something very particular?

It has been said that drawing and mark-making are especially powerful for young children in that the fundamental process involves 'representing the world and capturing reality through experience, imagination and reasoning' (Wright, 2010, p.78). It is one of the 'hundred languages of children' according to Loris Malaguzzi, pioneer of the Reggio Approach (Cagliari et al., 2016) (see also Chapter 3) and can help children give shape to abstract ideas, as well as being the vehicle by which they can express their growing awareness of themselves and the world in which they live.

The early twentieth-century artist Paul Klee (1879–1940) is famously quoted as saying, 'drawing is simply a line going for a walk' (Saccardi, 2014, p.64), and his continuous-line portraits and sketches certainly bear the hallmarks of this approach. This playful notion is fine on one level, but a deeper understanding of what is really happening when children draw and why, is required. It is also worth unpacking the very term 'drawing' to see what is really meant, how it might be defined and the different ways in which it can be used and interpreted, the 'uses of drawing' as it were. A helpful starting point is to consider the work of Eileen Adams, author of a series of books on *Drawing Power* for The Campaign for Drawing – a British charitable trust that now takes the form of 'The Big Draw' – an annual festival and national initiative. Amongst its aims is a desire to show how drawing can be valued more highly in education and everyday life as a medium for learning. The Big Draw stresses the importance of drawing in the intellectual and emotional development of young children, as Adams herself states very eloquently when talking about the power of the medium:

drawing is an experience

drawing draws on experience

drawing intensifies experience

drawing is a trace of experience

drawing makes sense of experience (Adams and Baynes, 2003, p.1)

Adams goes on to explore the different purposes of drawing, that is to say:

- Perception
- Communication
- Invention

Perception – In the sense that drawing assists the ordering of sensations, feelings, ideas and thoughts. This can be a very personal experience, done simply for the need, pleasure, interest or benefit of the individual.

Communication – Children cannot always express themselves using words and actions, so drawing is another important form of communication that assists the process of making ideas, thoughts and feelings available to others. Certain codes or conventions are likely to be used so that an individual viewer or other group can understand what is being communicated (more on this later).

Invention – Drawing that assists the creative manipulation and development of thought. Embryonic or partially formed ideas take shape when the drawer experiences the process of 'reflexive oscillation' between impulse, ideas and the marks appearing on the page, prompting further thought and mark-making (Adams and Baynes, 2003, p.2).

Reflecting on these different purposes, we might re-consider the everyday uses of drawing and mark-making by adults. For instance, a hastily drawn map on a scrap of paper to assist a friend in finding their way home; annotated diagrams in a biology textbook; architectural ideas that might inform the planning for a new development; a thumbnail portrait that captures a likeness; a cartoon storyboard; a full-scale representation of the form for a metal casting; a rubbing of a surface that captures the rough texture of a material; a colour sketch by a fashion designer that shows the inspiration for their new collection; gestural marks or abstract doodles that are an emotional or therapeutic response to a traumatic situation; an observer attempting to capture the speed and patterns of movement within a crowd; a representation of the coloured wiring within an electrical circuit. All these examples of drawing have a different purpose and we can clearly see the inter-disciplinary nature of its many and varied uses in the fields of science, technology, engineering, the arts, humanities and mathematics (see also Chapter 11: Children as researchers).

When adults pay attention to young children's drawing and mark-making, they are giving it the respect it deserves and acknowledging the attempts at communication and decision-making that are taking place, as the following case study illustrates.

■■■■■■■ Case study – Making your mark ■■■■■■■

Jacob has a large sheet of paper attached to a board in front of him that has been set up, so it stands vertically on a wooden easel at eye level. Standing still for a moment, he selects a thin, almost weightless piece of black charcoal from the tray in front of him and then starts to move it backwards and forwards across the page in large sweeping movements... 'what are you doing?', asks his carer Neena. 'I'm drawing me on the swing yesterday', says Jacob without stopping to look away. 'You're going ever so fast!', says Neena excitedly. Jacob's charcoal stick suddenly breaks with the pressure and makes a 'snap!' sound. He doesn't stop but instead uses his fingertips and the palm of his hand to continue the sweeping gestures in smudged grey lines whilst his hands become increasingly blackened and dirty. Neena encourages him to keep going and see what other marks he can make...

━━━━━━━ **Reflective questions** ━━━━━━━

- What type of learning and development might be taking place here?
- Why do you think Neena did not intervene more?
- How could this exercise help Jacob to make sense of his lived experience?

As mentioned in Chapter 3, Lillian de Lissa Nursery School based in Birmingham, UK, has its own artist in residence as part of the core staff team. On the Nursery's Instagram pages are numerous exemplars of successful expressive arts and drawing projects. Artist Lorna Rose describes the particular benefits of working on a large scale (Figure 5.1):

> We find that if a child is standing up when mark making they use the whole of their body in the expressive movements. It also allows marks ranging from tiny, to really big sweeping gestures. In terms of gross motor development this is really beneficial in building the muscles needed in children's bodies at this stage. (Lorna Rose, Lillian de Lissa, 2021)

Observational drawing, or drawing from life, is also a challenge that young children will rise to, given the opportunity and the right resources. 'We have been asking the children to look in the mirrors before they use fine liner pens to draw a self-portrait. Slowing the process down has allowed more details to be noticed and has included lots of nose wiggling, sticking tongues out and puffed-up cheeks' (Lillian de Lissa, 2021). This act of slowing the process down and taking time to really observe; 'looking, not just seeing', is what leads to deeper levels of understanding, as we shall explore in this next section.

Drawing for understanding

Drawing is necessarily a selective process because it cannot reproduce reality in the same way that a camera can, drawing is a process of editing, but it can deepen our understanding at the same time. In the act of recording, the selection of what we choose to represent is the first step in the process. As Adams explains, 'All understanding is selective, partial and interpretive. Drawing might help to achieve a more complete understanding' (Adams and Baynes, 2003, p.16). Drawing can help us to make sense of incomplete information and suggest connections and even alternatives to what is being viewed. Drawing can also encourage imaginative and playful responses, but most importantly for young children, it is a key strategy for being able to articulate their understanding of something. Used together with talking or writing it can provide a basis on which to base their views and opinions. These attempts at interpretation can be developed and refined most powerfully through conversation and discussion with others. It is drawing that provides the focus and opportunity for the development of personal value

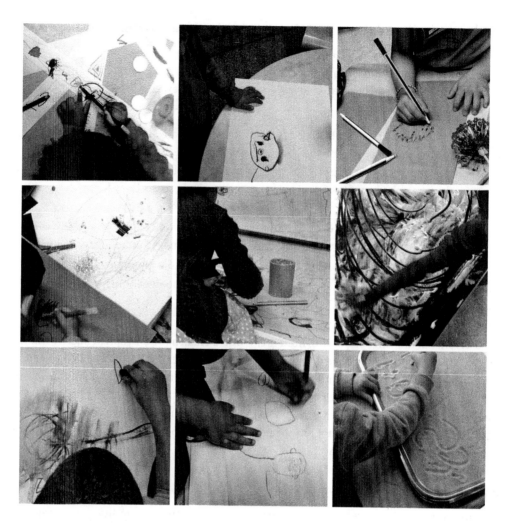

Figure 5.1 Expressive mark-making in a range of media
Source: Lillian de Lissa Nursery and Pre-school.

judgements, development of empathy and appreciation of other points of view. Through discussion of their drawings, children are required to make their thoughts explicit and to justify their opinions. This process can also encourage children to be comfortable with ambiguity and the possibility of different perspectives, multiple interpretations and multiple meanings, even from a single image. Critics might argue that the act of copying, a common practice amongst children's work, should be looked down upon as mere imitation, but it is Adams argues, a long-established tradition in learning through drawing as it focuses concentration and can facilitate understanding and remembering.

Parents… are very aware of the value of drawing in the life of their children. They see how excellent illustrated books encourage them to learn to read. They are aware how animated films feature importantly in their children's cultural experience. They witness their children's efforts to understand and explain their world and to process their experience of life through drawing. They see them succeed in mastering yet another code and set of conventions that allow them to engage with ideas, and which nurtures their powers of observation, memory and imagination. Children and their parents see drawing as positive and life-enhancing. (Eileen Adams, The Big Draw, 2021)

Drawing and language

For over three decades professor and linguist Gunther Kress (1940–2019) explored the link between children's early expression through drawing and the development of language and literacy. Kress was a social theorist who pioneered the fields of critical linguistics, critical discourse analysis and social semiotics (more on this later). In his book *Before Writing: Rethinking the Paths to Literacy* (1997), he put forward the position that a child's thinking or cognition is not dependent solely on language. His influential view was that 'all modes enable cognition', that is to say, thinking is possible and takes place in all modes of children's expression, but in different ways. The central point is that 'written language enables one form of cognition; drawing another; colour as a medium another; the production of physical objects and their interactive use yet others' (Kress, 1997, p.43). More recently there have been critiques of Kress's ideas on multimodality, including those who argue that drawing and early writing develop concurrently, not in sequence. Many feel very strongly that the intrinsic value of drawing should be appreciated in its own right, not just as a precursor to writing, but as a unique way of seeing (Hall, 2014) and as a way for children to develop their cognition (thinking) and meta-cognition (thinking about thinking) (Heaton, 2021). As practitioners, it is essential that we value all these different modes of a child's thinking and pay equal attention to their outputs.

Putting the debate about early drawing to one side for a moment, Kress developed a useful theory of children's meaning-making that included the following elements, each of which will be explored in more depth in this next section:

- Interest
- Transformation
- Multimodality
- Representation and communication
- Resources for making meaning
- Imagination and cognition

Interest

We must pay attention to children's interests as they are often invisible due to the dominant power of adult interests. As children's interests change, what is represented also changes. Their view of the world is affected by age, gender and cultural differences and as they get older, increasingly influenced by social conventions. Consider this example; why do three- and four-year-olds have a tendency to draw adult figures with long legs topped by a short body and small head, or with enormously oversized hands? Not because of limited competence, an inability to make something look 'right', but the fact that from *their* perspective, adults do look like that (see Figure 5.2).

Pablo Picasso, the renowned twentieth-century artist, is famously recorded as saying '. . .it has taken me a whole lifetime to learn to draw like a child' (Richardson, 2010). Rather than being a flippant, throw-away remark in response to critics of his style of work, this quote shows a profound respect for the child's perspective, their understanding of the world, and their uninhibited approach to creativity and mark-making. Throughout our lives, we have *our* view of the world. We may share common experiences but I will always see the world from *my* position, you will always see the world from *yours*, and that produces a difference of view (Kress, 1997, p.90) (my italics).

Figure 5.2   The child's perspective: 'Mummy holding flowers' drawn by Luke, aged four years and six months

Transformation

Children's creativity and making take place in a world that has the complex shape produced by all the previous producers of that culture. As a result, it could be argued that children and all members of a culture end up as 'acculturated' – all having the same cultural knowledge, the same values, the same recognisably similar traits and dispositions to a certain extent. An alternative view is that children, like adults, transform the things around them in subtle and barely noticeable ways (Kress, 1997, p.94). Examples might include children's unique and original use of language in their early years (see example in *Signs and Symbols* below) or their imaginative storytelling and play (see Chapter 4). This notion of transformation suggests that we arrive at a stage that is sufficiently similar to that of other members of our culture to make communication possible, but that we are able to open up the possibility of individual differences. It is important we respect these individual differences within the children in our care.

Multimodality

Children are used to making and communicating their ideas in a number of ways simultaneously and their approach to meaning-making is shaped and established in that way. Different 'modes' of expression (speech, gesture, writing, colour and music) are often combined in one activity, for example, making and decorating an object out of scrap materials which then becomes an instrument to make sound for spontaneous movement, dancing or performance. If we return to the quote from Picasso that opened this chapter, 'To draw, you must close your eyes and sing' (in Richardson, 2010) we can see this multimodal approach in action. To be truly creative we must not limit ourselves to one mode, or way of expressing ourselves, at any one time. Indeed, in our modern digital world with the increasing use of technology and artificial intelligence (AI) in our homes and schools, it could be said that each child who enters a classroom comes from a context, an environment, a world in which s/he is surrounded by multimodality (Kress et al., 2001); sound, texture, smell, touch and taste can all contribute to a rich environment for children beyond the visual modes of communication.

Representation and communication

Our view of representation or how we represent the world 'out there' has, until relatively recently, rested on the assumption that truth, fact, history, knowledge and progress are stable things and have characteristics that we all recognise. However, these big ideas or 'grand narratives' are being increasingly questioned as we move into a post-modern understanding of the world, with more diverse stories or narratives, alternative or 'hidden' histories, multiple perspectives and beliefs (Lyotard, 1984). Recent examples might include the re-examination of our colonial history and the role of slavery in the British Empire in the light of 'Black Lives Matter' protests and the removal of contentious statues in public spaces (see Chapter 10 for a more detailed discussion of 'decolonisation of the curriculum'). This complexity is, according to Kress, 'an inescapable characteristic of the communicational and representational world into which children are moving' (Kress, 1997, p.100), and it is our responsibility as practitioners to understand this and help children to navigate their way through.

Children form 'internal' representations from what they read or see and these then form the basis of new 'external' representations or signs (see the section below on *Signs and Symbols*). This internal representational system changes over time, and in this way, the child can participate in the constant re-making of systems of representation and communication and ultimately 'participate in changing her or his culture's system of representation' (Kress, 1997, p.102).

Signs for carrying meaning

Children will always surprise adults in the way they see the potential for making within materials that are to hand, often in entirely unpredictable ways. The preference for a particular cardboard box or set of buttons or shiny fabric may seem arbitrary and random; however, we must not underestimate the importance of the act of selection and pay attention to their choices. 'For young makers, the materiality of the stuff from which they make their signs matters; it is a meaning-carrying element...' (Kress, 1997, p.104) (see also Chapter 4: Story-telling, imaginative and symbolic play). The way children act on these materials is also significant. For example, a simple flat sheet of plain paper might be used for drawing, writing or mark-making, but once folded, its potential changes. Now it offers opportunities for cutting and re-folding, perhaps producing complex patterns and shapes: a snowflake or tree decoration. The folded sheet could also become a surface for receiving further 'representations' in the form of a picture book or birthday card. These transformations are also utilising children's abstract, cognitive and conceptual materials and resources that they have to hand. A story or narrative might emerge, or a link to a significant event in the child's life might become apparent; at that moment they are 'making meaning'.

Drawing, imagination and cognition

The boundaries to children's imagination, it goes without saying, are potentially unlimited and are not subject to the usual social constraints that we as adults have learnt. It could be argued that this is possibly due to the structure of formal education, with its focus on written language as our sole means of expression, fear of failure or giving 'the wrong answer'; the end result being that we are 'educated out of our creativity' as Robinson has said (2010). Kress asserts that children's imagination is dependent on and enhanced by the ability to engage in 'free movement among forms of (internal) representation – not confined, for instance, to staying within language, or the visual, or the tactile, but able to range freely across modes' (Kress, 1997, p.108). This free movement between modes is a central characteristic of the expressive arts, but the fact that they are treated as a separate domain indicates the extent of the problem. Different media make different kinds of imagination possible, and all have their own limitations and potentials. An important question for us to ask therefore is what the limitations and possibilities are of each medium. The visual seems to allow for more subtle grades of expression than the verbal;

language is constrained by units of meaning, words and sentences, nouns, verbs and adjectives, along with the rules of spelling, punctuation and grammar (SPAG). In the visual mode, there is no such limit and the apparent rules about distance, perspective, size and shape can all be broken. Similarly, the range of possibilities for signifying meaning through colour is infinite in the visual, whilst in our use of language they are relatively limited by the existence of colour terms.

Cognition also works within established boundaries and often with fixed units of thought; 'if I do this then this will be the result'. Imagination on the other hand goes beyond fixed units and exceeds boundaries. It is essential therefore that the forms of teaching we adopt do not, over time, create dispositions in children which impose limits to their imagination; a teacher saying to a child 'that's not right... what colour *should* the leaves be on your tree?' is a classic example. Instead, we should adopt forms of teaching which are designed to open up imaginative possibilities (see also *Teaching for Creativity* section in Chapter 1).

Visual literacy

Few would argue that the visual acts as a system of communication, but how many of us consider that it must be learnt like other systems of communication, such as language? The evidence within schools and early childhood settings often points to the general view that images made by children are decoration, perhaps expressing feelings and emotions, but not explicit communication.

This brings us to the idea of 'visual literacy', that is, the ability to discriminate and interpret gestures, objects, signs and symbols and other things in the environment. 'By creatively using these... the individual communicates with other people' (Debes in Charles and Boyle, 2014, p.52). According to Charles and Boyle (2014), a visually literate individual should be able to successfully decode (read) visual messages and to encode (write) or compose meaningful visual communications. There are many forms of visual communication that children are exposed to, and visual signs are everywhere, for example, dance, film, fashion, hairstyles, exhibitions, public monuments, interior design, lighting, computer games, advertising, photography, architecture and art. To be visually literate, children need to understand the subject matter of images. Our role is to help them develop the tools to be able to analyse them, including:

- Style and composition (the syntax or language of the image)
- Techniques used (how was the image made?)
- Aesthetic qualities (the 'look and feel' of the image)
- Purpose and audience (why was it made? and who is it for?)
- Impact (how does it affect you?)

(Charles and Boyle, 2014, p.53)

The latter is known as the 'affective dimension' and might be an expression of enjoyment, surprise, awe or wonder when examining images or exploring pictures. Clues can be found in children's gestures and facial features when engaged in discussion about a piece of work. The affective dimension also involves personal interpretation where a viewer brings their own experiences and aesthetic preferences to an image (Callow, 2008, p.618). The approaches outlined above are commonplace within museum and gallery education even with very young audiences (see Chapter 11), but they can equally be utilised within the nursery or pre-school setting.

Returning to the campaigning work of The Big Draw, Adams acknowledges that there are major challenges in her research and lobbying, surrounding the recognition of visual literacy as a vital educational tool. For her, the biggest challenge has been changing entrenched attitudes, in both education and government policy. Adams claims 'our notion of visual literacy tends to be too narrow. It is not merely about encoding and decoding images. 'Literacy' has a social value: it is also about shaping and sharing experience, ideas, meanings, values and prompting action' (The Big Draw, 2021). Her assertion is that through lack of vision, lack of understanding and disregard for evidence, successive governments have neglected a major area of education. The need is for policy changes to embed visual literacy – particularly through art, design and environmental education – in the school curriculum. The aim must be to give young people a voice to shape the ideas that shape society and the world in which they live.

Signs and symbols

To understand visual literacy and the language of children's drawings, it is essential to have some understanding of how we read images around us, especially signs and symbols, and how these are given significance in our culture and society. This is known as semiotics, from the Greek word *semeion*, meaning sign. Semiotics is the study of the meaning of systems of signs. For example, language is a system of signs (a word symbolises something), images are organised as a system of signs (think advertising or your favourite social media), and the clothing we choose to wear is organised as a system of signs (what does your outfit say about you?) (Kress, 1997, p.6).

The sign itself is a combination of meaning and form; if we consider a road sign for example, the 'meaning' of a circle with a straight red line across it is almost universally understood to be a command: 'Stop!'. The 'form' is that it is made of metal, is circular and has a pattern of red and white shapes within it. However, according to Kress and his approach, when children make their own signs they are often new combinations of form and meaning, 'often imperceptibly different, even to the maker, and rarely conscious, even to the maker' (Kress, 1997, p.7). Speaking from personal experience, our eldest son around the age of three or four would experiment with words as he got to grips with language (itself a set of 'signs'). A favourite activity of our family was going for a walk in, what he called, the 'crunchyside' – perhaps not simply a mistake or a mis-hearing of what the grown-ups were saying, but a word that better described his lived experience of being outside in nature, the different textures beneath his feet and new sounds in his ears. In the same way, we should not assume we just simply *use* language, but that we *make* it, Kress asserts that we make our new signs '...in the environment of our constant interactions' (Kress, 1997, p.8). His strategy is to 'trust children' and by paying attention to their actions, see what we might come to learn. In this way, we can attempt to understand how children themselves tackle the task of making sense of the world around them, and how they make their meanings in that world (Kress, 1997, p.3).

Cultural objects

Experience tells us that the child's appropriation of culture is a creative process in itself, rather than a mere reproduction of particular patterns they might see around them. Psychologists understand that cultural meanings may be attached to everyday objects, but certain objects, such as artworks, ceremonial or ritual objects, are special because they have 'an unlimited variety of human meanings and are open to creative interpretation by any person or child who uses them' (Kudryavtsev, 2011, p.50). Freire offers the very simple example of flowers in a vase, pointed out to him by one of his students; 'As flowers, they are nature. As decoration, they are culture' (1974, p.69).

We must also acknowledge the importance of social semiotics – culturally significant signs and symbols and their place in the creative and visual language of children (Kress, 2010). An example might be the trademarked logo or costume of a Marvel comic superhero or Disney film character; these cultural objects often form a symbol that is universally understood by children when they reach a certain age or stage of cultural awareness.

Pedagogical documentation - The Mosaic approach

A good practical example of this 'paying attention' to young children's interests through a range of visual media is the Mosaic approach. Described by its creators as 'a way of listening which acknowledges children and adults as co-constructors of meaning' (Clark and Moss, 2001, p.1), it is an integrated approach which combines the visual with the verbal. This methodology is an excellent example of participatory learning in action and grew out of the practice of participatory appraisal – a desire to empower communities from priority areas to have a 'voice' in changes within their local area. The Mosaic approach also takes inspiration from the 'pedagogical documentation' (Rinaldi, 2021) developed in the pre-schools of Reggio Emilia in Northern Italy (see also Chapter 3); it is responsive to the 'voice of the child' and recognises young children's competencies.

Based on the pioneering research and practical project work of Alison Clark and Peter Moss at the Thomas Coram Early Childhood Centre in the King's Cross area of London, this approach was originally developed with three- and four-year-olds but was adapted to work with children under two. As a tool, it has the potential to work alongside children for whom English is an additional language (EAL) and older children with speech and language or communication difficulties (SpLD). On a very practical level, this multi-method approach combines the visual with the verbal; children's own photographs, tours and maps are combined with talking, interviews and observations to enable adults to gain a deeper understandings of young children's lives. Techniques might include digital photography (see Figure 5.3) mapping and modelling, drawing and collage, child-to-child interviewing about who or what is important to them, drama and puppetry (Clark and Moss, 2001).

Figure 5.3 Paying attention to children's interests: digital cameras as part of a project using the 'Mosaic approach'
Source: Lillian De Lissa Nursery.

━━━ Case study – Lights, cameras and action! ━━━

Karam has been given a small digital camera to explore the nursery from his perspective as a three-year-old. He takes great care to seek out the spaces and objects that are important to him – the Lego table, the drying rack with the wet paintings, the outdoor play area, bikes and slides, and the trolley with the lunch boxes! The staff notice him lying down, looking up at the underside of tables, peering closely at plants in the flowerbed through the viewfinder and edging as close as he can to an insect perched on a leaf. Later the staff download his pictures and project them, so they appear as huge images on the wall. This gives Karam the chance to talk about his choices and share why he took these particular pictures. The staff pay close attention to his explanations and the other children seem to share his enthusiasm for these unusual points of view...

━━━━━━━━━ **Reflective questions** ━━━━━━━━━

- What does Karam's use of the camera reveal about his perspective on the world?
- Why do you think he was so engrossed in the task?
- How could this activity help us to understand a child's lived experience?

A framework for listening

The Mosaic approach has an underpinning framework for listening to young children that involves several different elements, according to Clark and Moss (2001), it is:

- **Multi-method** – Recognising the different 'voices' or languages of children
- **Participatory** – Treating children as 'experts in their own lives' (Langsted, 1994)
- **Reflexive** – Encouraging children, practitioners and parents to reflect on meanings through active listening, addressing the question of interpretation and perspective
- **Adaptable** – With a range of participatory tools which can be applied in a range of early childhood settings, a focus on relationships and process
- **Focused on children's lived experiences** – Looking at their everyday lives as members of communities rather than knowledge gained or care received as consumers or users of a product
- **Embedded into practice** – As an evaluative tool that also forms the basis for relationships in early childhood education and care settings

(Clark and Moss, 2001, pp.5–10)

Whilst this approach relies heavily on visual methodologies, what is the status of craft-based activities that have hands-on skill as their basis? This next section explores this often-undervalued avenue for creativity and creative 'thinking through making', in a field that could be considered as 'drawing in three-dimensions'.

Thinking through making

As biological beings we all have different dispositions, different preferences in relation to our senses and how we relate to the world. One child might prefer the distanced representation of painting, drawing, writing or mark-making, another might prefer to express themselves through the body in dance, movement and gesture, yet another might prefer physical three-dimensional representation. However, rather than trying to discover a preferred mode or 'learning style', which can be problematic for various reasons (see Chapter 4), I believe all children benefit from the opportunity to explore 'thinking through making' (Dormer, 1994). Thinking in three dimensions involves a very particular set of spatial abilities, visualising how something might look before it is even built, checking progress from different angles and trying out different structural options. If you have ever observed a child engrossed in building a rather precarious construction (using plastic bricks, wooden blocks or any other objects), you will see them very quickly develop their problem-solving skills, use of trial and error, resilience in the face of failure ('the tower collapsed... nevermind!') and joy at starting over afresh with a new plan.

Developing a 'tactile literacy'

Effectively what children are doing when they make something in three dimensions is learning about a new set of parameters: the balance, weight, texture, temperature and 'feel' of materials. Consider the humble ball of clay: is it soft and warm to touch or cool and hard to work with? Is it cold and wet from being stored outside or soft and sticky straight from the bag? Is the clay dusty and brittle because it was left to dry out overnight? Is it rough, textured or smooth? How heavy is it? How strong is it? can I use it to hold other things together? (see Figure 5.4). Importantly, when a child considers these questions, they are using their sense of touch, proprioception (their position in space) and developing 'muscle memory' as they handle unfamiliar materials. Over time, this knowledge becomes embodied through experience as 'tacit knowledge', that is to say, knowledge that is understood almost on an unconscious level without the need to state out loud or to think consciously about what is being done.

Figure 5.4 Drawing in three dimensions and developing 'tacit knowledge' through the use of clay
Source: Lillian De Lissa Nursery.

Sadly, the status of craft and material-based 'applied arts' have gradually diminished during the twentieth century to the point where they are now seen as below the 'fine arts' of drawing, painting and sculpture in the hierarchy of art forms. This is compounded in the twenty-first century by the lack of confidence and even basic knowledge of materials and techniques amongst early career teachers and practitioners. With our ever-increasing focus on theory and academic ability, even 'skill' itself is seen as secondary, or even an unnecessary hindrance to developing a conceptually sophisticated work of art. Peter Dormer, renowned critic and writer about contemporary art, craft and design explored this idea in his book *The Art of the Maker: Skill and Its Meaning in Art Craft and Design* (1994). He debunks the myth that craft, making and skill are somehow secondary to 'ideas' and points to examples of famous artists, such as Henri Matisse, whose apparent spontaneity was accompanied by a complex, rich expertise, developed over many years (Dormer, 1994). This 'expertise' starts at an early age and, I would argue, develops over time as tacit knowledge of materials and how they behave. Children only become familiar with material culture and how things are made by hands-on exposure to clay, ceramics (fired clay), fabric, textiles, metal, wire, glass and wood, in their early years.

Self-reflection and group critique

As we explored in Chapter 1, activity or active experimentation (making and doing) followed by review or self-reflection (stopping to evaluate) are key to creativity but also key parts of the experiential learning process according to Kolb (2015). Both these stages are essential to ensure children's creative outputs are appreciated, discussed and critiqued, ideally with their peers as part of a group. In this way, children come to appreciate other points of view and different interpretations of their own work. It is important to understand the role of the early years practitioner in facilitating this process with key questions and discussion prompts (see also Chapter 1: What is creativity? Definitions and debates).

The process of participation and reification (making real or tangible) can be seen as dimensions of both practice and identity. According to Wenger, there are two kinds of affordance for negotiating meaning: having some things in place (tools, plans, schedules and curricula) and the right people in the right kind of relation to make something happen (Wenger, 1998, p.231). For example, within the Reggio Approach practitioners create pedagogical documentation to 'make learning visible' (Guidici et al., 2001; Rinaldi, 2021); photographs and visual records of children's learning achievements, capturing moments as 'learning stories' which can be shared more publicly. According to Claxton and Carr, 'such reifications make concrete and visible for the student (child) and the family the kinds of responses that the teachers find valuable' (Claxton and Carr, 2004, p.94).

Conclusion

This chapter has explored how drawing and mark-making are especially powerful tools as they enable young children to represent their world, express their feelings creatively and make sense of their lived experience. We have looked at how drawing can support children's making of meaning, the development of language, communication and writing as well as having intrinsic value in its own right. Visual literacy is an essential life skill that should be developed from an early age so children can 'read' the cultural signs and symbols that surround them. Early childhood practitioners must pay attention to young children's interests and encourage activities such as photography, expressive mark-making, crafting and 'thinking through making' to support children's agency and to share their unique ways of seeing.

Further reading and resources

Plamper, S. and Wetterings, A. (2024) *How Children Learn and Create Using Art, Play and Technology*. London: Routledge.

The Big Draw Festival: annual UK-wide celebration of drawing https://thebigdraw.org/
Early Arts: resources, creative 'toolkits', training and inspiration for Early Childhood Educators https://earlyarts.co.uk/

6

MUSIC AND MOVEMENT

Communication and community

Children, of necessity, develop from both the inside out and the outside in Elliot
Eisner (2002, p.93)

======== **Chapter overview** ========

Personal experience has shown me that music and movement are powerful forms of creative
communication, and this chapter will make the case for the importance of encouraging spontaneous
music-making and musical behaviours in play and early years situations. It will argue for the benefits
of music to children's cognitive development, communication pre-language and literacy skills as well
as explore suggestions that academic achievement is significantly greater for those children who later
participate in formal music education.

Whilst it must be acknowledged that many practitioners face challenges when trying to organise
activities involving music, this chapter also explores creative and accessible solutions to inspire
children to become the next generation of music makers. We make links to the visual arts and look at
best practice in settings, including examples of music-making that use multi-sensory methods and
exploratory play. This chapter will also explore the collaborative nature of music and dance and the
positive effects on children's social and emotional development, health and well-being, looking in
particular at case studies of music-making with children using low-cost materials and inclusive
approaches.

Musical narratives from birth: 'Communicative musicality'

Kindergarten pioneer Friedrich Froebel (1782–1852) was one of the first education reformers to
see the value of sound, music and singing as a means of creative expression that had specific
educational benefits. He acknowledged the importance of songs and nursery rhymes for young

children and promoted a collection called 'Mother Songs', published in 1878. Froebel's influ-ence internationally has been profound and today few people would deny that music and singing are an inherent part of children's lives or ignore the evidence that learning and development can be encouraged using song, rhyme and movement (Greenhalgh, 2018).

Indeed, we now know far more about biological development before birth and the fact that the foetus in the womb, from at least the 25th week of gestation, is experiencing music and has the ability to respond to other sounds. As the auditory system continues to develop the brain is processing stimuli such as internal body sounds, including heartbeat and digestive system. Research indicates that in the latter stages of the third trimester babies are familiar with and respond to the maternal voice. Hearing is an integral aspect of musical development, so it is important to consider that musical development itself may begin in the womb (Burke, 2018). In support of this there is a growing body of research, led by Professor Colwyn Trevarthen, from the University of Edinburgh, which confirms the idea of young children's innate musicality:

> ...I have seen what power music has in communication with infants... songs, action games and dances, and instrumental and recorded music... appeal to young infants many months before words have any sense, pleasing them, animating them and calming them to peaceful sleep. Infants also participate musically with skill. They hear music and they join in. We are certainly born musical. (Trevarthen, 1997)

This idea that we are *born musical* has been reinforced by Trevarthen's research on babies' innate ability to communicate through sound from birth. By analysing video recordings of parents and babies during simple interactions when talking and singing together he discovered that right from birth babies were far from passive agents – they were often instigators of these new encounters or anticipated the parent's next sound or vocalisation. They were essentially social and sociable (Fawcett, 2009).

In a joint paper published in 2002, Trevarthen and Malloch made some fascinating claims:

- From the time of birth, infants are able to engage musically with parents and caregivers.
- Music is used differently in the stages of an infant's development: first to calm and arouse, then to provide an opportunity for performance and sharing.
- An infant may learn language patterns by first recognising musical patterns in a parent's or caregiver's speech.

(Trevarthen and Malloch, 2002, p.11)

Alongside this research, Malloch and Trevarthen collected evidence from neuroscientists, biologists, anthropologists, music therapists and others, essentially revealing that the qualities of a caregiver's speaking voice to their baby (infant-directed speech) are musical, with noticeable rhythms and patterns of melody. This led to the development of the concept of 'communicative musicality' (2002), the idea that humans use musical forms in their speech, for example, changes in pitch, rhythm, volume and tempo or speed. The baby imitates these musical ideas and communication goes back and forth between adult and child. It is now thought that this very early musical communication has been valuable in human evolution as it strengthens bonds between parent or carer and child (Fawcett, 2009).

If we accept communicative musicality as an idea to explain the use of music to converse emotionally with others, then the benefits are potentially deep and wide-ranging. In the UK, the All-Party Parliamentary Group on Arts, Health and Wellbeing has stated that '...music can relieve the pain and anxiety of childbirth, lead to weight gain in premature babies and encourage parent–child bonding' (2017, p.85). Perhaps more significantly it also goes on to say that 'art, craft and singing help mothers to overcome postnatal depression, promote parent–child bonding, and improve children's mental health and well-being' (2017, p.86). These wider health and well-being benefits will be explored later in this chapter, but first, we will look at the potential impact of music on a child's learning and development.

Music and child development

According to the Department for Education's non-statutory curriculum guidance for the Early Years Foundation Stage, *Development Matters* (2020, p.5), 'language is the foundation of children's thinking and learning', but it could be argued that music is the foundation of communication and language, and so is even more critical in terms of a child's development. Many early childhood practitioners certainly think so and music specialists such as Nicola Burke have worked with the National Foundation for Youth Music, Arts Council England and Early Education: The British Association for Early Childhood Education, to create some alternative guidance entitled *Musical Development Matters in the Early Years* (2018) in response.

This independent and expert guidance on aspects of musical learning and development is presented in the familiar format of the DfE's non-statutory *Development Matters* (DfE, 2020). It uses the familiar themes of 'a unique child', 'positive relationships' and 'enabling environments' to explore aspects of musical learning and development from birth to 60 plus months (five years of age). These three themes are detailed in terms of 'observing what a child is learning', 'what adults could do' and 'what adults could provide'. The key aspects of musical development are outlined by Burke using the categories of 'hearing and listening', vocalising and singing', moving and dancing', exploring and playing'. Table 6.1 shows a small selection of the typical observations, and a wide range of practical suggestions Burke has produced for each developmental age/stage. Note that these bands overlap and the level of sophistication of the activities increases significantly with age:

Table 6.1 Key aspects of musical development by age

Age	Birth to 11 months	8–20 months	16–26 months	22–36 months	30–50 months	40 to 60+ months
Aspects of Musical Learning and Development						
Hearing and Listening	Listens attentively when sung to and can anticipate phrases and actions of familiar rhymes/songs, e.g., 'round and round the garden...'		Musical preferences and favourites develop, can describe music, e.g., 'scary music, angry music and happy music'		Adults introduce a wide range of musical genres and invite children to be 'sound detectives' by providing recording devices to capture sounds	
Vocalising and Singing	Creates sound effects of animals, e.g., 'baa baa', roaring, etc.		Vocalising and singing whilst playing with instruments, creating sound effects for toys and props in their pretend play		Adults introduce large and small group singing sessions, plus opportunities for children to sing solo, children create their own songs, improvise or merge elements of familiar songs	
Moving and Dancing	Enjoys being moved gently to the pulse of music (live or recorded), e.g., being rocked or bounced, finger rhymes and songs that involve touch		Adults provide portable instruments, which lend themselves to movement and may enjoy dancing to music		Children move in response to rhythms heard, clap or tap to the pulse of the music they are listening to or singing, may physically interpret the sound of instruments or choreograph their own dances	
Exploring and Playing	Holds small instruments/shakers in each hand and brings them together to tap		Creates own patterns in music-making and experiments with ways of making and playing instruments		Create environments that invite children to make music together, e.g., dens/enclosed spaces, music tables, instruments hanging on a 'musical washing line', experiment with different genres, record children's pieces and play them back	

Source: Adapted from Musical Development Matters in the Early Years (Burke, 2018).

   Whilst not wanting to create a prescriptive template or age and stage-based checklist, Burke is keen to show how music threads through all areas of learning and can be a way of exploring, communicating and responding to experience. Making music with others can be a **social experience** with two or more children together or a parent/carer and baby. This interaction, whether one-to-one or in a group, is **personal** to each individual and is often combined with an expression of **feelings** (Burke, 2018).

However, Burke also sounds a note of caution acknowledging that music-making can be challenging to provide for in early years settings as 'it is noisy and can be difficult to document as it is live, invisible and once it has been created in that moment it disappears, unless we capture it' (2018, p.1). In the current evidence-based climate, the potential of music in early years' settings is often unrecognised or undervalued and it could be argued that spontaneous musical behaviours are not encouraged to the same extent that mark-making or drawing activities might be as there are few tangible or permanent outputs that can be assessed. This is a source of frustration for many music specialists, but potential solutions can be found.

According to Hanna (2014, p.293), if we consider musical documentation as another type of 'pedagogical documentation' within the Reggio Approach (Malaguzzi, 1998), examples might include a recorded performance of a child singing or playing instruments, a spontaneous dance interpretation to a particular piece of music, an original music composition, a dramatic play with musical sound effects, or a vocal or instrumental improvisation produced by a child. These recordings can be done digitally via a smartphone, tablet, iPad or other simple software and applications. The advantage here is the ability to share these musical 'documents', either publicly in the setting to allow teachers, parents and other children to provide constructive comments and encouragement or privately with parents and carers via online file-sharing software. However, Hanna also offers a note of caution, advising that whilst this documentation of musical expressions can take many forms, they should not be considered 'performances' in the sense that adults might look for evidence of musical ability or talent. The point of developing children's musical fluency is to help them create musical products that 'express a child's perspective, feelings, ideas and imagination' (Hanna, 2014, p.293).

> When we label a two-year-old an "artist", we don't expect this child to paint landscapes and create large sculptures; instead, we acknowledge the physical demands of controlling the crayons and creating the lines and circles known to us as scribbles... In the same way, identifying a two-year-old as a "musician" should not be based on expectations of precocious demonstrations of adult musical behaviours. Fox (1991, p.42)

Sandra Smidt, in her book *Introducing Trevarthen: A Guide for Practitioners and Students in Early Years Education* (2018), discusses how children create and inhabit imaginary worlds through their music-making. Since music is an affective art form, it is particularly valuable for expressing moods and emotions. Just as words and sentences are essential to meaningful expression in language, understanding the basic elements of music such as melody, rhythm, timbre, dynamics, tempo and harmony provides the essential building blocks that are necessary for children to express themselves musically. This next section will explore effective and creative strategies for engaging children with these fundamental elements of music.

The language of music

It is worth considering for a moment the core elements of music mentioned above, such as pitch, pulse, tempo and timbre and indeed music itself – these are quite abstract things in the sense that they are temporary, ephemeral and often difficult to describe. This can present problems for practitioners wishing to engage children in any structured way. However, it is this affective and experiential nature of music, almost beyond language, which can be particularly powerful, especially for non-verbal children or those at the pre-writing stage in the early years. Bateson's theory of 'meta-communication' (2000) was especially important to Malaguzzi in developing the Reggio Approach and is relevant here. According to Bateson, meaning is derived from interaction with others and does not depend on *literal* verbal meaning (Bateson and Bateson, 2000). When children interact, complex layers of communication occur at the same time that are not always visible. Bateson believed that multiple layers of learning provide the best type of education and inspired Malaguzzi's idea of an emergent curriculum which can embrace subjectivity, curiosity and creativity (Hanna, 2014). Malaguzzi also believed that Bateson's idea of 'double description' was particularly valuable in developing his vision of education, that is to say, the combining of multiple perspectives which gives a much more complete picture of knowledge (Bateson, 1982).

> Another consideration is that as children develop in their experience in music making the importance of providing them with a greater level of familiarity with key words and musical terms is also essential. We will now look in more detail at opportunities to develop this specialist vocabulary through regular use in group activities.

The case study that follows illustrates how the following keywords can be explored (the Italian terms used by professional musicians are in brackets):

- **Rhythm:** An arrangement of short/long sounds. These patterns are an arrangement of elements which are then repeated.
- **Pulse/metre:** The regular heartbeat of the music.
- **Tempo:** The speed of the music-fast (allegro) or slow (largo), gradually speeding up (accelerando) or slowing down (ritardando).
- **Pitch:** Ranging from high sounds to low sounds.
- **Structure:** How a piece of music or song is arranged, e.g., A-B-A-B (verse-chorus-verse-chorus).
- **Dynamics:** How do you play a sound – is it loud (forte) or soft/quiet (piano)? gradually getting louder (crescendo) or getting softer (diminuendo)?

- **Articulation:** Are the sounds light and separated (staccato), joined (legato), emphasised (tenuto) or heavy/stressed (accent)?
- **Sonority (Timbre):** How you might describe the colour, texture, quality or character of a sound, e.g., 'thumping', 'buzzy', 'clicky', 'swishing', 'popping', 'crackling'...
- **Texture:** Layers in the music, e.g., one sound or voice (monophonic) or several sounds or voices (polyphony) weaving together.
- **Melody:** A sequence of notes that form the main tune in a song or piece of music; a combination of pitch and rhythm.
- **Harmony:** Refers to specific moments in time where an effect is created by a combination of pitches which occur simultaneously. Consonant harmony is more pleasing to the ear, whereas dissonant harmony is more clashing.
- **Genre:** the type of music, e.g., pop, jazz, folk, rock, classical, world music, etc.
- **Notation:** Different ways of writing music down – this 'musical score' can be very creative and even take the form of a drawing or arrangements of objects (known as a 'graphic score') (see example below) (Figure 6.1).

Case study – Runner bean orchestra!

Emily, aged three, has been carefully placing different-sized fruit and vegetables on the floor to create a pattern. There are plenty of choices and staff have brought in a whole range that includes strawberries, runner beans and pumpkins – some grown at home and some grown in the outdoor learning space at the nursery. Emily has been creating a musical score using these vegetables where the large fruit represents loud sounds and the small ones quieter sounds. Runner beans of different lengths are lined up and represent notes of different duration... the big pumpkin shows everyone that Emily wants a pulse in her music lasting several beats and the strawberries are arranged in a particular shape that shows the notes of her melody rising and falling in pitch. Later that morning her teacher helps Emily perform her composition and encourages her to try playing it on different instruments.

Reflective questions

- How effective do you think this approach is for introducing complex musical ideas?
- What other objects could you use to create similar opportunities for musical exploration?
- Which directions could this activity go in next?
- What opportunities does it offer for individual and group involvement?

Figure 6.1 Musical score created using vegetables
Source: Rhythm Circle.

This example shows an innovative way to encourage a child to create their own **graphic score**, an inclusive and accessible approach to musical notation which could make use of any set of household items. It is inspired by the work of music educator Wai Sum Chong and her *Rhythm Circle* music education initiative. Chong has based her ideas on multi-sensory methods – an approach grounded in good practice from Early Years education methods and exploratory play, exploring ways in which musical concepts can be simplified and utilised in the home environment. In the case study above the child is exploring **melodic shape:** this is a little like the outline of the song or piece of music, picture a line that goes up steeply when the **melody** suddenly jumps to a much higher sound, or that goes down slowly when the **melody** gently falls. This 'line' gives the contour or shape of the melodic line.

> Rhythm Circle is the name I gave to my music education initiative which uses multi-sensory approaches to teach young kids about the elements of music… the methods I use have their roots in Early Years. We value and aim to nurture musical creativity/exploration amongst young children but know that most families and educators do not know how to do the same. We discovered that there was a lack of confidence and knowledge amongst educators when it came to musical activities for SEN/early years. (Wai Sum Chong, 2022)

Sound exploration

Similarly, Chong encourages children to use large plastic building blocks (e.g., 'Megablocks') to create 'towers of rhythm', with longer and shorter blocks representing different lengths of sound and gaps in the structure representing rests (silence) in the musical pattern. These three-dimensional structures could be collaborative, where children add their own individual sections together to create a larger piece. These constructions can then be 'performed' using instruments in the same way as if they were conventional music notation. The large size of the individual blocks makes this approach particularly accessible for children with visual impairments and in effect helps them to create their own sensory soundscapes (see Figure 6.2).

To promote concentration amongst my youngest students, I embraced some commonly used concepts in Early Years education. One of the most useful was the Montessori practice of 'isolation of quality'. This meant eliminating all other elements apart from the one which you wanted the child to learn. Very useful for children who are easily distracted as it promotes focus. (Wai Sum Chong, 2022)

Figure 6.2 'Towers of rhythm'- plastic blocks representing patterns in music
Source: Rhythm Circle.

Chong goes on to explain how this idea is incredibly helpful in her work with neurodiverse children: one of the common characteristics shared by those who have learning differences is that they experience sensory overload, and do not have the ability to filter out less important information. Consideration needs to be given to these children potentially experiencing auditory and visual overload during music-making, and so this activity is an effective alternative to a noisy group session (see also Chapter 9: SEND: Inclusion and creativity).

Musical play and art

There is a clear connection here between play-based experiences and the visual arts and importantly for practitioners and parents alike, these play-based approaches are considered much more appropriate for young children than formal music lessons (Hanna, 2014, p.288). Often referred to as 'musical play' research has shown that this approach can enhance social, affective and cognitive development (Fox and Liu, 2012). It also facilitates important physical development including gross and fine motor control and hand-eye co-ordination (Nyland et al., 2011). Problem-solving, concept development, divergent thinking and language development are also thought to be part of the musical play experience (Tarnowski, 1999).

Learning by sight and touch and familiarisation with musical symbols can all be developed by practitioners using a play-based approach which incorporates these symbols. Ideas might include:

- Tracing shapes in sand
- Musical 'Tic Tac Toe' or 'Noughts and Crosses'
- Musical Sudoku/Bingo
- Salt art

The standard visual art elements of line, colour, texture, value, space, shape and form correlate with the fundamental elements of music in interesting ways according to Hanna (2014). **Line** in art could be seen as similar to **melody** in music in the sense that it has a beginning and an end and can stand alone. On a very simple level, lines in art make 'pictures' and melodies in music make the 'song'. **Texture** in art is similar to **timbre** in music and is felt by children in a very physical way. In art, materials can be rough, smooth, bumpy, scratchy, hard or soft and in music texture is heard in the way sounds interact or voices, sounds and instruments feel. **Value** in art describes the point in the continuum between light and dark, whilst in music **dynamic** is also a point on a continuum between loud and quiet or soft, indeed, 'value, dynamics and tempo are particularly important for affective expression in both art and music' (Hanna, 2014, p.292).

As explored earlier in this chapter (see 'Sound Exploration'), the use of **space** in art has parallels with music's use of **rhythm**. Space in art refers to distances or areas around, between or within components of a piece (often referred to as 'negative space') whilst in music the material is time itself and the spaces are the silences placed within the rhythm, the pauses within the sound. Finally, **form** in art has three dimensions: length, width and depth. Similarly, **harmony** in music is produced when two or more notes are sounded together and so is also multi-dimensional. When different pitches are played or sung together it can be hard to distinguish between them and together they produce complex 'sound-forms' known as musical chords (Hanna, 2014, p.292).

Music and community

For young children who are pre-readers, possibly the most effective way to engage them with music-making is by using multi-sensory methods through musical games and activities. By learning through exploratory play, we can nurture young children's musical creativity, and promote musical independence and confidence. The main issue for many parents, carers and early years educators is that this musical independence and confidence can be quite hard to recognise. An example might be a child exploring rhythm, volume and tempo by using a wooden spoon on metal pots and pans in the kitchen; it might just be seen as a really annoying 'noise'!

However, these exploratory approaches with household and kitchen utensils have strong parallels with heuristic play, which is rooted in young children's natural curiosity (Goldschmied and Jackson, 2004). When toddlers make a discovery, for example when one item fits inside another, or an interesting sound is produced, they often repeat the action several times to test the result. This strengthens cognitive development as well as fine motor skills and hand/eye co-ordination. According to Goldschmied and Jackson, heuristic play involves adults offering a group of children a large number of different kinds of objects and receptacles with which they play freely without adult intervention. This supports children in making their own choices and discoveries and offers staff/carers an opportunity to observe the social interactions. If adults sit quietly nearby, children take assurance from their presence and there is an opportunity to witness the thought processes children display (Goldschmied and Jackson, 2004). The following case study shows how educators at home and in school can provide meaningful and progressive musical activities with little or no budget (Figure 6.3).

━━━━━━━━━━ Case study – My tissue box guitar ━━━━━━━━━━

Hannah is a university student on placement within a nursery setting. She has asked the other practitioners to keep behind any resources, from old tissue boxes to milk cartons and has provided rice, elastic bands, plastic cups, chickpeas, boxes and other simple resources for the children to create guitars, drums and shakers. Hannah has set up the activity on a table and calls the children over in groups of three. 'I'm going to play sunflower like spiderman on my guitar', says one girl. There is a mixture of preschoolers and toddlers in the class, and Hannah understands their different stages of development and wants to include all of the children in the activity. Younger ones who struggle to

(Continued)

(Continued)

create the instruments are given the opportunity to design and decorate them instead. Every child, no matter what their stage of development, is able to use their imagination to express themselves through the musical items they have created. Once the instruments have been made the group head over to the 'performance area' to play them and create music. They work together to create patterns, rhythms and melodies. The children are clearly proud of what they have created and the music they are making.

Reflective questions

- Why do you think this activity was so engaging for the children?
- What low-cost materials could you use to make instruments or graphic scores as a means of sharing musical ideas?
- How could you make musical learning multi-sensory in your setting?

Figure 6.3 Musical instruments made from recycled materials
Source: Hannah Moore.

The above case study is from an undergraduate student on an early childhood studies course and in her reflective writing she comments on the positive feedback she received from practitioners in the setting: 'Its lovely to see the children recycling resources to create something new'. Perhaps more significant are her reflections on the impact on the children themselves:

> I was so happy to see how engaged the children were with this activity and how they all added their own individual styles to their instruments. From what instrument they chose to make, how they decorated it or how they played, every child expressed themselves differently. A lot of the children were linking their instruments to experiences from home, one child said her dad had a guitar, so she was excited to take hers home and show him, and others recreated music from Spiderman and Trolls. I think they showed aspects of learning and developing in this activity. (Student Reflective Journal)

It is clear that the student wanted to show the children that music can be created in any way and that they are all capable of making music themselves, rather than it being beyond their reach. Her reflective writing also went on to make clear links with the Early Years Foundation Stage curriculum:

Unique child: Choosing which instrument, how to play and design it.

Positive relationships: Working with their friends to make a 'band' and perform musical patterns.

Enabling environments: Using resources they see on a regular basis around the classroom to create something they are all proud of.

Whilst the items needed for making music may be seen as a barrier for some, the materials used for dance and movement are very different in the sense that children use their own bodies as 'materials' to clap, stomp, move and perform. It is this 'embodied' experience that will be explored in the next section.

Dance and movement: Embodied experience and 'flow'

Music includes movement and drama in the sense that the body naturally responds to music through movement and because music often tells a story, there is often a strong dramatic play or 'make-believe' aspect to music and to many musical experiences (Hanna, 2014, p.294). This provides an effective opportunity for young children to learn holistically, using all their senses at once. For instance, one single music and movement session can support:

- **Physical development** by making body shapes that strengthen, co-ordinate and flex limbs
- **Emotional development** by building trusting relationships when practising balance or physical contact

- **Cognitive development** by counting jumps or devising rhythms and patterns of movement
- **Linguistic development** by articulating the sounds of movement (wriggle, jump, spring, etc.)
- **Creative development** by expressing their inner feelings and responses freely and innovatively

(EarlyArts, 2021)

This links to the concept of 'flow' and acquiring the state of 'optimal experience' (Csikszentmihalyi, 1990) that we first explored in Chapter 3. 'Flow' is the sense of satisfaction and intrinsic motivation that comes from challenging oneself and the positive experience of learning which becomes its own reward. By giving children the freedom to explore creatively away from having to focus on any specific outcome or end result provides an opportunity for practitioners to improve children's well-being. Here are some considerations in the context of music, dance and movement:

- Flow involves **giving children time** to become engrossed in an activity.
- Children need to 'feel at ease, self-confident and able to **act spontaneously**', according to Ferre Laevers (1994, 2004, cited in Fawcett, 2009, p.94).
- The predominant characteristic of flow is **concentration**, with a tendency to persist.
- Ideally, the **motivation** for continuing the activity is entirely intrinsic (self-motivated).
- **Sense of time** is distorted (time will pass rapidly).
- Profound sense of **satisfaction and fulfilment** (true 'happiness').
- Thinking ultimately moves to a higher dimension and '**mastery**'.

Flow is also associated with a strong sense of autonomy and is more likely to occur where people feel in control of their environment. Children in particular can then concentrate on their internal drives rather than the external demands of others. Flow decreases when there is pressure to achieve and when there are external, tangible rewards (Csikszentmihalyi, 1990).

Music and cognition

The benefits of music to children's cognitive development, language and reading skills have been explored widely in the literature (Bugaj and Brenner, 2011), but here we will explore suggestions that academic achievement is significantly greater for those children who later participate in formal music education (Hodges and O'Connell, 2005). Research shows how some **musical approaches can activate the same areas of the brain that are also activated during mathematical processing.** It appears that early musical training begins to build the same neural networks that are later used for numerical tasks (Sousa, 2006). In fact, a large body of evidence suggests that music-making in early childhood can develop the perception of different phonemes and the auditory cortex and hence aid the development of language learning as well as musical behaviour (Lonie, 2010).

Over the years, several music education methods, including Suzuki, Kodaly, Orff and Dalcroze have been designed to give children stage (not age)-based, structured musical activities from very young ages. The *In Harmony* programme, established by British cellist Julian Lloyd Webber in 2009 (and based on Venezuela's *El Systema* programme) illustrated how a large-scale approach to music-making in the foundation years can lead to **enhanced academic achievement and engagement in learning**, especially for children with special educational needs or those living in deprived areas for whom music opportunities would not otherwise have been available (EarlyArts, 2021).

Diverse musical perspectives

New Zealand's early childhood programmes have successfully integrated songs as a tool for language and numeracy literacy (Trinick, 2012), and in Israel music in early childhood education has been used to increase literacy in reading (Gluschankof and Kenny, 2011).

In the UK, the Oak National Academy has produced curriculum resources especially for music in the Early Years Foundation Stage (2021) which, like all their lessons, are described as 'knowledge and vocabulary rich, sequenced and coherent, evidence-informed, flexible, accessible and diverse'. The latter feature of their philosophy is particularly striking in the way it incorporates culturally diverse language, texts and media used, 'so all pupils feel positively represented' (2021, p.1). The following example lessons are from 'Unit 2: Journeys and Adventures' and illustrate this point perfectly:

1 **Walking on my street:** Using singing games to explore beat, note duration and rhyme. We will listen to a piece of music called 'Promenade: Walking the Dog' by George Gershwin.
2 **Sitting on the bus:** Singing games to explore note duration and improvise rhythms with a rapping bus driver. This lesson's imaginative listening will take us on a bus tour through the Queen's neighbourhood, as we listen to Eric Coates' 'Knightsbridge Suite'.
3 **Getting on a train (Part 1):** We will learn a new rhyme about trains and a fun counting-out game that children in India like to play.
4 **Getting on a train (Part 2):** We will continue working on rhythm and beat through the rhymes we learnt last lesson and we will also sing a Tamil Lullaby from Sri Lanka.
5 **Sailing on a boat:** We will be singing a song in French, with movement to mirror the rocking of a boat and making up some rhythmic rhymes in 'Ally Ally O'.

Music, health and well-being

According to the All-Party Parliamentary Group on Arts Health and Wellbeing, programmes like *Creative Homes* and *Developmental Dance Movement* increase school readiness, defined by the Government as the level of preparedness to succeed cognitively, socially and emotionally in school. However, school readiness is unevenly distributed across the social gradient. Two in five children in London are not ready for school (increasing to four in five in poorer boroughs outside the capital), yet £1 spent on early care and education has been calculated to save up to £13 in future costs. Sure Start Children's Centres could be sites for delivery of the arts for health and well-being, but one-third of them have been lost since 2010 (APPGAHW, 2017, pp.86–86) (see also Chapter 7: Creativity and the policy context). UCL's Institute of Education, Professor Susan Hallam reviewed evidence on the impact of music-making on the intellectual, social and personal development of children and young people. She concluded that 'There is considerable and compelling evidence that musical training sharpens the brain's early encoding of sound leading to enhanced performance on a range of listening and aural processing skills' (APP-GAHW, 2017).

Transformations in the brain develop quickly, but music practice needs to be sustained over time for these effects to be retained. Once developed, neurological shifts lead to improved motor skills and speech perception, contributing to language development, literacy and spatial reasoning, bearing a lifelong impact. Formal music practice requires sustained attention and the encoding of musical passages into memory while playing in an ensemble requires goal-directed, pro-social behaviour that heightens self-belief. People who have learnt to play a musical instrument score better on tests across subjects and display a high degree of conscientiousness, openness to new experiences and enhanced emotional intelligence. According to Hallam (2014), music education such as this improves skills such as self-esteem, motivation, and self-efficacy, along with improving mental health and social integration.

The UK Government has published a new ten-year strategy for 2030 and national plan for music education, *The power of music to change lives* (2022) with the intention to establish music hubs and a more co-ordinated approach for progression in music, from the early years through primary, secondary school and beyond. A good example of this kind of partnership working in the sector is the Birmingham Early Years Music Consortium (BEYMC) consisting of 18 partner organisations all committed to supporting and developing Early Years music provision. Supported by Youth Music Charity and Arts Council England, their project, called *Sounds of Play*, aims to improve provision for birth to five-year-olds and their families across the entire city. The project will target both early years practitioners and professional musicians to help provide a more co-ordinated approach to music-making opportunities for young children. Professional organisations such as B'Opera, Birmingham Contemporary Music Group, City of Birmingham Symphony Orchestra, Royal Birmingham Conservatoire and Midlands Arts Centre (MAC) have joined forces with Barnardo's, Spurgeons and the Early Years Alliance to develop a sustainable network of early years music practice that will support children's musical entitlement through a range of workforce development opportunities with specialists. The BEYMC will be working with a wide range of settings including children's centres; maintained nurseries; and private, voluntary and independent settings. The partners in the consortium have appointed project manager Nicola Burke (see **Music and child development** section above) to focus on training their own practitioners in early years music, impacting the work of teachers, practitioners and musicians. The whole project is being evaluated by the Centre for Research in Early Childhood (CREC).

> Children's lives in music-making must start as soon as possible. The evidence is overwhelming in terms of the positive difference this makes for their own personal, social and musical development and for their families too. (Matt Griffiths, Youth Music Chief Executive)

Engaging children with SEND

As mentioned earlier, Chong's *Rhythm Circle* inclusive music education initiative has also developed effective approaches to working with children with SEND that include making and playing simple instruments made from junk or waste materials. A good example is a 'spanner glockenspiel' made at virtually no cost by suspending metal tools on a cardboard frame using elastic rubber bands. These 'loose parts' (see also Chapter 4) encourage physical interaction and importantly, allow children to feel and sense the vibrations made by the sound. Other sensory approaches include the use of scent bottles with smells that might be very evocative and provide a starting point for musical compositions based on the personal reaction of each individual child.

Chong uses an inclusive approach to communication with children with SEND who are non-verbal using Curwen Hand Signs (Mayo, 2023). This is a well-established convention for representing the notes in the musical scale (Do-Re-Mi-Fa-So-La-Ti-Do) that has similarities to British Sign Language and is an excellent way to foster an accessible classroom environment in the spirit of universal design for learning (UDL) (see Chapter 9: SEND: Inclusion and creativity). In addition, for children with limited mobility, 'lap trays' are an ideal solution to enable them to engage with sensory items that evoke different musical textures (known as 'timbre'), such as felt, fabric, metal, corrugated cardboard, etc. Staff can also develop a 'sensory board' with these different materials, surfaces and textures, particularly effective for visually impaired children. A musical idea such as 'legato' (smooth) could be evoked by a particularly fine piece of satin or cotton that is smooth to the touch for example (Chong, 2022).

Conclusion

This chapter has explored how music-making, dance and movement can be powerful forms of communication and creativity for children in the early years. Research shows us that babies have an innate ability to communicate with parents and carers through sound from birth. Giving children the freedom to explore musically can improve brain connections and academic ability as well as support their personal and social development, health and well-being. Sensory and play-based musical explorations have particular benefits for children with special educational needs and disabilities. Opportunities to develop professional networks and music hubs with specialists can improve the quality of musical provision in early childhood settings.

Further reading and resources

Musical Development Matters: a free downloadable resource written by Nicola Burke (2018) to complement the English, Early Childhood framework, the Early Years Foundation Stage (EYFS). https://www.musicforearlyyears.co.uk/musical-development-matters/

Family Arts Campaign: Birmingham Early Years Music Consortium https://www.familyarts.co.uk/birmingham-network/

Rhythm Circle: music classes for children who learn differently https://rhythmcircle.co.uk/

Youth Music: national charity supporting children and young people's access to musical opportunities https://youthmusic.org.uk/

SECTION III
CREATIVITY, POLICY AND INCLUSION

7
CREATIVITY AND THE POLICY CONTEXT
Key debates and policy milestones

The arts teach children that problems can have MORE than ONE solution and that questions can have more than one answer. (Elliot Eisner, 2002)

━━━━━━━━━ **Chapter overview** ━━━━━━━━━

The value placed on creativity within the early years' curriculum has been in a constant state of flux throughout the twentieth century and its status should never be taken for granted now in the twenty-first century. Why is this the case? What changes have there been historically? What drives current priorities within the early years' sector? Ball (2021) in the fourth and most recent edition of his seminal book The Education Debate, looks at how education policy in England is constantly evolving and becoming increasingly incoherent. According to Ball, it is becoming harder to keep up with and make sense of all the changes, as the UK increasingly becomes a social laboratory for global education policy.

This chapter will argue that in order to navigate our way through these changing tides of policy, politics and ideology, as an early years' practitioner, it is essential to have a good knowledge of the historical and social construction of childhood and a clear understanding of how policy is developed and decisions are made. Walker et al. (2017, p.67) define policy in general terms as a 'framework or a guideline for behaviour'. Sometimes, this can take the form of legislation; sometimes it is in the form of guidance that is open to interpretation by practitioners. I am keen to show early childhood education in the context of the wider educational sector in the UK, rather than view it in isolation. So, this chapter will give an overview of the current debates and some key policy milestones along the way (with the proviso that each of the devolved administrations of Scotland, Wales and Northern Ireland has its own curriculum for children) (see also Chapter 2 for an overview of more recent early years' education policy development). As we develop our practice as professionals, we need to consider our own personal philosophy and values and look critically at educational policy and its impact on pedagogy, creativity and the child.

(Continued)

(Continued)

This chapter also provides practical examples of ways in which practitioners could influence future directions for policy and practice, including facilitating positive change in settings. It will argue that rather than being passive recipients of policy within a top-down system, practitioners can help shape the system from the ground up and become agents of change.

Origins

Taking the long view and situating current practice within the historical policy context is an essential way to discern the changing value placed on creativity and to understand why it is such a contested area. In fact, any writing on child development reveals dominant discourses about power, the role of the adult and the invisibility of the child often traced back to Locke's idea of the 'empty vessel' waiting to be filled. Wyness (2012) draws our attention to the ways in which adults and the institutions they represent, regulate every aspect of children's lives. Owen (2021) claims that this even manifests itself in children's play, which must now be 'purposeful' and is instrumentalised to serve the curriculum and notions of 'school readiness'. However, this was not always the case, and it is worth pausing for a moment to explore some historical antecedents; key educational thinkers who have influenced our modern understanding of the child. We shall look briefly at several contrasting and influential concepts of early childhood which have come from the likes of Jean-Jacques Rousseau (1712–1778), Friedrich Froebel (1782–1852), Maria Montessori (1870–1952) and John Dewey (1859–1952), to see how their ideas have influenced current theory and practice.

Jean-Jacques Rousseau, the French enlightenment philosopher, developed thinking within the eighteenth century and promoted new ideas about the nature of childhood in his treatise on education 'Émile' (1762). The autonomy of the (male) child was seen as essential so that they could become self-governing free individuals. More broadly, education was seen as a way to bring out a child's full potential through their natural abilities and talents, directing passions rather than suppressing them. Very much a product of the 'age of reason', Rousseau's emphasis is on science and reasoning, but his ideas on distinct gender roles (women should be submissive, men dominant) are very problematic to the modern reader. Despite this, perhaps his greatest legacy today is the idea that children have autonomous inner lives of their own that cannot be controlled, only nurtured by adults.

Pioneering nineteenth-century educator **Friedrich Froebel** developed this thinking further, recognising that children have unique needs and capabilities. He recognised the importance of play when he opened the first kindergarten in 1836 (for children under the age of 7) and believed that play was the principal means of learning in early childhood. For Froebel, play should be child-centred, sensory and open-ended, thus enabling children to construct their understanding of the world through direct experience with it. We have already discussed the strong links between play and creativity, but Froebel's legacy is seen in the free-flow open-plan design of many nurseries where children have a degree of choice in self-directed games and activities, both indoors and outdoors in the environment, and a strong commitment to integrating arts, science and humanities in the curriculum (Churchill Dower, 2020).

Maria Montessori's name is now known internationally from the schools that have adopted her approach and principles in the twentieth century and right up to the present day. These institutions provide an environment that supports children's natural curiosity and innate interest in the world in order to encourage development and prepare them for life beyond school. According to the Maria Montessori Institute, 'Montessori schools promote hands-on, self-paced, collaborative, joyful learning. Children in Montessori follow their interests, wherever that passion leads...' (2022). Other notable characteristics of these nurseries and pre-schools are the mixed age groups that enable peer-to-peer learning and communication, freedom for children to work at their own pace without (adult) interruption, choice and exploration so children find out for themselves, make mistakes and correct them independently. The latter phenomenon is a key aspect of creativity, as we have explored previously. There is a notable respect for each child as an individual personality with unique talents (Isaacs, 2018).

The influence of American philosopher, psychologist and educational reformer **John Dewey** can be seen throughout the early twentieth century, but his progressive ideas and child-centred approach came into conflict with traditionalists during his lifetime and have fallen out of favour with policymakers in the UK in recent decades. This is even more apparent in England currently with the move back towards a more traditional, prescriptive, curriculum-centred model. His philosophy of education (Dewey, 1938) highlighted the central importance of learning situated in lived experience rather than abstract thought, with the pupil as an active agent in the process of constructing their own learning (Eisner, 2002), rather than a passive recipient of knowledge (a 'tabula rasa' or 'blank slate').

This idea of experiential learning has been hugely influential in the subsequent models developed by the likes of Kolb (2015), but Dewey himself warned against discussing education in terms of 'isms', even 'progressivism' for which he is largely credited. Dewey realised that this merely set it up in opposition, as a reaction to 'traditionalism' and other 'isms' and so would be unknowingly controlled by them. Instead, Dewey advocated 'a comprehensive, constructive survey of actual needs, problems and possibilities' in order to create a new movement in education (1938, p.6).

We shall see how this cycle of action and re-action, played out in the post-war policy debates and educational milestones that have marked the last 70 years. In terms of social policy, West (2020) claims that early years legislation during the twentieth century saw a fundamental shift in emphasis from a focus on targeted Nursery Education for the poorest children to one of universal childhood education and care to support parents back into work. Not only have ideas about childhood changed during this time, but so have funding models and types of provision. Maintained nursery schools and classes have shown some degree of continuity, but with the additional layering of private-for-profit and not-for-profit institutions to fill gaps in provision. This complex picture has provided an increase in parental choice but, at the same time, has seen the state taking increasing control of publicly funded early childhood education (free entitlement and voucher schemes), creating a mixed economy that many smaller providers are struggling to turn into a sustainable business model (West, 2020). What are the potential barriers to creativity in this context? How can creative practitioners thrive within the system? In order to address these questions, we must first take the long view to understand the political principles and ideologies that have underpinned these key changes during the course of the twentieth century.

Post-war innovation and consensus

After the Great Depression of the 1930s and during the Second World War (1939–1945), the economist William Beveridge identified five 'Giant Evils' in society; these were 'want (poverty), disease, ignorance (lack of education), squalor (poor housing) and idleness' (unemployment). The Beveridge Report (1942) ultimately led to social reform in the era of post-war reconstruction and the establishment of *the welfare state*, most notably:

- A National Health Service (1948) – medical treatment for all (free at the point of delivery)
- 'Social security' benefits (National Insurance) and 'cradle to grave' protection
- Full employment
- Social housing

Perhaps most importantly, it also led to the 1944 Education Act and its central tenets of free primary and secondary education for all, equality of educational opportunity and the tripartite system of grammar, technical and secondary modern schools.

Undoubtedly, these changes transformed the life chances of many children, but grammar schools favoured middle-class pupils, few technical schools were built and streaming by ability with the eleven plus exam proved an unreliable measure of potential and disadvantaged certain groups (in particular girls and working-class pupils). Over time, the system proved increasingly unpopular and a non-selective comprehensive approach was seen as a more progressive, democratic and socially just way to organise secondary education (Power and Whitty, 2015). In 1972, the school leaving age was raised to 16 years and the 1970 Education (Handicapped Children) Act signified a more inclusive approach (see Chapter 9: SEND: Inclusion and creativity for an analysis of the changing language of difference and disability):

Local Education Authorities... responsible for severely handicapped children hitherto considered to be 'unsuitable for education at school'. Now for the first time in history all children without exception are within the scope of the educational system. (Margaret Thatcher, Secretary of State for Education, 1970-1974)

Despite these advances, the late 1960s and early 1970s were marked by a gradual breakdown in consensus amongst policymakers in education and the public more generally. This was characterised largely as a battle between 'traditional' and 'progressive' views, that is to say, knowledge and curriculum-centred versus child-centred approaches to learning (and parenting) (Tisdale, 2017).

On one side of the debate, the 1967 Plowden Report *Children and their Primary Schools* exemplified a progressive, child-centred philosophy (largely inspired by Dewey) and included important recommendations for Nursery Education (pp.291–343). 'Towards freedom of curriculum' (Ch. 16) highlighted the value of flexibility, discovery and the use of the environment – all of which have echoes of Froebel and Montessori as mentioned earlier. On the other side of the debate, a series of articles known as the 'Black Papers' was published (1969–1977) highly critical of these progressive methods as encouraged by Plowden. These papers typified 'New Right' thinking and focused on a perceived national decline in standards, both morally and economically. These fears were realised in the high-profile 'William Tyndale affair' (1975) – essentially a tabloid-media 'storm' that focused on William Tyndale Primary School in Islington, London. Articles in the press and news media preyed on parents' fears about poor behaviour, lack of discipline, chaotic leadership and too much informality in the classroom (no restrictions on movement and children addressing teachers by their first names). This fuelled the public perception that education was in crisis, whether this was true or not, and strengthened public mistrust of teachers, teaching methods and the amount of control teaching staff had over the curriculum (Bartlett and Burton, 2020).

Within the wider context of a global economic crisis, rapid inflation, rising unemployment, strike action, power cuts and shortages (known as the 'three-day-week') the UK Government realised it had to take action. In October 1976, with the Tyndale affair very much still in the news, Prime Minister James Callaghan made his keynote speech at Ruskin College, Oxford, raising doubts about what he described as, 'the new informal methods of teaching, which seem to produce excellent results when they are in well-qualified hands but are much more dubious when they are not' (Haigh, 2006). This echoed the concerns of some teachers themselves when confronted with new ideas emerging from the developmental psychology of Bowlby (1969) and Ainsworth (1969). These ideas challenged the authority of the adult and foregrounded the needs of the child and child-centred innovation, often to the detriment or even in conflict with the needs of the parent. In doing so, they placed very heavy demands on the patience, humour, energy, knowledge and skill of teachers forced to abandon behaviourist approaches to classroom management (punishments and rewards) that had, on the surface it seemed, served them so well in the past (Tisdale, 2017).

All these issues and concerns contributed to what is known as *The Great Debate* about education: What was its fundamental purpose? Was it a social good? Was it about personal development and the individual? or should it serve the economy, leading to wider growth and prosperity? This debate about what shape education should take going forward was taken up by Shirley Williams, Secretary of State for Education (1976–1979). Notably, the debate featured parental involvement for the first time and its legacy can be seen in the major reforms that took place in the following decade.

Reform and the first National Curriculum

In the 1980s, against a backdrop of industrial disputes with teaching unions, national political unrest and high unemployment, the Conservative Government under Prime Minister Margaret Thatcher (herself a former Minister for Education) made sweeping reforms and changed the educational landscape in a way that had not been seen since 1944. The Education Reform Act (1988) introduced the first standardised National Curriculum and signalled a reduction in the autonomy of teachers and a move towards more Government control over what was taught in the classroom (Ball, 2021). A key idea that underpinned these changes was the introduction of market forces, namely competition and choice, into the education system for the first time. These changes were influenced by the persuasive power of economists and business and driven by neoliberalism, an ideology (a world-view or set of beliefs) that was rapidly gaining momentum in the United States and other parts of the world. Neoliberalism is a little under-stood term and has manifested itself in different ways in different locations around the globe (Bockman, 2013), but it is key to understanding the fundamental changes that have taken place within the educational landscape over the last few decades, including early childhood education and care. Whilst left-wing thinkers such as Freire warned of the dangers and Chomsky branded neoliberalism the 'single greatest threat to democracy' (Sims, 2017), mainstream political thinking has accepted this ideology almost without question, driven as it is by the demands of capitalist free-market economics, individualism, consumer choice, privatisation, de-regulation and a significantly reduced role of the state and government interference in people's lives (Bockman, 2013). The irony here is that most neoliberal governments have increased the level of central control they have over policy areas in education, including teacher training, SEND and early years' provision.

Many of the neoliberal policy changes in education in the UK happened during the era of New Labour, under the leadership of Tony Blair. New Labour came to power in 1997 using the memorable mantra of 'education, education, education...' to describe Blair's three priorities for Government. Massive investment in early years' provision was combined with an increased role for the private sector. From the flagship policy of Sure Start in 1998 (tackling disadvantage) to the integrated multi-agency approach of new Children's Centres, from the reforming proposals within 'Every Child Matters' (2003) to the 2006 Childcare Act that enshrined the idea of childcare in the UK as a market. Whilst some see these changes as a policy failure, others see a natural shift in emphasis from targeted interventions to a more universal approach (Lewis, 2011). Under the banners of diversification, increased opportunity and parental choice new facilities were combined with the re-branding of certain institutions, including arts and music specialist schools and new academy trusts (no longer under democratically elected Local Authority control). This approach became known as the 'third way' (Giddens, 1998) – a curious and, on the surface, contradictory re-branding or 'renewal' of left-wing social democracy, combining social inclusion with privatisation and marketisation in the era of globalisation (Bockman, 2011) (see Table 7.1 for a more detailed analysis of different political ideologies and their impact on education).

All our futures - Re-asserting the value of culture and creativity

If creativity is viewed in its widest sense, then cultural education policy becomes just as relevant as social or educational policy. Whilst the 1980s were characterised by neglect and a gradual decline in state support, the late 1990s and early 2000s were notable for the substantial investment in arts and culture by the New Labour Government in the UK, with many capital projects planned to coincide with the millennium. These included new art galleries such as TATE Modern, museum extensions, national events and year-long celebrations of varying size and quality, from the local and impactful *Year of the Artist* (ACE, 2000) to the international and much more maligned *Millennium Dome* in London, now the O_2 Arena (Hewison, 2014).

Commentators have since criticised politicians and policymakers for the 'misuse' of arts and culture in an attempt to address wider social problems such as poverty, youth unemployment or anti-social behaviour (known as 'instrumentalism') (Holden, 2006), but it could equally be argued that the inspiration behind much of this investment was the work of academics, museum and gallery professionals, artists and individuals from the creative industries who came together before the turn of the millennium to discuss the value of culture and creativity in the country's schools. The National Advisory Council for Culture and Creativity in Education (NACCCE) chaired by Ken Robinson made a powerful case for cultural learning in its report *All Our Futures* stating '...creative development is intimately related to cultural development' (NACCCE, 1999). Early childhood specialists such as Ellyatt (2010, p.93) note that classrooms, 'by their very nature, express the values, preoccupations and fears found in the culture as a whole...' but the problem is that our continual focus on (curriculum) content rather than context may have 'profoundly eroded the essentially joyful nature of human learning and development' (2010, p.93) (see also Chapter 1 for a discussion of creativity and culture).

Learning through the arts and culture also came to be re-framed during this period as a way of opening up opportunities for children and young people whilst also boosting the country's economic output through the newly dubbed 'creative industries' (Hewison, 2014).

Whilst many of these initiatives fell victim to the change of administration in 2010 (to a Liberal Democrat-Conservative coalition), others have endured. For example, *Artsmark* turned 20 years old in 2021 and has involved 5,000 schools and 1.9 million children participating in the programme over that period (CLA, 2023). The *Early Years Artsmark Feasibility Study* (Sandbrook and Churchill Dower, 2018) aimed to help inform future policy for the provision of arts and culture in the early years. This consultation document identified that in early years' settings:

Table 7.1 Political ideologies and their impact on educational policy

Ideology	Conservatism/Neo-conservatism	Neoliberalism	Liberal-progressivism	Social-democratic	Socialism/Marxism
	'Right Wing'		'Centrist' (aka The 'Third Way')		'Left-Wing'
Characteristics	Tradition, order, control, hierarchy, elitism, meritocracy and family values	Capitalism, free-market economics, privatisation, individualism and reduced role of the state	Tolerance, mutual respect, diversity, multiculturalism and equality of opportunity	Income redistribution, positive action, state intervention and welfare support	Critique of capitalist society, collective action, dismantling of barriers and addressing injustice
Impact on Education	Knowledge-based curriculum, standards and behaviour, selective schooling, streaming by ability, and private/ fee-paying schools and nurseries	Standardised testing, competition, marketisation, league tables, diversification of provision, de-regulation and increased parental choice	Child-led curriculum, support for vulnerable groups e.g., children with SEND, EAL, neuro-diversity and gender diversity	Targeted interventions, 'allyship', free school meals, breakfast clubs, free childcare, after-school provision, and subsidised trips and residentials	Critical pedagogy, intersectionality, critical race theory: exposing structural inequalities, e.g., racism, sexism, homophobia, disablism, and poverty and social class

- Arts and culture are not a high priority for most settings, although creativity is important.
- Skills migrate due to high staff turnover in private/voluntary settings.
- Staff confidence in arts is often very low, especially in music and dance.
- The early years' sector often feels disconnected from the rest of the education landscape.
- Often settings need to discover the resources and experiences to which they already have access.

Sandbrook and Churchill Dower (2018, pp.5–7)

Recommendations from this report have influenced the direction of Arts Council England's new 10-Year Strategy *Let's Create* (2020) and include: the development of an online professional learning platform for early years' arts and cultural practice for staff and managers to learn and develop skills; to strengthen networking and awareness-raising with expert mentors sharing practice in settings; training for staff; and developing relationships with arts and cultural organisations and other EY settings in the form of local action learning networks.

Changing the discourse

Fast forward (or back) to 2012 which saw both the Olympics come to London (with an associated surge in funding and provision for cultural learning) and the publication of the independent *Henley Review of Cultural Education in England* (DCMS, 2012), commissioned by both the DfE and the DCMS (Department for Culture, Media and Sport). The author of this report, Darren Henley (now Chief Executive at Arts Council England) provided a 'clear checklist of experiences that all children should have at different stages of their development' (CLA, 2023) and proposed a 'Cultural Education Passport' which would record children and young people's cultural activities and most importantly, a *National Plan for Cultural Education* that reflected the breadth of the creative industries. Despite the recommendations in the Henley Review, the new National Curriculum in England published by the Coalition Government in 2013 omitted film, digital, or any recognition of drama and dance as subjects in their own right.

A critical discourse analysis (Denscombe, 2021, p.341) of the language used for the Primary Curriculum for Key Stages 1 and 2 reveals certain cultural assumptions and meanings, including as it does the new aim:

> to provide pupils with an introduction to the essential knowledge that they need to be educated citizens. [The National Curriculum] introduces pupils to the best that has been thought and said; and helps engender an appreciation of human creativity and achievement. (DfE, 2014, p.6)

The language used for the Music 'Purpose of Study' is even more revealing in terms of underlying ideology; 'As pupils progress, they should develop a critical engagement with music, allowing them to compose, and to listen with discrimination to the best in the musical canon'

(DfE, 2014, p.196) (see Table 7.1 for a discussion of political ideologies). Contrast this with the language used in earlier curriculum guidance for Primary teachers published in 2000:

> Music is a powerful, unique form of communication that can change the way pupils think and act. It brings together intellect and feeling and enables personal expression, reflection and emotional development. As an integral part of culture, past and present, it helps pupils understand themselves and relate to others, forging important links between the home, school and the wider world. (DfEE/QCA, 2000, p.14)

A different view of children's creativity starts to emerge here, one that is perhaps more inclusive and democratic in its outlook. This interpretation focuses in particular on children's active participation and links it with their culture and identity. The guidance goes on to say that the subject 'encourages active involvement in different forms of amateur music making, both individual and communal, developing a sense of group identity and togetherness. It also increases self-discipline and creativity, aesthetic sensitivity and fulfilment' (DfEE/QCA, 2000, p.122).

In contrast, the more recent curriculum guidance prioritises the 'essential knowledge' that a traditional curriculum should offer, but the question must be asked, who judges which knowledge is 'essential'? It could also be argued that the new guidance only encourages a passive appreciation of 'the best that has been thought and said' which to my mind implies a values-based judgement and perhaps a much more elitist view of creativity. Basford (2019a) asks the legitimate question: whose knowledge and whose values are we talking about? (see also Chapter 1 for more on 'Definitions of Creativity')

━━━━━━━━━━━ **Reflective questions** ━━━━━━━━━━━

- Which of these interpretations do you think we should prioritise in early childhood education?
- What knowledge is 'essential' in your opinion?
- Which set of skills and abilities will children really need to prepare them for the future?

Creative and cultural skills

Even if we view the purpose of education in purely economic terms (as many policymakers do) and think of the children in our care merely as the workers and employees who will form the society of tomorrow or 20 years' hence, then it is useful to consider which skills these children might need. In an ideal world, we can and should go beyond these rather narrow expectations and, in the words of Darren Henley 'create a generation of fully rounded individuals' (DCMS, 2012, p.41). Interestingly, a report from the Times Education Commission (2022) uses this economic 'lens' to review the situation in schools, but nevertheless promotes a more holistic view to tackle the perceived issues facing the country:

> The commission has highlighted the importance of taking a serious, long-term approach to education, from the early years, through school, to further and higher education and lifelong learning, to better prepare young people for the challenges they face. The changing world of work, stalled social mobility, the growing mental health crisis and new technology means that reform is more important than ever to capitalise on all the country's talent. (Times Education Commission, 2022)

Looking deeper from this perspective, a separate 2022 *Future Skills for Innovation* report revealed research on what UK employers want their employees to have to remain globally competitive over the next 10–20 years. Not surprisingly, these include problem-solving, communication and creativity (Kingston University, 2022). Interviews with businesses and universities highlighted over 20 skills that they felt were important in protecting the UK's global competitiveness. These were put to the YouGov Business panel of over 2,000 senior decision-makers from a representative sample of firms in the UK who selected the top 10 as follows:

- Problem-solving – 60%
- Critical thinking – 55%
- Communication skills – 54%
- Digital skills – 51%
- Analytical skills – 48%
- Adaptability – 46%
- Resilience – 45%
- Creativity – 44%
- Ability to build relationships – 44%
- Initiative – 43%

It is easy to see the disconnect between these skills and those that are prioritised within formal education frameworks that teaching professionals are expected to deliver, right from the early years' foundation stage. Indeed, Kenneth Baker, former Secretary of State for Education under Margaret Thatcher, who oversaw the introduction of the very first standardised National Curriculum back in 1988, has criticised the lack of vocational pathways available to young people and the undermining of technical knowledge and design skills in favour of an increasingly narrow range of academic subjects (Baker, 2022).

This disconnect strengthens the argument for creativity within the curriculum at every key stage. We can, without much difficulty, cross-reference the research about future skills with the

perceived benefits of a creative, arts-based education as highlighted by many prominent edu-
cationalists, including Elliot Eisner. Eisner (2002), draws our attention to the particular benefits
of arts-based teaching and learning, including competencies such as; attention to relationships,
flexible purposing (adaptability), using materials as a medium, shaping form to create expressive
content, the exercise of imagination, learning to frame the world from an aesthetic perspective
and the ability to transform qualities of experience into speech and text (Eisner, 2002,
pp.75–92). Table 7.2 lays out these competencies and compares them with the findings of the
Future Skills Report (2022):

Table 7.2   Comparison of arts-based competencies and future skills

'What the arts teach and how it shows' (Eisner, 2002)	*Future Skills* Report (2022)
• Attention to Relationships	• Ability to build relationships
• Flexible Purposing	• Adaptability
	• Problem-solving
	• Resilience
• Using Materials as a Medium	• Digital skills
• Shaping Form to Create Expressive Content	• Initiative
• The Exercise of Imagination	• Creativity
• Learning to Frame the World from an Aesthetic Perspective	• Critical thinking
	• Analytical skills
• The Ability to Transform Qualities of Experience into Speech and Text	• Communication

It could be argued that the 'materials as a medium' of the twenty-first century are indeed
within the digital realm, with software, programming and online social media skills becoming
increasingly essential for employability. These, combined with a 'questioning mindset' and
'critical thinking' (that come from an 'aesthetic perspective' or arts-based education) are the
skills that children and young people will need to navigate their way through the forthcoming
decades of unpredictability and rapid social and technological change, so they know 'how to
live critically in and across new learning spaces' (Savin-Baden, 2021).

What next?

Looking ahead to the next 10 years and beyond, De Montfort University's ground-breaking
longitudinal research study Talent 25 is working closely with young families and diverse
communities in Leicester. Launched with Arts Council England in 2020 the project will
stretch over 25 years and began with workshops exploring music, stories, messy play,
movement and other creative activities for babies aged one and under. Initial findings from
interviews with participants reveal some key benefits: 'The parents... recognised and highlighted the potential of creative activities to enhance the acquisition of a number of skills for
their babies, including the following skills: curiosity, confidence, creativity, and imagination'
(Ochieng et al., 2020).

The Cultural Learning Alliance's Briefing Paper (2022) 'Early Years and The Arts: Why an arts-rich early years' matters' makes reference to this ground-breaking project, and it is my sincere hope that this research will feed into the new Ofsted early years' Strategy 2022–2027 *The best start in life*. Ofsted's stated aims are to:

- Develop the evidence base around the early years' learning and development curriculum through our research and insights programme
- Develop specialist training on early years' education for our workforce to enhance their understanding of what high-quality early education looks like
- Raise awareness and promote a better understanding of education and care in children's early years

(Ofsted, 2022)

Ofsted has launched an accompanying Early Years blog *Giving Children the best start in life* announcing that they are doing so at a time when they claim to have 'placed early years' education at the heart of their new 5-year strategy'. It claims that this new blog aims to shine a spotlight on the early years and give it the attention that it deserves. Amanda Spielman, Ofsted's Chief Inspector spoke at the Nursery World Business Summit 2022 and summed up the situation in the early years' sector, admitting; 'It's absolutely fair to say that early years doesn't get the attention you'd expect given the size of the sector and the importance of your work' (Ofsted, 2022). Ofsted's strategy goes on to state 'Although many children do well in the early years, over a quarter are not where they should be in their learning and development by the age of 5, a situation that has been exacerbated by the COVID-19 pandemic' (Ofsted, 2022).

Reflective questions

The above statement by Ofsted begs several questions about children's learning and development:

- Where *should* they be...?
- Should we even be focusing on developmental stages?
- What about their health and well-being or social and emotional state?
- How about a recovery curriculum with a different set of priorities other than literacy, numeracy and 'school readiness'?
- What is the most important thing we can do for families and children after the collective trauma of the global pandemic and a cost-of-living crisis?

Finding your voice

There is growing concern amongst early years' practitioners and academics alike about the tension between the values of those working in the sector and the expectation that government requirements will be addressed without question. Gibbs and Gasper in their book *Challenging the*

Intersection of Policy with Pedagogy (2019) talk about the struggle to balance compliance requirements with innovation and professional practice. Sims (2017) goes further and argues that the growing push for the professionalisation of early childhood creates demands for discretionary decision-making that is in tension with the top-down compliance that has become a hallmark of neoliberalism. How can graduate practitioners use their skills to interpret policy and their newly acquired status to inform and influence practice (Basford, 2019b)? If and when should they question policy decisions? Can they provide an alternative narrative to the dominant discourse? Where is the voice of the early childhood education and care sector?

Developing a personal philosophy and values

Whilst we might subscribe to certain ideologies (political, religious or other), they do not always provide a coherent set of beliefs or frameworks as we have seen, and the ways in which they are interpreted are subjective and inconsistent (Robertson and Hill, 2014). Perhaps a more useful approach as we develop our priorities and refine our practice as professionals is to consider our own personal philosophy and values with regard to how educational policy is enacted on the ground, by looking critically at its impact on pedagogy, creativity and children themselves. Walker et al. highlight the importance of 'day-to-day interactions between professionals in the setting and what children and families actually experience as a result of a policy decision' (2017, p.68), in that sense staff are the very real face of policy and practice. What a child or parent experiences may be guided by government regulations or curriculum design, but it will also be about positive interactions, the 'warmth, kindness, concern for others, professional behaviour and the quality of planned learning opportunities, which include teaching and learning' (Walker et al., 2017, p.68). These are the elements of policy which a child can actually 'see' and have a direct impact on their well-being and development.

In order to look critically at policy and practice it is worthwhile using different viewpoints to assess the potential impact. Carey-Jenkins (2015) advises using six perspectives to assist in this process;

1   **The child's perspective:** does the policy support an entitlement to a quality education? what will be the child's experience? how does it meet their needs?
2   **The political perspective:** what will be the wider impact on society? Is the policy sustainable? How will it be regulated and inspected?
3   **The parent/carer perspective:** how will the policy be viewed through the eyes of a parent/carer? Are everyone's voices being heard?
4   **The international perspective:** examine wider views and approaches which may accept or challenge a particular policy
5   **The learning perspective:** is the policy rooted in a process based on research or theory? Does it have educational integrity?
6   **The moral perspective:** what are the underlying values of a policy? How do they relate to your educational beliefs and core values?

(Carey-Jenkins, 2015, pp.193–205)

These perspectives are a useful starting point; however, one potential critique of the 'moral perspective' is that some would ask if there are 'classed assumptions' within early years' settings? Is there a danger that practitioners might imply that all children should share the same behaviours and values? Is the function of education in society simply to produce individuals with 'appropriate values' (by implication 'middle-class values')? (Stirrup et al., 2017).

■■■■■■■■ Case study - Creative policy-making ■■■■■■■■

Siobhan is a third-year undergraduate student studying early childhood education and care at University. She is feeling nervous but is looking forward to making a 10-minute presentation in front of her class after several weeks of research and preparation. Her proposal is for a new policy on a creative curriculum for the early years. She believes passionately in the value of child-led learning and whilst on placement Siobhan has observed that some children struggle with the transition to mainstream school; her ideas include providing more continuity in terms of creative teaching and learning approaches from pre-school to Reception and beyond. The rest of the students in the cohort listen attentively and offer feedback and constructive criticism in the discussion afterwards when she has finished.

■■■■■■■■ Reflective questions ■■■■■■■■

- What might be the benefit of generating new policy ideas and receiving feedback from your peers?
- What proposals do you have for improving early childhood education policy and practice?
- Have you considered your own philosophy or set of core values? Try to articulate them and write down some keywords.

Students and practitioners may feel that changing the education system from within, no matter where they find themselves working, is beyond their sphere of influence. However, the final chapter in this book explores the role of the early years' practitioner as an 'agent of change' (see Chapter 14: Conclusions and next steps), and the late Ken Robinson has some clear advice on this matter:

> Education is a human system that is dynamic and changing. As teachers **you are the system**... there is much more room for innovation within the system than most people realise. (Ken Robinson, 2021)

Conclusion

The value placed on creativity within the early years' curriculum is constantly changing and its status should never be taken for granted. In order to navigate a way through the changing tides of policy, politics and ideology, as an early years' practitioner it is essential to have a good knowledge of the history of early childhood education and to understand the current debates. Early childhood practitioners need to develop a values-based practice and have the confidence to evaluate and critique the current policy context that they are working in. Practitioners should consider ways in which they can change the system, with the understanding that they have a voice because *they are the system...*

Further reading and resources

Ofsted (n.d.) *Ofsted strategy 2022–27, GOV.UK.* Available at: https://www.gov.uk/government/publications/ofsted-strategy-2022-to-2027/ofsted-strategy-2022-27

'Imagine if' Festival: Continuing Sir Ken Robinson's Legacy of Creativity and Innovation. Available at: https://www.sirkenrobinson.com/imagine-if/

Centre for Research in Early Childhood https://www.crec.co.uk/

Cultural Learning Alliance (CLA) champions a right to art and culture for every child https://www.culturallearningalliance.org.uk/

Talent 25: De Montfort University's longitudinal research study in Leicester https://talent25.org.uk/

8
GLOBAL PERSPECTIVES ON CREATIVITY

Janet Harvell

Creative individuals have developed a capacity to take risks, to tolerate ambiguity, possess openness to experience and a freshness of perception. (Frank Lilly and Gillian Bramwell-Rejskind, 2004)

▬▬▬ Chapter overview ▬▬▬

This chapter will encourage you to question your current understanding of creativity from a global perspective, understand how different socio-cultural factors inform a country's response to developing a creative pedagogical approach and apply different perspectives when reflecting on the challenges faced when developing a curriculum that promotes creativity and critical thinking. This chapter will also introduce you to some of the issues faced by international communities when developing their current curricula and pedagogical approaches to promote a more child-/ student-centred approach, which values creativity and critical thinking.

Introduction

Promoting creativity within children's learning and development is now widely accepted as a critical key twenty-first century skill (Kupers et al., 2019). In addition, further benefits identified by research into social and emotional learning following coronavirus disease 2019 (COVID-19) have shown that '… creativity can be beneficial for mental health and can [also] help build critical skills such as empathy and introspection' (The Teaching Factor, 2021). When exploring this at a global level, taking into account different socio-cultural contexts, it is key that there is a shared understanding of what is understood by the term 'creativity'. Not least when considering how to include this within existing/new curriculum initiatives.

As discussed in earlier chapters, creativity has often been linked to the creative arts and artistic expression, with Lilly's (2014) summary recognising the more generic definition that it is:

> ... something unique or novel that [has] external value, the result of purposeful [behaviour], and a result of sustained duration'. Although, for this chapter, the author prefers Lilly's own definition of creativity as having a '... sense of curiosity and wonder, inventiveness, flexibility, exploratory behaviour, imagination, and originality. (Lilly, 2014)

When exploring global engagement, the differing education systems do not always leave room for creativity. The subjects deemed most important to teach are the result of current national and state curriculum aims (Lilly, 2014), with a focus on testing and skills being blamed for diminished opportunities for children to engage in activities that support the development of their creative thinking (Kupers et al., 2019). Nevertheless, globalisation has had a role in opening up the world to different perspectives, and the role of play and child engagement in appropriate activities has long been recognised as critical to the support of early creativity; with early theories such as Vygotsky's belief that the origins of children's creative imagination are embedded in their play (Penfold, 2019). This has led to the role of creativity being included as an important agenda item in a range of international public policies (UNESCO, 2023a). The historical background to these policy changes and initiatives that have informed these will be explored in the following section of the chapter, with specific reference to the Chinese perspective.

Global strategies/initiatives

The United Nations Convention on the Rights of the Child (UNCRC, 1989) was one of the first global policies to identify the right of a child to 'play and artistic opportunities'. Specifically, Article 31.1 (UN, 1989) which recognises '... the right of the child ... to engage in play and recreational activities appropriate to the age of the child and to participate freely in cultural life and the arts'. Whilst Article 31.2 provides further detail citing the need for '... the provision of appropriate and equal opportunities for cultural, artistic, recreational and leisure activity'.

This was the beginning of a series of international strategies which began with the facilitation of a global commitment to providing quality education for all and has resulted in the current attention on the value of promoting creativity and critical thinking. Initially, *Education for All* (EFA) launched in 1990, primarily focused on widening school attendance, particularly linked around equality and gender and the more traditional education targets such as access to a basic education (UNESCO, 2023b). This initiative was followed by the *Millennium Development Goals* (MDGs) (UN, 2015) in September 2000, with world leaders committing to addressing poverty, hunger, disease, illiteracy, environmental degradation and discrimination against women. The MDGs were followed by the *Sustainable Development Goals* (SDGs) (UN, 2022a) in 2015, which widened the scope, building upon the sustainability movement. The key aims are focused on promoting prosperity and protecting the planet and, in addition, to a continued commitment to reducing poverty, hunger and health, and improving well-being, quality education and gender issues. This initiative recognises that these aims go hand-in-hand with societal reforms that address increased job opportunities, climate change and environmental issues.

Unfortunately, the global pandemic of COVID-19 has had a detrimental impact on the progress that has been made, with data suggesting that, '… 147 million children missed more than half of their in-class instruction over the past two years [and that] this generation of children could lose a combined total of $17 trillion in lifetime earnings in present value' (UN, 2022c). Although a creative curriculum was not specifically identified in the SDGs, goal number 9 'Industry, Innovation and Infrastructure', subsection 9B specifically addresses 'Support[ing] domestic technology development, research and innovation in developing countries'. Within this context, 'innovation' focuses on the development of new ways of working, seeking '… to build resilient infrastructure, promote sustainable industrialisation and foster innovation', recognising that more diverse countries are better able to recover faster (UN, 2022a). This highlights the benefits to a population of being able to be innovative and think creatively.

Reflecting this, the *Programme for International Student Assessment* (PISA) has recognised the significance of assessing creativity as a key subject area that promotes a '… way of thinking that leads to the generation of valuable and original ideas' (OECD, 2022). PISA was originally introduced in 1997 as a global method of comparing 15-year-old children's attainment in reading, mathematics and science, every three years. Sjøberg suggests that this has had severe consequences in exam-centric regimes wherein creativity, innovation and entrepreneurship in schooling disappear (cited in Mullen, 2017b). Subsequently, the *Creative Thinking Framework* has been introduced in order to include it within the assessment cycle. Originally approved in 2019, the final version was delayed until 2022 as a result of COVID-19. Of note is the change in assessment methods that have traditionally focused on a written response or the use of multi-choice questions. Creativity is challenging to measure and to better reflect this, students will be asked to produce a visual artefact with open-ended questions, although opportunities to assess the success of this will be delayed until the first set of results which are due to be released in 2024 (OECD, 2022). This addition to the PISA curriculum areas is the result of the growing importance being placed on creativity and critical thinking within a global focus, and governments recognising the criticality of building a creative workforce if their countries are to be/continue to be leaders and successful in the future. Where the key focus had previously focused on STEM subjects of science, technology, engineering and maths, the speed of change and advances has seen the international community appreciate the crucial role that 'creativity' will play, and is playing, in the continued progress and success of their economies (see also Chapter 11: Children as researchers).

Unfortunately, as touched on earlier, the past decades have seen the education system focusing significantly on a narrow range of curriculum subjects: literacy and mathematics in primary education, and STEM subjects in secondary education. This has been to the detriment of creativity/critical thinking with accountability and the assessment process reducing the learning environments to one that is unconducive to creativity. For example, consider the current curricula followed by settings in England, the Early Years Foundation Stage (EYFS) (DfE, 2023b) and the National Curriculum (DfE, 2014b). The EYFS curriculum identifies three prime, and four specific areas of learning with creativity only being mentioned in the specific detail of the area of learning 'expressive arts and design'. Here the only reference to creativity is the expectation that children have opportunities to experiment, share creations and be imaginative (DfE, 2023b, p.15). Interestingly, previous iterations of the early years curriculum had a specific area of learning for Creative Development; with clear guidance on what this meant for practitioners:

> Creativity is about taking risks and making connections and is strongly linked to play ... [it] emerges as children become absorbed in action and explorations of their own ideas ... [it] involves children in initiating their own learning and making choices and decisions ... Being creative enables babies and children to explore many processes, media and materials and to make new things emerge as a result. (DCSF, 2008, p.105)

▬▬▬ Reflective questions ▬▬▬

- How effective do you consider the curriculum followed in your setting is in promoting the development of creative, inquisitive, critical thinking children?

International education programmes

In order to bring such radical changes to existing programmes there is a need to bring about a wider change in perception around creativity in order to gain universal acceptance for such key changes. Not least the value that parents and carers (and teachers) place on developing this aspect of the curriculum. In many countries, parents/carers may challenge such changes, particularly when reflecting on their own cultures and societies.

Nevertheless, the key role of 'creativity' within the global context has been recognised by many countries seeking to reflect this within their educational programmes. One initiative run by The Lego Foundation (2020) supported a number of countries (the state of Victoria in Australia, Japan, Thailand, Scotland and Wales), to develop their educational programme, founded on the premise that learning through play is key when supporting creativity. Common findings highlighted the importance of supporting their professionals in having an agreed understanding of what is meant by creativity and the necessity for a clearly articulated curriculum that staff would be able to follow and implement. When Japan revised its curriculum in 2006, creativity was identified as one of the four goals to be enshrined in the *Basic Act of Education*, justifying this by stating that the country '... will face a lot of challenges such as the depletion of resources and destruction of the environment, and will need creative ways to address these issues' (The Lego Foundation, 2020, p.8).

As referred to earlier, some of the challenges faced in implementing a more creative curriculum can arise from parental concern about the value of such practices, and the impact of these on their child's/children's future success, achievement and progress. This is particularly sensitive where neoliberal policies are in practice and settings must sustain parental confidence to maintain a viable business (see also Chapter 7: Policy context). The following discussion will explore the challenges and successes of developing a creative pedagogical approach in China.

China
Historical perspective

In this section, there is an opportunity to reflect on the role of creativity and critical thinking within the Chinese context. Consequently, it would be helpful at this point to gain an understanding of the historic philosophies that have informed existing educational practices, supporting an understanding of some of the fundamental differences between Asian and Western approaches. Originally founded on Soviet models, and often run by factories and revolutionary committees, pedagogical approaches were informed by Confucianism and Pavlov's behaviourism, with an 'emphasis on conditioning children's behaviour' (Tobin et al., 1989). Confucianism is based on living in harmony with others, incorporating the key aspects of co-operation and respect for elders and authority which still underpins current practices, together with an emphasis on academic achievement (Harvell, 2013).

The development of globalisation and China's engagement with the international community introduced Western approaches to the Chinese people and government who were committed to developing a modernised society. Recognition of the importance of education, and the early years, saw the Ministry of Education release the *Standards for Kindergarten Education* (MoE, 1996), followed by the introduction of nine years of free, compulsory education as a result of education reforms which focused on the acceleration of education provision (MOE, 2010), influenced by the UNCRC, EFA and MDG initiatives. This included a commitment to developing an appropriate early years' provision (MOE, 2001, cited in Harvell, 2013), not least informed by the human capital theory which recognises that economic prosperity is dependent upon effective national education policies (Olaniyan and Okemakinde, 2008).

With the end of Mao Zedong's Cultural Revolution in 1976, China was also grappling with the challenge of a population that was approaching one billion, the potential economic consequences of which presaged the controversial one-child policy introduced by Deng Xiaoping in 1979 (Chen, 1985). Apart from its success in reducing the population, there were a number of unexpected consequences that emerged. With the traditional family make up of extended families living together, 'only' children grew up in an environment that saw both parents and two sets of grandparents focus all their aspirations on their only child/grandchild. The emergence of these 'Little Emperors', also referred to as the '4-2-1' generation highlighted the fact that with **four** grandparents and **two** parents all focusing their hopes on the fortunes of **one** child, leading to spoilt and over-indulged children (Harvell and Ren, 2019, p.74). The consequences of this appeared when the first generations of children born under the 'one-child' policy entered the workforce. This suggests some interesting issues have arisen where some 'employers may discriminate against only children as a result of reduced social skills, poor teamwork and risk-adverse attitudes' (Harvell and Ren 2019, p.74).

Ultimately, despite realising the goals of population control, this controversial policy has had wider ramifications. As with many Western countries, one of the key issues that is troubling the current government is that of China's rapidly ageing society and predictions that by 2050 one-third of the population will be aged 60 plus years (Campbell, 2019). In an attempt to rectify this, the one-child policy was relaxed to a two-child policy in 2015, and then extended to three in 2021. Despite this, Chinese families are reluctant to take advantage of these changes not least due to the new middle-class expectations and prohibitive costs of bringing up children (Attané, 2022). The adoption of neoliberal practices has seen the marketisation of childcare provision and a move towards private care, with significant cost implications for parents when choosing provision.

Confucianism informs the aspirations of parents and grandparents, focused on the importance of education and social mobility in such a vast country that has such disparity of economic well-being, and ensuring their children have all possible opportunities to become successful adults. A creative curriculum could be seen as a paradox when considering the Confucian ideology that underpins Chinese culture which does not promote individuality, with Lockette (2012) noting that '... Confucian philosophy [ ] does not allow secondary students to act divergently or question any authority'. This can bring challenges when attempting to change practices and so, for creativity to be accepted and embedded within the education system, this would also suggest the need for cultural change. Consequently, parents have high expectations of providers in providing care and education, and immense pressure is placed on children to pass the entry examinations that will see them successful in getting into the school of their choice. There are nine years of compulsory education, comprising six years of primary school and three years of lower secondary school; with a further three years of senior secondary school also available dependent upon ability (Harvell, 2013; Nord Anglia n.d.). In addition, in order to progress to university students must achieve a certain standard of written and spoken English (the second official language), which places further pressures on students and parents.

Consequently, children's achievement is high on the agenda for parents when choosing their childcare provision, from early years through to high school. With globalisation, the emerging middle-classes have become exposed to Western approaches, although some are concerned at the 'chaos' observed in Western preschools, they look to see many of these practices emulated within their chosen provider. Nevertheless, in the early years, the focus on learning through play can form tensions when settings try to deliver this, whilst also being expected to ensure a successful transition through entry examinations to the school of their choice (Harvell and Ren, 2019). From personal experience gained over four years of researching early years' provision in China, most settings recognised the value of play but were also managing parent expectations, with many examples of observed practice tending to show staff providing highly directed activities with limited resources to support freely chosen play opportunities. One teacher stated, 'Some grandmothers will tell me – will you let my child learn more English, more knowledge, 1,2,3,4 [numbers], or they will [tell the] mother not to choose our kindergarten' because of the lack of teaching. Following Confucianism grandparents play a strong role within the family. This has resulted in significant pressure on both the settings and the children, with children taking part in a range of extra-curricular activities, at substantial cost to parents, to provide them with additional tuition and skills to facilitate progress within their educational journey. These are mainly linked to speaking English, music, arts, crafts and sports; many parents take on additional jobs to fund these. The news channel CNBC (Ye, 2021) interviewed one parent who described that the additional tuition attended by her children was in order to help them compete for 'very limited' high-quality education available in China. Her older child spends three hours daily attending an online group class, supplemented by one-to-two hours of personal tuition; whilst her younger child, who has just completed the first year of elementary schooling, attends a daily online group session for 30 minutes a day (Ye, 2021).

Parental expectations that their children should be given homework are reinforced by a discussion with a staff member who spoke about '... the amount of pressure on the children to achieve [being] enormous, if a good mark was not gained, the choice of next provision would be limited' (Harvell, 2013). This provides some context to the challenges of providing a creative and stimulating environment which parents want for their children, whilst at the same time wanting their children to pass the range of examinations within such a test-centric culture, that begin with examinations for entry to school, university and eventually jobs of their choice. As one teenager explains, 'They put so much love on us that love becomes a reason to do everything .... One of the things that happens when you're an only child, the thing that happens in China is that everything is focused on your grades, every aspect of expectation is focused on your grades. If you don't have good grades, you aren't a good child' (Bennett, 2011). Likewise, Kirkpatrick and Zang (2011, p.33 cited in Mullen, 2017b) reflect on education in China '... as nothing more than merely passing examinations'. It may not be a surprise that China accounts for 25% of worldwide suicides, and it is the fifth highest cause of death in the country (World Population Review, 2023).

Reflective questions

- How does the socio-cultural environment impact on the settings in your area?
- How much influence do parents and carers have in the running of your setting?
- How would you address their concerns?

China's challenges and changes

The Chinese government is aware of these issues and since 2001 has recognised creativity as an important component of education policy, where innovation is seen as synonymous with creativity, with a revised draft copy of *The National Guidelines for Medium and Long-Term Educational Reform and Development, 2010–2020* being released in 2010 (Mullen, 2017b); a key document on how China intends to transition from the current labour-intensive market to an economy based on creativity and innovation. Interestingly, the document recognises the negative impact of testing on students as a result of '… letting the result of one round of exams decide the destiny of a student's life' (Gu, 2010, p.301). Debroy (2018) explains how the Chinese are keen to integrate '…elements like innovation, flexibility and creative thinking into the curriculum … [through a range of strategies, such as] … problem-based learning'.

Nevertheless, Gu (2010, p.37) suggests that in order for this to be successful, China faces a number of challenges including 'antiquated educational ideas, outdated contents and methods, weak adaptability of school leavers, and a shortage of trained personnel who are innovative, practical or possessing multiple qualifications or skills'. Challenges related to class sizes are also problematic when supporting a creative approach. These can vary drastically between 50 and 100 students in formal education, and this can be further exacerbated in rural areas where provision is basic, uptake limited and the quality of teaching problematic, with many still following a passive and rote-style of teaching (Chang et al., 2017). Equality of access to quality provision is also challenging, with well-qualified staff tending to work in urban areas and where, from personal experience, many nursery settings had 200–1000 children on roll. Teachers can be reluctant to facilitate a creative environment and are prone to regarding the resulting '…nonconformity as rebellious and expressive behaviour as arrogant' (Lockette, 2012). Unsurprisingly, he reflects on the ongoing dominance of the Chinese examination system, which focuses on getting the right answer in order to progress onto the next stage, and that '… open-ended answers are challenging for a population that has always sought the correct answer … [where] rote memorisation and recitation [are] the standard teaching methods'. As a result, there are limited prospects for students to participate in creative activities or experience an open-ended curriculum. Instead, an expertise at rote learning and tests has developed to the detriment of a creative learning environment, with 'Chinese graduates [emerging] with a strong memory, math, and science skills but impoverished creative capacities' (Mullen, 2017a).

Conversely, Hong Kong, a Special Administrative Region of China, has had more positive experiences in developing a creative approach. This could be seen as evidence of the impact that the socio-cultural environment can have, when considering that Hong Kong was a British colony between 1841 and 1997 before returning to Chinese rule, but those years were strongly influenced by Western approaches and ideologies, in partnership with Confucian philosophy.

Within the early years, although there is no specific curriculum, there are guidelines which teachers are expected to refer to when planning. The current early years' guidelines are intended to promote the holistic development of young children, '… including physical well-being, cognitive growth, moral strength, and aesthetic sensibility' (MOE, 2012, p.3). In particular the encouragement of children's confident engagement with learning, resulting in children who are, 'curious, taking initiative, focusing attention, being willing to try, persisting, exploring, imagining and creating' (MOE, 2012, p.4). The guidance recognises five focus areas: Health, Language and Early Literacy, Social Development, Sciences and Arts.

Focusing on the Arts, this is subdivided into 'Perception and Appreciation' and 'Expression and Creation', with Benchmark 2 including 'creativity' in its title: 'Possess Beginning Artistic Expression and Creativity' (MoE, 2012, p.49). From personal experience, many of the settings visited were keen to include some aspects of Western ideology, with Gardner's Multiple Intelligences' (1999), Montessori's and Reggio's approaches being popular choices among parents. Often this was expressed in the format of a separate session focused on the approach that is favoured by the setting, but the daily routine was also constrained by external regulations which placed expectations on sleep provision (2 hours per day) and guided outdoor activities taking up a further 2 hours, leaving limited time to cover curriculum activities and more play-based opportunities. Creative activities tended to be organised to achieve specific outcomes and support staff in assessing children's development, rather than encouraging/promoting innovation. In one setting, creativity was promoted in the form of a visiting artist, similar to the Reggio Approach, who supported children in the making of clay models. Children followed the artist's demonstration and developed their own replica items, which they worked on during subsequent sessions. This provided an opportunity for children to engage in aesthetic appreciation, but limited individuality. In secondary schools visited, art was highly prized and there were well-equipped pottery rooms with some exquisite items being made by students, linking back to China's historic excellence in working with ceramics. From personal observation, creativity was seen more as an artistic expression with the rest of the curriculum being tightly managed and regulated; the result of parental expectations and testing that has been discussed earlier.

The following Case Study is compiled from a series of personal observations following 25 visits to 15 different kindergartens, including government and private provision, with the numbers on roll varying from 130 to 1,000 children (Harvell, 2013). As English is the official second language of China, with students needing a certain level of English skills in order to enrol on higher level courses, all settings provided English classes of varying quality. A further two hours of outdoor play and two hours of sleep for all children (during which staff plan activities, write up records and update learning diaries) leave a limited amount of time for a more creative curriculum. Although, as the Case Study shows, there are opportunities for additional activities such as music and roller-skating.

Case study – The Chinese Kindergarten experience

Chun 春, whose name means 'spring' in Chinese, is four years old, and an only child who lives with her mother and grandmother on the 10th story of a large block of flats in a busy urban area. Her mother works from 08.00 to 18.00, six days a week, in a local factory which makes plastic cutlery.

(Continued)

(Continued)

Her father has gone to earn a better salary in Beijing, the capital of China, and comes home once a year during the Chinese New Year to spend time with the family. Chun misses him a lot but is able to talk to him and see him during regular telephone calls. Chun attends a large kindergarten which is a short walk from her home, and she can see the building when she looks out of her bedroom window.

The kindergarten, called No. 66, has 600 children on roll and is located in a former high-rise office building. Chun's grandmother walks her to kindergarten for an **8.00** start and then waits with the other grandparents/parents until the children line up and walk to their classroom. As she walks, Chun likes to look at all the pictures on the walls that have been made by different children, this is also where lesson plans can be found for grandparents/parents to understand what the children will be doing throughout the day. There are 50 children in Chun's class, with one early years' teacher, one assistant and another staff member who supports the children and staff. There is no heating in the building and so in the winter months, when temperatures are well below freezing, Chun will wear lots of layers of clothing and keep her coat on during the day. Her grandmother makes sure she has a clean set of 'sleeves' which are pulled over the sleeves of her coat to keep this clean during play and mealtimes.

For the first hour, Chun has her breakfast and plays with toys before her first lesson at 9.00. This is English language and Chun practises saying familiar English phrases such as 'Good morning ... my name is ...I like to play ...', as well as being shown different picture cards which she identifies in Chinese and then tries to remember the English word. This is followed by Circle Time at 9.30 when the teacher encourages the children to take turns talking about anything that interests them. At 9.50, Chun then has a Chinese class which includes picture cards and repeating words; she particularly enjoys singing Chinese rhymes with her friends. On Fridays, they have Music Class instead and practise playing with a range of instruments as they learn the words to classic Chinese songs. Chun is ready for her snack at 10.20 when they all sit down for water and fruit, before going to play outside. There is no green play area, but the roof of the building is a large playground where they take part in organised physical play activities. During this time, the assistant is getting the classroom ready for lunch at 11.20 when the children return to their classrooms before lining up in small groups to collect their food, and bottles of water, which they then take back to their tables to finish. Afterwards, Chun goes to the toilet and brushes her teeth before returning to the classroom where she helps the other children to move the tables and chairs to the side of the room, before pulling out their sleeping mats where they all go for a sleep at 12.30. Everyone has to be quiet during sleep time and sometimes Chun goes to sleep straight away, but other times when she is not so sleepy, she fidgets and daydreams until it is time to get up at 14.30. She is ready for a snack before going up to the roof for free play until 15.30. On returning to the classroom, Chun likes being able to play with the toys, although on Tuesdays there is a roller-skating session in the main hall which she really enjoys; and on Fridays, they go to the library instead where they are read a story and are able to choose a book to take home. After this, it is time to clear up the classroom ready for the next day and then they have dinner before going home. During the last hour of the day, some children will attend extra-curricular activities, but Chun's grandmother makes sure she is collected before the kindergarten closes at 18.00. When she gets home, she has a wash and gets ready for bed, looking forward to seeing her mother before she goes to sleep.

━━━━━ **Reflective questions** ━━━━━

- How challenging would it be to promote a learning environment to support children's creativity, within these time management restrictions?
- What ideas do you have for engaging such large numbers of children creatively?
- How would you address the issue of a lack of 'green space' for the children?

'Lightening the burden'

In an attempt to redress the balance of home life, the authorities advised limiting the amount of time spent on homework. 'Jiǎn fù', abbreviated from 'jiǎnqīng fùdān', is a word that has entered popular discourse and translates as 'lightening the burden' in consideration of children's homework (Pasden, 2021). Although Pasden is more sceptical when considering the motives, suggesting that it could be related to the cost of childcare in China which is seen as a key factor in persistently low birth rates (mentioned earlier), particularly the extra-curricular activities that children engage in to increase their chances of success when sitting national examinations. During my research in China, it was common for parents to have two to three jobs in order to afford additional tuition and provide the best educational foundations for their children. At the same time, the government released a 'double reduction' policy which began to limit the amount of extracurricular tuition in maths, Chinese and English, that could be offered, resulting in local authorities and provinces suspending '... online and offline tutoring for classes for children from kindergarten to 9th grade' (Ye, 2021). The new school year that started following this edict, saw homework significantly reduced to 30 minutes or less for elementary students, with no homework for younger students. However, this has been received badly by parents who were already complaining about the lack of homework when the new policies were first introduced (Jingnan, 2018). At the same time, social media discussions, stating that many universities and selective schools still mainly offered places based on test scores (Jingnan, 2018).

However, there are some areas of innovative pedagogical practice that embrace the principles of learning through play. Anji Play is an approach developed by Cheng Xueqin in 2001 and located in the rural Anji province (anjiplay.com). Xueqin was given responsibility for the 130 public preschools and village sites within the county, looking after 14,000 children between three and six years. When implementing the *Chinese Kindergarten Education Guidance Programme* (Trial) in 2001 (Zhu, 2009), she observed what she termed as 'false play' informed by adult expectations and goals. This prompted reflection on her own childhood, and that of other practitioners, and analysis of these reflections identified that their prized memories of play were '... defined by risk, self-determination, and that meaningful play took place on a grand scale' (anjiplay.com). The resulting Anji Play approach, informed by Western values/theories of experiential learning and, in particular, the role of the practitioner, was grounded in love, risk, joy, engagement and reflection recognising the importance of the resources available and the environment and the involvement of parents (anjiplay.com; Coffino and Bailey, 2019). Xueqin questioned the appropriateness of planning developmentally appropriate activities for a whole class of children. Instead, she recognised that when children were given the autonomy and time to engage in 'self-determined and risky play', with teachers observing and not intervening, children worked successfully through the challenges that arose. She also recognised that 'true play' needed time for children to develop their ideas and increased the outdoor play sessions from one to two hours. This resulted in 'true play' which saw children challenge themselves more, reinforcing that '... the most effective learning takes place when a child owns her own experiences and discoveries' (anjiplay.com, n.d.). Of particular interest was parental reaction to the approach when first introduced. Parents and grandparents were very concerned about the impact of a play-based approach and that this would disadvantage their children in the future. Consequently, Xueqin had copies of the MoE kindergarten guidance (1996) printed and sent out to all carers who were then invited into their settings to observe their children and grandchildren playing, whilst making links between what they saw and the guidelines. The results were overwhelming as they recognised '...that their four years olds were possessed of such high levels of bravery, compassion and intelligence brought many of the parents to tears'. Overnight, once resistant parents had become adamant supporters and took on the role of training incoming parents on the skills of observation and documentation' (anjiplay.com, n.d.).

Reflective questions

Reflect on how you support parents/carers to understand the value of your practice.

- How would you support those whose cultures are different from your own?

Conclusion

This chapter has encouraged the examination of the recognition, globally, of the key importance of promoting a creative curriculum in order to develop effective workforces that have the creativity and critical thinking skills required to meet future needs. This was explored through the change in policies and initiative starting with the initial recognition of a child's right to play enshrined in the 1989 UNCRC, through to the recent updates to PISA which now includes creativity as an area of assessment. The challenges that can be faced when implementing such changes to pedagogical approaches have been explored within a Chinese context, supporting the reader to understand some of the ideological and socio-cultural influences that can be challenging to reformers. It is hoped that this has supported the reader by providing a more informed understanding of the holistic challenges faced when implementing change.

Further reading and resources

Carol A. Mullen (2017) *Creativity and Education in China: Paradox and Possibilities for an Era of Accountability*. New York: Routledge.

Anji Play www.anjiplay.com.
Childhood Education International https://ceinternational1892.org/innovation/the-anji-play-ecology-of-early-learning/

9
SPECIAL EDUCATIONAL NEEDS AND DISABILITIES

Inclusion and creativity

Human differences are normal... learning must accordingly be adapted to the needs of the child rather than the child fitted to preordained assumptions regarding the pace and nature of the learning process. (UNESCO, 1994)

━━━━━━ Chapter overview ━━━━━━

This chapter will look at the wealth of opportunities that creativity offers when engaging children with special educational needs and disabilities (SEND), including those with specific learning difficulties (SpLDs) and autistic spectrum conditions. It will examine different definitions and models of disability, avoiding labels and deficit language. We examine the idea of 'special rights' rather than special needs and an inclusive 'pedagogy of differences' in which adults recognise the different potentials of each child. We discuss 'hidden needs' and the challenges of diagnosis in early years alongside the benefits of creative multi-sensory spaces, play-based therapy and arts-based learning. Changes in our understanding of disability and inclusion over the last few decades, equality and diversity and children's rights will also be explored, including the move towards a more inclusive pedagogy; enabling environments, 'reasonable adjustments' and the idea of universal design for learning.

Models of disability

Most important at the outset is to have an awareness of the different models of disability and the different perspectives that they offer about the individual and society. The medical model is based on a scientific approach to identifying symptoms in order to assign a particular condition or disorder so a diagnosis can be made. What is significant here is that this model clearly places the causes of the disability 'within' the individual (Sewell and Smith, 2021, p.7). The medical model may even take the approach of seeking treatment or even a 'cure' for disability.

In contrast, the social model places the causes of the disability in the external environment, including the political and social context. Instead of seeing disability as a deficit or lack of ability within the individual, any difference in functioning is seen as an impairment which may not automatically lead to a disability but may be exacerbated by the environment and its design (Sewell and Smith, 2021, p.7). The impact of design and the environment will be explored later in this chapter when we look at the idea of 'universal design for learning'.

More recently, a third model, known as the affirmation model (Swain and French, 2000) has been emerging from the disability rights movement and related literature that sees impairment and disability in an affirmative way. In this model, disability is seen as a positive social identity with its own benefits that are worthy of representation, rather than a type of personal tragedy (medical model), a constant struggle for social change and acceptance (social model), or even worse, a charity model where individuals are viewed as objects of pity and in need of support and assistance from the 'able-bodied'. High-profile examples of the affirmation model might include the paralympic athlete and swimmer Ellie Simmonds and the comedian, writer and actress Rosie Jones.

Special needs or 'special rights'?

Alongside these different models of disability are different terms of reference, including those who work hard to avoid labels and deficit language and others who believe passionately in a rights-based approach, using the term 'special rights' rather than 'special needs'. This has its origins in the Reggio Approach and the strong belief in an inclusive 'pedagogy of differences' in which adults recognise the different potentials of each and every child (Malaguzzi, 1998). It could be argued that if we define a child's special needs as 'special rights' and we are aware of which model of disability we are using, then our interactions will be more inclusive and equitable.

Policy context for SEND

In terms of the policy context, legislation in the form of the Children and Families Act (2014) and the *Special Educational Needs and Disability Code of Practice* (DfE and DoH, 2014) have seen a progression towards supporting improved equality of access for those with disabilities. The latter document refers to a growing number (approximately 'one-fifth') of pupils with SEND in schools in England. This document classifies the different 'dimensions of need' of children and young people into the following categories:

- **Communication and interaction** – may include autism spectrum condition (ASC) and Asperger's syndrome
- **Cognition and learning** – a range of learning difficulties from moderate to severe, including dyslexia, dyscalculia and dyspraxia

- **Social, emotional and mental health difficulties** – may be displayed through challenging behaviour, disorders such as attention-deficit hyperactivity disorder (ADHD), attachment disorder or anxiety, depression, self-harm and eating disorders
- **Sensory and/or physical needs** – may include visual impairment, hearing impairment or multi-sensory impairment and physical disabilities requiring specialist equipment and support.

(DfE and DoH, 2014)

In response to a recent consultation, *SEND review: right support, right place, right time* (2022), the Government in England has acknowledged that the process of having a child assessed for special educational needs can be a long, drawn-out and stressful experience for parents/carers and can involve a confusing array of education and healthcare professionals and specialists; typically a child psychologist, a teacher with responsibility for SEND, speech and language therapists and possibly a physiotherapist, depending on the child's needs. Ideally, this single co-ordinated assessment process will result in an education, health and care plan (EHC) with associated funding and a requirement for schools to respond to any recommendations (DfE and DoH, 2014). The Government has responded to criticism and feedback with a new *SEND and alternative provision improvement plan* (DfE, 2023) which includes recommendations for more joined-up planning and strategic implementation between departments for children, families and well-being, mental health and women's health.

A particular problem within early childhood education and care is the challenge of early diagnosis as SpLDs such as dyslexia, ADHD and ASC may not reveal themselves clearly until later in a child's development, either through communication, language, motor movement or emotion (Wearmouth, 2017). This may mean that specialised interventions to address their learning needs do not start until later when they enter the primary school stage.

With all these potential barriers to learning that children may face, how can practitioners incorporate creativity into their planning in a meaningful way? Wearmouth (2017) recommends that 'However much is known about their sensory or physical difficulties, (children) all have their own personal strengths and needs, interests, experiences, family backgrounds...' (2017, p.108) and so any planning must involve the child and parents/carers in the process. The following case studies might provide some inspiring examples of creative projects working with children with SEND in a range of contexts. Some of these projects are based in specialist SEND settings, but the principles and ideas I believe are valuable and highly transferrable to any early childhood education and care (ECEC) context.

Case study - Thinking differently

Esmé is five years old and attends a special school for pupils aged 2-19 with sensory impairments and mild, moderate, severe or SpLDs. For some of the children, this is in addition to physical disabilities such as a visual impairment. The majority of children have an Education, Health and Care Plan (EHCP) and Esmé herself is neurodiverse and has been diagnosed with autism. Today, she is especially excited as she is working in a small group with Sally, the artist in residence who

(Continued)

visits the school every week. Today's activity is felt-making and Esmé loves the calming feel of the soft wool as she and the other children work as a group to rub the soap and warm water into it. Sally, the artist, is encouraging their teacher to be bold and fill their classroom walls, floor and ceiling with all the artwork they have made over the term and the colourful pieces spill out of the door and along the corridor of the school. Esmé says it feels special and 'safe' when they enter the art room, and it is her favourite space in the school.

Reflective questions

- Why do you think these activities and interventions are so beneficial to children with severe learning difficulties and disabilities?
- In what ways do neurodiverse children and artists 'think differently'?
- How have the staff used the environment to create a 'safe space'?
- Consider how many children there are with SEND in your setting... what creative activities could you design for them?

The above case study comes from a project designed by Meadow Arts, a small regional arts organisation based in the rural parts of the West Midlands with a strong track record of placing professional artists in classrooms to deliver bespoke arts-education projects for children and staff. This particular project was based in three SEND schools and was designed to explore and test the potential link between how contemporary visual artists express ideas and the way children with special educational needs and disabilities uniquely approach the world.

The participants were a neurodiverse group of children and young people, some with social, emotional and mental health issues, some with autism spectrum disorder (ASD) and others with severe or complex learning difficulties or physical disabilities and complex health needs. All three settings had experienced teachers or art specialists, but as education practitioners, they received little or no subject-specific or arts-based professional development and were working with pupils who all faced barriers engaging with the traditional curriculum (Taylor et al., 2022).

Three arts professionals were employed as artists in residence, each with experience in delivering high-quality workshops using textiles, mixed media, sculpture, ceramics, recycled materials and the outdoor environment. It was agreed that a child-led creative co-enquiry inspired by the Reggio Approach would be most appropriate, especially for the older primary-aged children with SEND who were working at P-Scales (pre-National Curriculum levels with descriptors used to monitor progress and achievement of pupils with SEND) due to their developmental stage which often does not match the usual age-related stage.

Key concepts

A key element of any project is the continuing professional development (CPD) that should be embedded throughout to support staff and provide a framework for the creative co-enquiry that is taking place. The model used for *Thinking Differently* was that of whole day or twilight sessions, facilitated by the *House of Imagination* (HOI), an arts-based charity and research organisation based in the Southwest of England. HOI aims to support children's exploration, communication, and expression of creative ideas and to develop creative skills for life, with a focus on children's and young people's creative and critical thinking (HOI, 2023).

A key concept of *HOI* places children and young people at the heart of a creative 'listening pedagogy' (Rinaldi, 2021) as co-creators and co-enquirers. This is a collaborative learning approach that helps develop critical thinking and communication skills. Crucially, it places value on the process of learning rather than pre-defined outcomes (Bancroft et al., 2008).

HOI provided mentoring for the artists and introduced key concepts and the importance of the **Creative-Reflective Cycle** as a process of reflection, co-research and project development (Aguirre-Jones and Elders, 2009) (see Chapter 13: The creative and reflective practitioner). These sessions also explored how individuals make personal connections between objects and how each of us develops unique ways of seeing the world. This modelled the process of supporting neurodiverse pupils with their emerging questions, interests and obsessions or lines of enquiry, and discovering less obvious themes that might emerge through conversation and dialogue (Taylor et al., 2022).

Evidence and impact

The power of the arts for learning is evident across *Thinking Differently*. Education staff have benefitted from working alongside professional artists and have started to see the arts as wider than just painting and drawing. Children and young people with SEND have also begun to see themselves as artists in their own right. Themes, such as identity and relationships, significant to the children and their well-being have been explored through the power of the arts and creativity. This approach has also supported the pupils' social and emotional needs. Project artists and educators have reported seeing the rebuilding of confidence and children and young people working through anxieties post-lockdown. There emerged a better attitude to learning – a 'growth mindset' rather than a 'fixed' outlook (Dweck, 2017) and an emerging ability to be receptive to learning again, a form of creative 'recovery curriculum'. One of the artists has described this as 'a transitional experience' for the children as they were making sense of where they are at that particular moment in time.

Connection and reconnection

Participants in this creative project have reflected upon how the approach has supported children with SEND to reconnect with school, the whole class and education, post remote learning from home, and how it has supported social interaction, group dynamics and well-being. 'We are using this opportunity to integrate our young people back into full-time education' (educator, Regency SEN School). There is evidence of improved social interactions and group dynamics, and the creative opportunities for re-connecting and re-socialising after the isolation of lockdown have been described by one of the teachers as 'a joyous thing' (Taylor et al., 2022).

Encouraging connections to out-of-school interests and popular culture is also a reoccurring theme that can be of great benefit to children with SEND. Evidence from this and other projects shows many occasions where children were seen to be 'animated about their outside interests' when the adults were not judgemental about their interest in popular culture. The importance of connection to the familiar where the children really respond to things they recognise in terms of making art cannot be underestimated. *Thinking Differently* also produced tangible evidence of improved attainment, communication and self-confidence (measured through SOLAR, an online pupil assessment tracker for SEND children enables easy recording of pupil progress for assessment frameworks). There is clear evidence of some pupils making above-expected progress in terms of raised attainment, improved communication skills and self-confidence:

1 **Raised attainment**

In terms of art, all children made good or outstanding progress. This isn't necessarily reflected in other subject areas. They all learnt new skills and experienced new techniques and processes. Lynne, educator (Regency SEN School)

2 **Improved communication skills**

Some of them have shown improvement in communication e.g. XX has speech therapy interventions but increasingly could have a conversation about her Masked Singer. I spent more quality time with her so could also understand her more.

XY's target was to slow down speech so he is understood - I saw how well he communicated with his peers when asked to interview them about their work using the iPad. (Lynne, educator, Regency SEN School)

For those children using **assistive technology**, for example, high-tech electronic devices such as a voice output communication aid (VOCA), the use of creative approaches can be particularly effective in providing yet another type of augmented and alternative communication (AAC), a 'multi-communication approach' combining high-tech with low tech (or 'no-tech'):

> There has been real progress in their communication with each other and with us as the adults in the room. We have seen more signing, use of symbols, VOCA machines and vocalising. Through this multi communication approach, everyone is included, and everyone has a voice. Julia, educator (Chadsgrove SEN School)

3   Improved self-confidence

> Some of the pupils became more independent as the project progressed and irrespective of amount of adult direction, all were more confident in their attitude as they knew that…they had the opportunity to explore their own creative ideas if they wanted to. (Lynne, educator. Regency SEN School)

Valuing uncertainty

Thinking Differently has encouraged educators to adopt the mindset of 'thinking and acting like artists' (Ofsted, 2009, p.11). This involves developing a sense of adventure as they navigate into the unknown, trusting the process and employing creative habits of mind (Lucas et al., 2013). It also emphasises the importance of valuing multiple perspectives and different voices, with a focus on observation rather than teaching. The challenge for educators is their multi-faceted role and perhaps uncertain status, being at once both inside and outside the process, as artists/facilitators/recorders/observers.

For artists and educators, the project, whilst perhaps not producing radical change to their practice, has helped to embed approaches, empowering educators and giving them the confidence to make the case for the value of the arts in schools and creative approaches to the curriculum. *Thinking Differently* has brought 'new ingredients for a classroom culture', providing inspiration and ideas so 'the spark comes back' – for long-serving teachers this can diminish over time (see Figure 9.1).

Trusting the process

Artists have the ability to introduce what might be termed transgressive activities or 'teaching to transgress' (hooks, 1994). These provocations include inking on tables; whole-school interventions and installations; exploring the idea of the environment as the third teacher, so that 'everywhere is art and creativity' and 'wow!' moments; encouraging teachers to be bolder and broadening their creative horizons – essentially helping educators deal with their own self-imposed constraints and fear of failure (Taylor et al., 2022). These words from one of the educators and art specialists based at one of the SEN schools reveal the true impact:

> From my point of view, working alongside (the artist) has been an amazing experience. We bounced thoughts and ideas off each other and she gave me the confidence to be much freer with my approach to art teaching as a whole. She

Figure 9.1 Thinking Differently: New ingredients for a classroom culture

taught me to trust the pupils and go with their creative directions. We as facilitators, the pupils as the creators. (Her) confident, calm, brave approach has also helped the teaching assistants to trust in the pupil's creative direction. As we have been allowed a whole morning time slot, we have all been able to take time and step back occasionally to watch the work grow and take shape... I feel braver now... I feel empowered. (Julia, educator, Chadsgrove SEN School)

Other feedback has highlighted the importance of giving the proper status to art specialists within any setting and the added value that working with professional artists can bring:

It has confirmed my view that as an art specialist we should have an invaluable role to play in children's education and that the learning climate... where there were two art specialists with very different skills, but similar values (it) benefitted them greatly. (Lynne, educator, Regency SEN School)

Multi-sensory approaches
Earlier in this chapter we looked at the different 'dimensions of need' that a child with SEND might experience, including social, emotional and mental health difficulties, and sensory

and/or physical needs, which may include multi-sensory impairment. These dimensions of need can be addressed effectively using multi-sensory spaces or sensory rooms designed to engage all the senses. These spaces are often found within specialist provision, but it is possible to create a similar experience for children within a mainstream classroom or even cultural settings. Sensory approaches to arts-based learning have been used effectively in 'A SENsory Atelier' (Christer, 2021) – a SEND schools project with Attenborough Arts Centre at the University of Leicester. This project uses the Reggio principles of an 'emergent curriculum', dialogue with materials and the environment as a third teacher within a museum and gallery space:

> This approach gave us good guidance on setting the environment as a blank canvas to build on, selecting materials or activity, that can be introduced in stages, and that provoke curiosity and experimentation. In short, in order to truly work collaboratively with young people (or Artists or Teachers for that matter) we need to allow space for them to set the pace, and use that momentum to build on. (Bob Christer, Programme Manager)

A key thread in this work is the idea of making a safe space whilst at the same time leaving enough space for the children themselves to fill, 'joining them in their explorations and supporting them by encouraging the development of their own hypotheses on learning through testing and experimentation' (Christer, 2021).

Benefits of music

Research has shown that children with additional needs are able to express themselves through music. The connection between music therapy and ASD has been explored since the 1970s, and a recent review of the literature in this area found that 'music therapy may help children with ASD to improve their skills in primary outcome areas that constitute the core of the condition including social interaction, verbal communication, initiating behaviour, and social-emotional reciprocity'. Music therapy is recognised as a psychological therapy by NHS England, NICE and Ofsted (APPGAHW, 2017, p.87) (see also Chapter 6: Music and movement).

With a diagnosis of ASC, there may also be verbal delay or speech and language issues which may lead to difficulties in being understood as a child will develop their own way of communicating and expressing their needs and emotions. Every child has their own individual strengths, but with ASC there also come challenges to daily living which many parents find stressful and exhausting. Non-verbal communication through music and music therapy may be a particularly useful method to help modify challenging behaviours sometimes associated with ASCs (Brownell, 2002).

Play-based therapy for children with autism

We have previously discussed the value of learning through play and its links with creativity, but play can also have important therapeutic benefits for children with special rights. Indeed, Carla Rinaldi has declared 'it was and is necessary to not only declare play as a right for children but... as an essential element defining human identity in the digital age' (Rinaldi, 2021, p.180). Research by LeGoff et al. (2014) has explored how Lego-based therapy can build social confidence by establishing Lego-based clubs for children with autism and related conditions. 'Lego therapy' can also have significant benefits in terms of mental health and well-being as children can work through post-traumatic stress and process difficult experiences (Altman and Esber, 1995).

Hidden needs

One issue that my occur within any setting is the accommodation of children with 'hidden needs' that may present barriers to their communication, learning and development. These needs might include deafness and hearing loss or even English as a second or other language (ESOL). It is essential that a personalised approach be adopted in every case: meeting with the family, exchanging information with healthcare or other professionals, mitigating distances and ensuring the school or setting is a welcoming place for everyone to meet. Useful strategies might include:

- Peer-to-peer support (by older children): works equally well for 'new starters' as for children with special rights
- Projects that explore common interests (e.g., drawing/graphical language)
- 'Silent invitation' to be part of a smaller group of children

The benefits of small groups include:

- Allowing for proximity
- Getting to know group members and knowing themselves better
- Reciprocal relationships
- Learning to co-exist with different personalities
- Living with 'the other' and others
- Divergent thought processes, including:
  - Fluidity
  - Flexibility
  - Originality

The latter benefits can help to mitigate against any 'rigidity of thinking' that might exist within the child, especially if they have an autistic spectrum condition where they can very quickly come to rely on repetition or familiar routine. However, having said that it is essential to pay attention to the characteristics and personalities of every child (Rinaldi, 2021).

Changes in our understanding of disability and inclusion

The quote that opened this chapter comes from UNESCO's 1994 World Conference for *Action on Special Needs Education: Access and Quality*, known as 'The Salamanca Statement'. Representatives from 92 countries called for inclusion to be the norm for all children with disabilities and created a framework that included the right for all children to attend their local neighbourhood school regardless of their needs (UNESCO, 1994).

   This statement was significant in that it indicates the distance travelled and the changes in our understanding of disability and inclusion that have taken place over the last century, especially since the ground-breaking *Warnock* Report (1978). The biggest change introduced by Baroness Warnock's Report was the introduction of the term Special Educational Needs (SEN) and a rejection of the word 'handicapped' and a deficit approach. According to Smith and Sewell (2021) 'this reconceptualised our understanding of educating those with difference and disability' and 'acknowledged the role of environmental factors in improving or exacerbating disability and learning difficulty' (2021, p.26).

An inclusive approach

Acknowledging the potential 'barriers to learning' that children with SEND might face is a useful metaphor (Sewell and Smith, 2021, p.61) and an important way to ensure equality and the rights of all children to a quality education, as enshrined in the United Nation's 17 *Sustainable Development Goals* (Goal 4: Quality Education) (UN, 2015). The move towards a more inclusive pedagogy is a theoretical approach that can be used when seeking to remove these barriers to learning. This perspective takes the view that effective teaching for children with SEND is also effective teaching for all pupils (Sewell and Smith, 2021). According to this theory, the needs of all children can be met through 'quality first teaching' (EEF, 2020), differentiation and good practice in a mainstream classroom and so specialised interventions and strategies are not needed for those particular children with SEND. Inclusive pedagogy does not identify children with SEND as different or needing separate educational provision. It also does not assume that ability is fixed or innate, so high expectations of all children are appropriate; an idea which perhaps relates to Claxton and Lucas' idea of learnable intelligence' (2010) (see also Chapter 1: What is creativity?).

   The alternative point of view is that specific disorders require specialist interventions and strategies, particularly for children with profound or multiple learning difficulties and disabilities who may require a combination of education and healthcare professionals with specialist knowledge and training. The argument for specialist provision in SEN schools, separate from mainstream provision, is that some children require a bespoke approach, with personalised interventions and a curriculum that is designed to meet individual needs (Lewis and Norwich, 2004).

Environmental factors

When discussing potential barriers to learning, it is important to also acknowledge that environmental factors may also have an impact. In Chapter 2, we discussed the benefits of 'potentiating environments' (Claxton and Carr, 2004) and in the context of SEND these might be called 'enabling environments' where the products, systems, procedures and the physical environment are as 'user-friendly' to as many people as possible. This practice can be seen to be continued in the idea of universal design for learning (see below).

Educational organisations also have a duty to make 'reasonable adjustments' to accommodate disabled students and make sure they can fully participate in education and any other benefits, facilities and services provided for children and young people. This duty was introduced in the Disability Discrimination Act (1995) and taken forward into the Equality Act (2010), so organisations must take reasonable steps to avoid putting disabled students at a substantial disadvantage and provide a truly enabling environment, rather than just 'do the minimum' (Sewell and Smith, 2021, p.80).

Universal design for learning

This idea of creating an 'enabling environment' has been taken forward in the theory of universal design for learning (UDL) which originated in the Universal Design movement in architecture in the 1980s (Rose, 2000). The idea is that the design of any building or technological device should be developed so it is useable and accessible to all individuals from the outset, not as a retrospective modification. This approach understands that what is useful from a design perspective for those with a disability, such as ramps, lifts and adjustable furniture, will ultimately benefit all users. UDL takes this approach and applies it to the educational context, addressing the disability of the school rather than the pupil (Meyer et al., 2014, p.5).

The principles of UDL include diverse ways of representing information, the design of inclusive teaching strategies with a range of experiential learning activities, flexible opportunities for expression and multiple means of engagement that will benefit all learners. These principles, as outlined by Bracken and Novak (2019) for transforming higher education, could equally be applied to early childhood education to minimise barriers and maximise learning. The following table illustrates the potential crossover between UDL's principles, associated neurological elements or 'learning networks' and guidelines (the 'why', 'what' and 'how' of learning) (Rossi, 2021) with creativity, (Table 9.1).

Table 9.1 Universal design for learning principles and networks (Rossi, 2021)

The Universal Design for Learning Guidelines

Provide multiple means of **Engagement**	Provide multiple means of **Representation**	Provide multiple means of **Action & Expression**
Affective Networks The "WHY" of Learning	Recognition Networks The "WHAT" of Learning	Strategic Networks The "HOW" of Learning

CAST | Until learning has no limits

Access

Provide options for
Recruiting Interest
- Optimize individual choice and autonomy
- Optimize relevance, value, and authenticity
- Minimize threats and distractions

Provide options for
Perception
- Offer ways of customizing the display of information
- Offer alternatives for auditory information
- Offer alternatives for visual information

Provide options for
Physical Action
- Vary the methods for response and navigation
- Optimize access to tools and assistive technologies

Build

Provide options for
Sustaining Effort & Persistence
- Heighten salience of goals and objectives
- Vary demands and resources to optimize challenge
- Foster collaboration and community
- Increase mastery-oriented feedback

Provide options for
Language & Symbols
- Clarify vocabulary and symbols
- Clarify syntax and structure
- Support decoding of text, mathematical notation, and symbols
- Promote understanding across languages
- Illustrate through multiple media

Provide options for
Expression & Communication
- Use multiple media for communication
- Use multiple tools for construction and composition
- Build fluencies with graduated levels of support for practice and performance

Internalize

Provide options for
Self Regulation
- Promote expectations and beliefs that optimize motivation
- Facilitate personal coping skills and strategies
- Develop self-assessment and reflection

Provide options for
Comprehension
- Activate or supply background knowledge
- Highlight patterns, critical features, big ideas, and relationships
- Guide information processing and visualization
- Maximize transfer and generalization

Provide options for
Executive Functions
- Guide appropriate goal-setting
- Support planning and strategy development
- Facilitate managing information and resources
- Enhance capacity for monitoring progress

Goal

Expert learners who are...

Purposeful & Motivated	Resourceful & Knowledgeable	Strategic & Goal-Directed

udlguidelines.cast.org | © CAST, Inc. 2018 | Suggested Citation: CAST (2018). Universal design for learning guidelines version 2.2 [graphic organizer]. Wakefield, MA: Author.

Conclusion

Creativity and creative approaches can offer a huge range of therapeutic, health and well-being benefits for children with SEND. There are different models of disability and special needs, but if we define those special needs as 'special rights' then we can use a 'pedagogy of differences' to ensure our interactions will be more inclusive and equitable. Neurodiverse children think differently in a way that has strong parallels with the way creative artists think. Removing barriers to learning and adopting the theory of universal design for learning (UDL) has the potential to benefit all children, not only those with SEND.

Further reading and resources

Cultural Health and Wellbeing Alliance – https://www.culturehealthandwellbeing.org.uk/

The National Autistic Society (2023) *What is Autism?* – https://www.autism.org.uk/advice-and-guidance/what-is-autism

Meadow Arts *'Thinking Differently'* Arts Project with SEND Schools – https://meadowarts.org/learning/thinking-differently-project/

10

SOCIAL INCLUSION, CREATIVITY AND GLOBAL CITIZENSHIP

Art helps us identify with one another and expands our notion of we - from the local to the global. Olafur Eliasson, Artist

━━━━━ **Chapter overview** ━━━━━

In Chapter 8, we started to explore different global perspectives on creativity and the challenges to engagement that many children face in particular contexts. In this chapter, we will look at social inclusion, creativity and global citizenship with a different lens and argue for the importance of intercultural dialogue and the 'culturally literate child'. Whilst Chapter 8 looked at the international context and discussed the relevant articles and agreements that outline a child's right to a quality education, this chapter looks at other changes that are taking place to raise the profile of creativity internationally. Case studies explore practical ideas for promoting children's rights and cultural diversity through creativity, and we start to unpack the challenges we face when tackling issues of social inequality. The chapter examines more recent demands for transformative action for arts education as being integral to sustaining communities and meeting the needs of all people in the face of critical global challenges most notably, sustainable development and the climate crisis.

A new social contract

UNESCO, the United Nations Educational, Scientific and Cultural Organisation is also the UN's special agency for education and claims to take a humanistic approach to its work. UNESCO's recent report, entitled Reimagining Our Futures Together: A New Social Contract for Education (2021) is the result of a global initiative, The International Commission on the Futures of

Education, established in 2019 to 'reimagine how knowledge and learning can shape the future of humanity and the planet' (UNESCO, 2021, p.2). The initiative involved extensive engagement with the public and experts alike exploring how education needs to be rethought in a world of increasing complexity, uncertainty and fragility. With thousands of participants and hundreds of focus groups across 193 countries, this huge collaborative effort showed there is a clear need to create 'a new social contract for education that can repair injustices while transforming the future' (UNESCO, 2021, p.3). The report advocates the renewal and transformation of current education practices to help build peaceful, just and sustainable futures. Three key questions were asked about the practice of education to establish a clearer focus:

- What to continue?
- What to abandon?
- What should we reimagine? (and how?)

These questions could usefully be asked in any educational setting to help the process of self-reflection, joint practice development (JPD) and renewal. Of particular interest to those wishing to promote arts-based practice and creativity in their setting are the statements that refer to 'building imagination, judgement and possibility through arts education'. It goes on to say:

> Education in the arts – music, drama, dance, design, visual arts, literature, poetry and more – can greatly expand students' capacities to master complex skills and can support social and emotional learning across the curriculum. It can enhance our human abilities to access the experience of others, whether through empathy or the reading of non-verbal clues. (UNESCO, 2021, p.73).

We can trace the origins of these ideas back to the Seoul Agenda, a report published 10 years earlier by UNESCO (2010), in particular GOAL 3 which recommended that countries should 'apply arts education principles and practices to contribute to resolving the social and cultural challenges facing today's world' (2010, p.8). The report contained accompanying strategies and actions, for example; applying arts education to enhance the creative and innovative capacity of society and, of particular relevance to the early years, promoting arts education 'throughout schools and communities to foster the creative and innovative capacity of individuals and to cultivate a new generation of creative citizens' (2010, p.8). The Seoul Agenda has been a particular inspiration to a new generation of researchers, such as CARE (Connecting Art with Real Life Issues), an international Erasmus-funded project based at Frederick University in Cyprus (see case study in the next section).

More recently, in 2019, the Frankfurt Declaration for Arts Education demanded transformative action for arts education as being integral to sustaining communities and meeting the needs of all people in the face of critical global challenges, most notably, sustainability and the climate crisis. UNESCO publishes regular Global Education Monitoring Reports and, in 2020, it focused on Inclusion and Education: All Means All (2020) assessing the progress that has been made towards Sustainable Development Goal 4 (SDG 4) to 'Ensure inclusive and equitable quality education and promote lifelong learning opportunities for all' with its ten associated targets (UN, 2015).

The report addresses inclusion in education, drawing attention to all those excluded because of identity, background or ability, and the discrimination, stigmatisation and stereotyping that many marginalised groups face; issues which we will explore later in this chapter. UNESCO declared that they are motivated by the explicit reference to inclusion in the 2015 Incheon Declaration, and the call to ensure an inclusive and equitable quality education in the formulation of SDG 4, the global goal for education, stating that it reminds us that, no matter what argument may be built to the contrary, we have a moral imperative to ensure *every* child has a right to an appropriate education of high quality (UNESCO, 2020).

The report also explores the challenges holding countries back from achieving this vision and demonstrates concrete policy examples from countries managing to tackle them with success. These challenges include differing understandings of the word inclusion, lack of teacher support, absence of data on those excluded from education, inappropriate infrastructure, the persistence of parallel systems and special schools (see Chapter 9: SEND: Inclusion and creativity), lack of political will and community support, untargeted finance, uncoordinated governance, multiple but inconsistent laws and policies that are not being followed through (UNESCO, 2020).

Creativity, sustainability and climate change

If these are the priorities on a global level, then it is useful to reflect on priorities on a more local level. The Department for Education in England has published a draft strategy entitled Sustainability & Climate Change: A draft strategy for the education & children's services systems (2021b). The strategy outlines the following aims with the vision of making the United Kingdom the world-leading education sector in sustainability and climate change by 2030:

- Excellence in education and skills for a changing world
- Net zero
- Resilient to climate change
- A better environment for future generations

(DfE, 2021b, p.26)

Whilst some commentators such as Naomi Klein have criticised the aim of 'Net zero' as the wrong priority (a country might achieve 'net zero' but still not make a positive contribution to green energy, cease the use of fossil fuels or get big business to invest in long-term sustainable solutions for example) (Klein, 2014), it could be argued that the main thrust of these aims is to be applauded, despite the distinct lack of detail. The question remains, how might these aims be translated into actions on a more practical level? The gap between policy, rhetoric and the everyday reality of the classroom can seem daunting, however, the following section illustrates how practitioners might ensure 'excellence in education' and 'a better environment for future generations' (DfE, 2021b, p.26) using creative methodologies and the visual arts.

Visual art education for sustainable development

Recent research from the University of Exeter has focused on connecting art education with the principles of education for sustainable development (ESD) in partnership with schools in Cyprus, Malta, Greece and England. The project *Visual Art Education in New Times: Connecting Art with REal life issues (CARE)* resulted in the Teachers' Handbook: *Enhancing Visual Arts Education with Education for Sustainable Development: A Handbook for Teachers* (Pavlou, 2022) (also available in Greek) featuring in-depth discussions to encourage critical thinking and environmentally-themed projects with a range of children and young people, including 5- to 6-year-olds. This publication also asks some important questions of us as educators:

- How do/can contemporary art practices influence art education today?
- How can we transfer important competencies to our learners to prepare them for the future (particularly when we don't know what that future will look like)?
- Is it possible to promote amongst learners an attitude towards openness, critical inquiry and willingness to contribute to the well-being of their societies?
- How can we give 'voice' to their concerns and provide a means to them for action?

(Pavlou, 2022, p.5)

Whilst not strictly aimed at an early years age group, these creative project ideas are linked to different Sustainable Development Goals (SDGs) and I believe provide some inspiring starting points for investigating these key questions with pre-school children (see Table 10.1). It could be argued that the word 'sustainable' in itself is inadequate to describe the sophistication of these ideas and we need to go beyond sustainability to encourage a regenerative culture (Wahl, 2016), one that must be linked to a regenerative and distributive economics fit for the twenty-first century (Raworth, 2018). This regenerative approach could help us to be more healthy, resilient and adaptable as we face the challenges of the future and try to maintain the planet in a condition where life can flourish.

These activities are an effective way to make visual art lessons more meaningful and engaging for children and can play an important role in promoting 'a regenerative culture' as they create a platform for us to reflect on the future through our day-to-day activities. More importantly, engagement in visual art education (VAE) can encourage children to feel a personal sense of responsibility and gradually transform their 'ways of seeing' (Berger, 1972) and acting to bring about individual and collective changes to their external environment. The potential for good is generated by helping children nurture different qualities in themselves while understanding their ways of interacting with one another (Macdonald, 2014).

Table 10.1 Visual art education for sustainable development

SDG	Theme	Visual art education for sustainable development	Media/techniques/project ideas
3	*Good Health and Well-being*	Rebalancing our relationship with nature	Create junk sculptures/ collages made from materials found during a nature walk/ litter pick/clean up
7	*Affordable and Clean Energy*	Making the change to renewable sources	Make and decorate 'sun catchers' for your windows using old CDs and recycled plastics to harness solar energy
9	*Industry, Innovation and Infrastructure*	Ideas for new buildings/new interventions for old buildings	Make a drawing/take photo of your nursery/pre-school building; draw the changes/ special features that you could add to change the environment
11	*Sustainable Cities and Communities*	Using sustainable transport and green spaces/community gardens	Take photographs of a local park or open space and make a collaborative artwork/3D model that depicts your vision for its public use in the future
12	*Responsible Consumption and Production*	Challenging the production, consumption, and disposal of everyday items such as food, toys and clothes	Create colourful parcels from reused materials for donations; filling them with extra clothes, old toys, accessories etc. to be donated to those in need
14	*Life Below Water*	Appreciating the effect of man-made pollution on ecosystems and marine life	Draw sea creatures using chalk pastels on newspaper on the floor, then cover them with recycled plastics
15	*Life on Land*	Understanding the life cycle of plants	Plant seeds/beans and make paintings of the stages of growth as you observe changes in the roots, stems and leaves
15	*Life on Land*	Learning from nature's great builders, connecting with the outdoors, using organic materials	Nest Building: 'Big make' – weave a sculpture/installation piece large enough to move around, within and manipulate 'Mini make' – individual woven work developing fine and gross motor skills Drawing/mark making with natural materials – developing aesthetic sensibilities

Source: Adapted from: Enhancing Visual Arts Education with Education for Sustainable Development: A Handbook for Teachers (Pavlou, 2022).

Issues-based art education

Issues-Based Art Education (IBAE) is a broad term that goes some way to explain the shift in emphasis in recent years away from a more traditional interest in art-specific knowledge and skills to increasingly focus on topics broader than the subject itself. This could be seen to reflect a 'global' educational perspective coupled with a desire to underline art's versatility and universal relevance (Hall, 2022). According to Hall, it is essential to consider that in emphasising the role and value of the extrinsic learning of IBAE we do not compromise the intrinsic value of VAE. Lindström's (2012) four-way learning model draws a useful distinction between learning in, through, about and with art. According to Hall (2022), it reveals the versatility and universal relevance of VAE and 'helps to untangle the intrinsic from the extrinsic' (Hall, 2022, p.85), intrinsic learning in the subject and extrinsic learning through the subject.

Global context for creativity

How is creativity viewed in an era of globalisation, interconnection and economic inter-dependence? One of the guardians of global comparative standards, the Programme for International Student Investment (PISA), recognised its importance by making creative thinking the 'innovative assessment domain' to supplement their testing of 15-year-olds' core capabilities in English, maths and science. Lucas and Spencer's work on the key capability of creative thinking has provided research of international significance (OECD, 2019) and, in 2021, this new area of assessment was added to these international comparisons. As discussed previously in Chapter 8, this new definition and 'test for creativity' measures how children might show their thinking through creative expression in the written and visual domains and explores knowledge creation and problem-solving through the domains of the social and the scientific. This combination of art and science is significant and the emphasis on social problem-solving has links with creative social entrepreneurship (OECD, 2019). The associated 'competency model' for the PISA test of creative thinking assesses children and young people's ability to:

- Generate diverse ideas
- Generate creative ideas
- Evaluate and improve ideas

However, the model also acknowledges that the skills demanded by the cognitive processes of idea generation and idea evaluation and improvement are partly defined by context. They compare the example of composing a poem and developing viable scientific hypotheses in a laboratory – both could be considered acts of 'creative idea generation', but they make the important point that the actual cognitive and domain-relevant skills an individual needs to successfully think creatively in these two activities are different and 'rely on a different set of domain knowledge and experience' (OECD, 2019, p.23). My argument would be that these different sets of domain knowledge and experience often cross-over in a child's mind and their creative 'working theories' do not make the distinction between arts-based creative thinking, science-based creative thinking or maths-based creative thinking (see Chapter 11: Children as researchers).

Culturally relevant pedagogy

How can we adapt our work with children to ensure it is relevant to their cultural backgrounds whilst at the same time exposing them to the diversity and wealth of cultures that exist in our pluralist society? The idea of **culturally relevant pedagogy** was introduced by Ladson-Billings (1995) to inform and develop professional practice, to improve pedagogy when working with children and young people from different cultural backgrounds. They define this approach as, 'a pedagogy of opposition not unlike critical pedagogy but specifically committed to collective, not merely individual, empowerment, (Ladson-Billings, 1995, p.160)' (see later sections on De-colonising the Curriculum and Chapter 13: The Creative and Reflective Practitioner).

Many practitioners find that membership of a professional organisation helps them to keep their own professional development (often self-funded) alive and up to date with the latest research and developments in the field. The International Society for Education through Art (InSEA) are a global community of art educators and their manifesto states that they believe 'education through art inspires knowledge, appreciation and creation of culture' and that all learners are entitled to an art education that deeply connects them to their world and to their cultural history. This type of education is essential as it 'creates openings and horizons for them to new ways of seeing, thinking, doing and being' (InSEA, n.d.). The following Case Study shows how this 'knowledge, appreciation and creation of culture' might be encouraged and how animated films and drawings can help children develop empathy and be used to explore themes of belonging and identity.

■■■■■■ Case study - The culturally literate child ■■■■■■

Anya has been watching a short, animated film called 'The amazing little Worm' by Anna Gentilini, from Austria. It features colourful drawings of a character who wants to be different and more like the other creatures he meets but does not realise he is already amazing as he is. . ... There are no words in the film, just music; it lasts three and a half minutes and makes everyone laugh. Afterwards, the children learn to talk together about what they have seen with their teacher. They have generated some agreed 'Rules for Talk' so they can show they are listening and thinking carefully when sharing ideas. 'We are all amazing like worm!' announces the teacher and asks them 'What is amazing about you?' Anya thinks hard about how she might answer as she has just arrived at the nursery and doesn't yet feel a sense of belonging... 'Now', the teacher says, 'listen carefully to each other's ideas about what makes them amazing too'... Later, they all paint a picture of what they think is amazing about themselves and make a display entitled 'It's great being me!'. Anya is proud to reveal she and her family are from Estonia (adapted from https://dialls2020.eu/cllp-amazing-little-worm-ks1/).

━━━━━━━━━ **Reflective questions** ━━━━━━━━━

- How do you think this creative approach might benefit children?
- What is the value of children generating their own 'Rules for Talk'?
- Why is it so important to develop the skill of empathy?
- Which other values and ideas could you explore using this method?

This example comes from a great model of intercultural dialogue and creative pedagogy in an international context – the Europe-wide learning programme developing children's cultural literacy and awareness of their international neighbours entitled Dialogue and Argumentation for Cultural Literacy Learning in Schools (DIALLS, 2020). This programme teaches children how to be tolerant, empathetic and inclusive through talking together. DIALLS is an EC-funded project of nine countries working with schools to understand and develop how young people make sense of Europe and its differing cultures. The project includes a Cultural Literacy Learning Programme of lessons (CLLP) to teach children dialogue and argumentation skills in order for them to better communicate with each other and understand each other's perspectives. These skills include empathy, building on and being sensitive to the viewpoints of others, critiquing perspectives thoughtfully and thinking about shared values and ideas (DIALLS, 2020).

Cultural literacy

'Cultural literacy' is a term coined in the 1980s by Hirsch to mean the bank of knowledge, customs and norms that it was felt people should have to be able to operate and communicate effectively in any society, certainly before they can begin to understand the other, more traditional forms of literacy – reading and writing (Hirsch, 1983). Some of these might be visible and obvious, such as food, festivals, clothing and language, whilst others are not so obvious and might be more culture-specific, for example, heritage, values, perceptions and beliefs, such as gender roles or behaviours, such as personal space. Most people have fluent cultural literacy in their culture of origin as they will have absorbed this assumed knowledge from childhood. However, individuals need to develop new cultural literacies when they enter a new culture or interact with members of that culture (Western Sydney University, n.d.).

With the DIALLS programme, the approach is slightly different. Whilst there is general agreement that having a grasp of the histories and ideas of cultures around us is important, the approach moves beyond viewing cultural literacy simply as knowledge (DIALLS, 2020). In this context, the term 'cultural literacy' is used to include the attitudes and skills that people need to get along with each other in everyday living. Empathy is key to being culturally literate, as it enables us to understand and include differing perspectives and values that are reflected in people's lives. The skill of collaboration is also essential and that requires practice: to collaborate well, people should value diversity, respect others and be willing both to overcome prejudices and to compromise. According to the European Union (2006), these are amongst the key competencies for lifelong learning which all individuals need for 'personal fulfilment and development, active citizenship, social inclusion and employment' (2006, p.13), including communication, learning to learn, social and civic competencies, cultural awareness and expression. These key skills are seen as especially important in the context of globalisation and the shift to knowledge-based economies where people are seen as the main asset (2006, p.10).

Empowering teachers

The DIALLS learning programme uses wordless short films and picture books to empower teachers and stimulate classroom discussions about social responsibility and living together in twenty-first century Europe. Students have also created artworks as creative expressions of their values and ideas in response to the texts. An important outcome of the project is the open-access resource, professional development sessions, discussion prompts and a vast multilingual body of more than 100 projects in pre-primary, primary and secondary classrooms.

The project co-ordinator, Dr Fiona Maine, from the University of Cambridge, says 'discussions about social responsibility and how we can live together have been at the forefront of the cultural literacy learning programme that the children have engaged in...' (DIALLS, 2020). The project team includes researchers and teachers from nine countries who each bring their own specialism to work together and encourage people to think beyond geographical borders and consider issues of culture, heritage and identity. This collaborative approach allows them to draw on cultural studies and civic education experts, teacher educators, psychologists and literacy specialists.

The use of visual texts and dialogic or discussion-based techniques (Maine, 2015) is what makes this particular project so relevant to our exploration of creativity in the early years. In supporting children to develop skills in dialogue and discussion teachers will see a progression over time, from beginning, to developing, to sophisticated levels of thinking, speaking and interacting. Maine et al. (2021) have produced a 'Dialogue Progression Tool' to assist teachers in planning and developing these essential skills with children. What is clear is that this process supports and challenges children to think more critically, elaborate and explain ideas, provide evidence for their arguments and accept responsibility for their role. It also encourages them to relate better to their peers, deal with multiple perspectives, negotiate, accept plurality and appreciate the power of community, collective ideas and action.

Other notable global initiatives include UNESCO's International Arts Education Week (20–26 May) each year, which aims to increase the international community's awareness of the importance of creative education and learning about the arts, which it claims can lead to more prosperous and peaceful societies, stating 'art speeds up social inclusion and tolerance in our multicultural, connected societies' (UNESCO, n.d.). However, society might not achieve this level of social cohesion if there are large and increasing disparities between rich and poor and the opportunities that children have are largely determined by external forces and factors. This latter issue is important to consider in more depth and leads us to our next discussion – tackling inequalities in early childhood and the potential long-term impact of a child's environment on their opportunities in later life.

Tackling inequalities

While there is widespread agreement in societies like the UK that every child has the right to a secure childhood and opportunities to develop to their full potential, this does not match with reality for many of the four million children under the age of five currently living there. A recent report from the UK's Institute for Fiscal Studies (IFS) and the Nuffield Foundation entitled Early Childhood Inequalities (Cattan et al., 2022) draws attention to this sobering fact as part of the larger five-year Deaton Review of Inequalities, established in 2019, chaired by renowned economist and Nobel Laureate Professor Sir Angus Deaton. This report highlights the key facts about socio-economic differences in children's development and the environments they grow up in, and the importance of their early experiences in shaping later life. The impact of a child's environment on their cognitive and socio-emotional development is significant but in terms of policymaking there has been, in recent years, a relative shift away from spending on the most disadvantaged families and towards families in work. Much policy has focused on children aged two years and older, despite evidence of the first three years, starting from conception, being a crucial developmental period. Also, real-term cuts in benefits through measures such as the two-child limit and the reduction in the overall benefit cap in England have led to increases in relative child poverty (Cattan et al., 2022).

A lack of progress in reducing early inequalities may not mean that early years' policies aimed at supporting families with young children have been ineffective in reducing inequality, quite the opposite. They may have in fact prevented further increases in inequality. Evidence from the IFS Report suggests that policies need to tackle inequalities in income and/or inequalities in the home environment at a much earlier age (Cattan et al., 2022). Viding and McCrory (2022) looked at longitudinal data stretching back to the 1970s using a cohort study. They highlight that some children are disadvantaged on multiple fronts and that this requires that several factors must be addressed simultaneously for such children/families. Viding and McCrory also point out that although there is a strong imperative for intervening early, it is also clear that the effects of some early interventions decrease over time. The focus on early intervention should not detract from the importance of investments throughout childhood and adolescence (Viding and McCrory, 2022). The multi-faceted nature of disadvantage that some children face can be linked to the idea of 'intersectionality' where different areas of disadvantage intersect and create bigger challenges that can only really be overcome through wider systemic change, as we shall discover in the next section.

Intersectionality

The phenomenon of individuals facing multiple areas of disadvantage on many fronts has been developed by feminist academics in the US since the 1990s, in particular Kimberlé Crenshaw, who defined the term 'intersectionality' as a provisional concept linking politics with post-modern theory. She focused in particular on the intersection of race and gender in black women's experience of the legal system in America (Crenshaw, 2017). The field has expanded since in the last two decades to incorporate all areas concerned with racial justice and gender equality and wider issues of social justice and addressing inequality.

Intersectionality recognises that the solutions to these problems often require fundamental change to the very structures and systems that constitute civic society, such as the problem of systemic and structural racism that has been reported in certain national institutions in the US and Britain, such as the judiciary and the police (Crenshaw, 2017) and was the subject of protests by the *Black Lives Matter* (BLM) movement in the wake of high-profile miscarriages of justice. These problems are often compounded by the phenomenon of 'white privilege' (Bhopal, 2018) where the system is maintained and reinforced 'to perpetuate and self-perpetuate whiteness in access to jobs, housing, income and wealth' (Bhopal, 2018, p.159). In this way, inequalities in education and elsewhere have 'a cumulative effect on the lives of black and minority ethnic groups' (Bhopal, 2018, p.159). In Britain, the picture is complex, and there are other minority ethnic groups that face prejudice and potential social exclusion. Bhopal (2018) draws our attention to certain types of whiteness which are not privileged, for example Gypsy, Roma and Traveller (GRT) communities which remain marginalised and disadvantaged in society, especially in regards to their experience of the education system (Hamilton, 2021).

Fundamental values

In Britain there have been equally high-profile cases of racial injustice and BLM protests, despite an integrated multi-ethnic, multi-faith and increasingly diverse population, especially in large urban areas such as the West Midlands and the city of Birmingham; recently confirmed by the 2021 census data to be the first majority ethnic-minority city in Britain (ONS, 2022). However, some commentators have questioned the success of this supposed integration, and there is little agreement about multiculturalism itself as a 'project': What is its central philosophy? Has it been a success or a failure? Why are some people still ambivalent about living in a diverse country? Should new arrivals be forced to adopt British customs or keep their own cultural values? How should early years practitioners celebrate cultural diversity in this problematic context? (Baldock, 2010)

Perhaps in response to concerns about this lack of social cohesion and the perceived failure of multi-culturalism, the UK Coalition Government (2010–2015) introduced the anti-terrorist Prevent Strategy (Home Office, 2011) and the duty to 'actively promote' *Fundamental British Values* (DfE, 2014a) in education settings. It could be argued that rather than 'fix' a perceived problem or risk, this policy has instead caused more confusion, controversy and a lack of clarity for many practitioners as to their roles and responsibilities. Whilst it is hard to disagree with the overarching aim of improving the **spiritual, moral, social and cultural** development of pupils or the fundamental values of democracy, the rule of law, individual liberty and mutual respect and tolerance for those with different faiths (or none) (DfE, 2014a), some have argued 'what is so "British" about these values?' – surely they are simply fundamental 'human values' shared by people in all nations? (Rosen, 2014).

Instead of providing clarity, these policies have often contributed to a growing sense of unease amongst teachers and practitioners who are now instructed to look for signs of 'radicalisation' amongst children and young people who might be at risk of being drawn into extremist ideology. It could also be argued that this policy unfairly targets urban areas (due to the uneven distribution of ethnic populations across Britain) or particular faith communities. Others have highlighted the potential issues in majority white settings where there might be unconscious bias and so the 'potential for intercultural competence' has to be acquired by children and staff with a bespoke approach and specific interventions in terms of staff training before children from ethnic minorities arrive for the first time (Baldock, 2010, p.70).

Some practitioners might ask how these debates are related to their early years context if they live in a predominantly white area? If we do not perceive a problem with injustice or racism, then why do we need to find a solution or re-train our staff? If families and parents are happy with our curriculum and ideas for creative projects, then why do we need to change them? However, we must recognise the fact that just over one-fifth of children and young people living in the UK are from a diverse ethnic community background and are a part of the global majority (NSEAD, 2021) and so should not be 'minoritised' through oppressive structures (Devarakonda, 2012). Others have argued that it is not enough simply to take a passive or even a reactive approach to these issues, and there is a growing movement towards 'anti-racist education' in the early years that takes a more proactive approach (Sue et al., 2019).

Examples of this anti-racist approach might include: educating yourself on your biases and deconstructing stereotypes of ethnic groups you may have internalised; 'allyship' or becoming an ally (proactive use of your voice or dominant position to challenge prejudice and injustice) (Sue et al., 2019) and 'decolonising the curriculum' (making significant changes to the sources of knowledge that you use as inspiration and the resources that you offer to children to create a more inclusive pedagogy), an idea which we will continue to explore in the next section.

De-colonising the curriculum

Efforts to address systemic racism and injustice in education have been made recently through a process termed 'decolonising the curriculum' (Arday et al., 2021). Educators, students and academics are trying to re-address the historic imbalance created by seeing education, history and even society as a whole through a Eurocentric lens of empire, 'whiteness' and colonisation. Changes that have resulted in wider civic society include re-naming buildings and removing public statues, whilst within the academy (university) we have seen the re-writing of courses, changing set texts and reading lists so they are less narrow, and introducing a much wider and more diverse set of non-European, non-white, (non-male!) authors, books, films, (art) histories and teaching resources to lecture halls and classrooms (Arday et al., 2021).

Professor Vini Lander, from the Centre for Race, Education and Decoloniality (CRED) at Leeds Beckett University, has produced a series of podcasts for those who are committed to promoting anti-racism in education and want to learn evidence-based strategies and practices for challenging structural race inequalities in their school or organisation. Originally designed as a professional development programme for pre-service and in-service teachers nationally and internationally, these resources are invaluable to anyone who is serious about developing their racial literacy, including those working in early childhood education and care I would argue. This is done by providing case studies, discussions, seminars and debates about the issues with experienced education professionals, and asking difficult but important questions, for example, what is the curriculum for adults in your organisation and how do you bridge gaps in knowledge? (CRED, n.d.) (see also useful websites at the end of this chapter).

What else can we do on a practical level? Many practitioners who feel strongly about these issues and wish to become 'allies' may struggle to find appropriate resources or suitable creative starting points. Helpfully, the National Society for Education in Art & Design has produced discussion prompts to help practitioners and teachers critically review their teaching resources in a spirit of allyship, *Anti-racist art education* (ARAE) (NSEAD, 2021). The table below shows a set of key questions to start a conversation around anti-racism in your school context with your staff and students; questioning who is seen (practitioners), what is used (art, craft and design) and how it is being positioned (Table 10.2).

Social mobility

Another facet to tackling inequality is the issue of social mobility – to what extent are children's life chances and opportunities limited or supported by their socio-economic situation and immediate environment? UK Government's Social Mobility Commission produces regular *State of the Nation* reports and the 2022 report was entitled *A Fresh Approach to Social Mobility* (2022). Although driven in the past by a particular view of social mobility in terms of access to elite universities or privileged working environments, the report acknowledges the need for a broader understanding of the term 'social mobility' that is not so limited. It also paints a mixed picture that shows some long-term positive changes over the last two decades that are unfortunately counteracted by other areas of growing challenge:

- Trends in the drivers of social mobility over the last 20 years are generally positive.
- The conditions of childhood have tended to improve over the past two decades, in terms of both finances and parental education levels.
- Levels of social capital (trust and community relationships) in the UK compare well with those in other countries, although civic engagement has declined since the 1990s, and feelings of safety have decreased sharply from 2020 to 2021.
- There are different trends in household finances when we consider the longer term because income inequality and relative child poverty rose significantly in the 1980s and have never fallen back to the levels seen in the 1960s and 1970s.
- The full effects of the coronavirus disease 2019 (COVID-19) pandemic are still unlikely to be shown in the data.

(Social Mobility Commission, 2022)

Table 10.2 Anti-racist art education discussion prompts to start a conversation in your setting with staff, parents and children

WHO	1. Are the artists, makers and designers from ethnically diverse communities? For example: What percentage of practitioners included in your resource are from the various identities and ethnicities?
	2. Within all of us our identity is made up of intersections between our race, sexuality, disability, gender, age, class and so on. How does your resource talk to every child so that their personal identity is strengthened?
WHAT	3. The terms 'African art', 'African artist' or 'Aboriginal' conflate many diverse and varied countries and communities often thousands of miles apart. Have you avoided such terminology and researched the specific origin of the art, craft or design you are using?
	4. If historic Western art, craft and design are chosen as stimulus, has there been a questioning of how those works, or practices are currently positioned? For example: By using them could you be unconsciously promoting racist and sexist ideologies? If so, can you challenge this legacy through the works? Or could alternatives be used?
	5. Where museum objects are chosen for your resources, has there been a questioning of where they came from? What narratives surround them, if any and how they were obtained?
HOW	6. How do you talk about global communities? Is there an awareness of pre-colonial names and communities in your resource? For example: North American Indian is not acceptable. Use terminology such as 'Indigenous Peoples' or preferably self-chosen names.
	7. When discussing African-American, Indigenous American or Australian art do you also situate white artists, makers and designers as European-American or European-Australian?
	8. How will this resource be encountered by; black, Asian, dual heritage and white students for example? Will this resource support learning or discussions of possibly uncomfortable topics? Have you considered how you might manage racist comments?
	9. Does the positioning of the artworks or the artists, makers and designers selected in your resource build positive identities of diverse ethnic communities?
AND	10. In your own context and setting, what other questions need asking?

Source: Adapted from NSEAD (2021).

Conclusion

This chapter has highlighted the fact that all children have an internationally recognised right to education, as well as opportunities for leisure, culture and play. Creativity can play an important role in education for sustainable development as we respond to the global climate crisis and try to generate solutions for the future. We have also explored how practitioners can help children to develop their 'cultural literacy' through a culturally relevant pedagogy that uses dialogue and discussion to encourage empathy and cultural awareness through creative use of the visual arts. However, there are systemic and structural issues that might prevent inclusion and tackling inequality is key; we must be aware that not all children have the same access to creative opportunities due to social, cultural, economic and other factors such as gender, race and ethnicity. Practitioners can and should adopt a proactive approach to improving racial literacy and promoting anti-racist art education.

Further reading and resources

Dabiri, E. (2021) *What White People Can Do Next: From Allyship to Coalition*. London: Penguin.

Daniel, V. (2023) *Anti-Racist Practice in the Early Years: A Holistic Framework for the Wellbeing of All Children*. London: Routledge.

Kendi, I. (2019) *How to Be an Antiracist*. Boston: Bodley Head.

Art in Early Childhood: International Network and Conferences https://www.artinearlychildhood.org/

Centre for Race, Education and Decoloniality (CRED): https://www.leedsbeckett.ac.uk/research/centre-for-race-education-and-decoloniality/

DIALLS: Europe-wide Cultural Literacy Learning Programme https://dialls2020.eu/

NSEAD: *Anti-racist art education* (ARAE) resources. Available at: https://www.nsead.org/resources/anti-racist-art-education/

The Black Nursery Manager: resources and blog posts by Liz Pemberton: https://www.instagram.com/theblacknurserymanager/?hl=en

Maine. F. (in press) *More than Talk: Teaching Dialogue to Build Learning Communities*. Cambridge: UKLA.

SECTION IV
CREATIVITY, RESEARCH AND PEDAGOGY

11

CHILDREN AS RESEARCHERS

Supporting children's natural curiosity through science, technology, the arts and mathematics

Once children are helped to perceive themselves as authors or inventors, once they are helped to discover the pleasure of inquiry, their motivation and interest explode... (Loris Malaguzzi, 1998)

▬▬▬▬ Chapter overview ▬▬▬▬

'The child is a born researcher' according to Malaguzzi (1998) and this chapter examines the links between creativity and research: the idea of children as researchers, researching the world. Underpinning principles include the importance of working across disciplines, turning STEM into STEAM and the opportunities offered when using digital technologies as a tool of inquiry. It will argue that the natural world and cultural spaces including museums, galleries and collections offer often untapped creative opportunities for learning outside the classroom. As creative practitioners, we will explore some of the theories that underpin research-based practice and how children go about creating knowledge.

Practitioners and children as researchers

In Chapter 2, we discussed the importance of developing children's aesthetic sensibilities to learn how to look and observe. According to British artist Bob and Roberta Smith (real name Robert Brill), an ability to understand the possibilities afforded by science and technology needs both imagination and creativity and ideally, an understanding of how to look and observe the world around us; an ability which starts very young. Their point is that everything we use in our daily lives has been designed and made. They go on to argue that these conversations about design start with a drawing. In this sense, a pencil is a technological tool for observing, translating thoughts and communicating ideas in the same way that a camera, tablet or smartphone is a tool. There is a growing argument and an increasingly strong case to be made that, rather than teaching STEM in our primary and secondary schools (Science, Technology, Engineering and Maths), we should be teaching STEAM (Science, Technology, Engineering, Arts and Mathematics) to acknowledge the vital interplay between them and the essential combination of skills that children and young people will need for the future (CLA, 2017). This chapter will showcase innovative examples of Early Childhood Education (ECE) practitioners, researchers and artists incorporating STEAM in education programmes from around the world.

Recent reports by the British Educational Research Association (BERA) highlight the importance of interdisciplinary approaches, combining science with the arts and humanities in order to support children's research and scientific curiosity in a creative way, and by appreciating the wider role of science in society (BERA, 2016). Indeed, former President of Reggio Children, Carla Rinaldi advises that 'when researching into the world of children, it is really the children who must be the main protagonists of that research' (2021, p.130). In this sense, even the word 'research' demands to go beyond the laboratory and rather than being the privilege of the few, become the attitude with which teachers approach making sense and meaning from the whole of life, in effect 'living ourselves in a permanent state of research' (Rinaldi, 2021, p.100).

As we have explored in previous chapters, the idea that children are active in their learning and the co-construction of meaning rather than passive recipients of pre-determined knowledge is central to our discussions of creativity and its value within the early years' curriculum. As Malaguzzi states,

> either education is a situation of research and this research produces new pedagogy, or it is the provision of a service that is delivered to young children, subjecting them in a message which is already completely prefabricated and codified in some way. (Loris Malaguzzi, 1998)

Art versus science: A false dichotomy

Children do not see the world in terms of dualisms or opposing ideas, for example, objective facts versus personal experience, rational ideas versus imagination, science versus superstition or 'magical thinking' as psychiatrists call it (Dalton et al., 2020). And so, rather than view art and science as being in opposition to each other, children instinctively know this a false dichotomy (irreconcilable difference) and naturally want to explore the world in all its complexity in an active and creative way. Their 'why?' questions are the clearest sign of that curiosity and as we shall see, there are many ways to construct **hypotheses** and verify theories whilst retaining a sense of awe and wonder, fantasy and imagination. The affordances of new technology and digital media, as well as the attitudes of early childhood practitioners, are particularly relevant in this regard, as we shall explore in the next section.

Technology and creativity

With regards to the subject of new technology and in particular, digital media, there has been much discussion of early childhood practitioners' assumptions or beliefs and the success, or otherwise, of integrating technology into a child-centred classroom environment. Some practitioners have been found to be sceptical about the value of digital technologies for very young children whilst others, quite understandably, lack confidence in their ability to integrate it into early years' pedagogy or have concerns about excessive screen time on mobile devices (Muller and Goldenberg, 2021), passive/sedentary behaviour, physical inactivity and the potential impact on verbal and social development (Vidal-Hall et al., 2020). Indeed, if we re-consider the socially constructed nature of childhood then it could be said that we are constructing young children as users of technology ('digital citizens') without perhaps considering the problematic nature of implementation and potential barriers to embedding it in the curriculum, its appropriateness and potential in child-led or play-based curricula (Johnston et al., 2018).

Digital landscapes

Some critics have argued that there is an over-reliance on learning 'packages' and commercial software when 'educational technologies' are used to support teaching and learning in the early years (Jack and Higgins, 2019). Solutions can be found, however, by taking a completely different approach and by integrating digital technology with analogue resources and physical materials to create interactive environments that are an invitation for children to explore possibilities in a generative and open-ended way. An excellent example is the approach taken by the artists and teachers ('aterlieristas' and 'pedagogistas') in the infant-toddler centres and pre-schools of Reggio Emilia, Italy. The approach is exemplified in the model of the 'Digital Landscapes Atelier' at the Loris Malaguzzi International Centre but can be found to a greater or lesser degree, in every pre-school and infant-toddler centre in the city (Figure 11.1).

Here digital tools – such as computers, video projectors, webcams, miniature digital microscopes and graphic tablets are combined with more traditional materials like marker pens, construction materials ('loose parts'), everyday objects, mirrors and Perspex structures. These resources are offered in combination and 'stand in close connections in the same context, their interactions activating the kinds of exploration that take children and adults by surprise' (Reggio Children, n.d.). This is a perfect example of 'generative creativity' (Rinaldi, 2021, p.129) that reinforces 'children's sense of the possible' as Bruner referred to it (2004, p.27). The combination of physical materials with digital tools opens up entirely new worlds of possibilities that are not limited to a child's familiarity with a particular app or an adult's knowledge of a particular piece of commercial software. There is freedom to experiment within this approach that is collaborative, joyful and allows ideas to evolve overtime.

This approach embodies Malaguzzi's idea of 'nothing without joy' (1998), but equally it could be said that there is 'nothing without planning'! A key part of the success of this approach is the attention to detail in the planning and use of templates to capture children's responses and the

Figure 11.1 Interactive environment generated by adult participants in the 'Digital Landscapes Atelier', Loris Malaguzzi International Centre, Reggio Emilia
Source: Simon Taylor.

keywords that they use to describe the different 'provocations' or contexts that they are experiencing. By encouraging careful thought and the use of adjectives or 'describing words' adults can help with language development relating to science and technology, for example:

- Light
- Shadow
- Reflection
- Refraction
- Colour
- Magnification
- Distortion
- Image
- Projection

Digital cameras

As mentioned above, it is essential in the early years that technology should not be experienced passively, but actively. Give a child a camera and they will quickly prove that their snapshots show an eye for detail and that their choices are never random. Images are taken with awareness; every single shot is a glimpse of the world through children's eyes. The process can be collaborative-invite the children to create a title for each image and listen carefully to the keywords, phrases or **visual metaphors** that they use (see also Chapter 13). This dialogue can then be followed up with drawing and creative writing which allows them to elaborate key themes based on their view of the world (see Figure 11.2). Collating and printing hard copies of these images, words and thoughts is an important part of the creative process as it allows for reflection and review whilst also providing essential **documentation**, the importance of which will be discussed in the next section.

Figure 11.2 Photography created by children aged 3-6 years at the Tondelli pre-school in Reggio Emilia
Source: Simon Taylor.

Documentation

A key part of the Reggio Approach to early years' education is documentation (in its many forms) which reveals children's research interests, **makes the learning processes visible** and gives value and purpose to their work. Consisting of sketchbooks, folders, booklets and photographs, documentation combines expressive languages with pedagogical languages. It also allows practitioners to interpret their role and share experiences as teachers with colleagues. Documentation also becomes an important legacy/archive of a particular group or cohort and when shared with parents and families, offers insights into what is happening in the setting (see Figure 11.3).

Science and creativity

What happens when professional educators approach science in a creative way? Rob Kesseler is a visual artist and Emeritus Professor of Arts, Design and Science at the University of the Arts

Figure 11.3 Pedagogical documentation produced by the infant toddler centres and pre-schools of Reggio Emilia
Source: Simon Taylor.

London, a former NESTA Fellow at Kew and Research Fellow at the Gulbenkian Science Institute, Portugal. His work exemplifies the creative cross-over between science and the arts. During the past eighteen years, he has collaborated with botanical scientists and molecular biologists in an exploration of the plant world at a microscopic level. Reflecting the way in which the natural world migrates into many aspects of our daily lives, images are translated into a wide range of contexts and media, including ceramics, glass and textiles, video and photography. Kesseler asserts that since the nineteenth century technology has changed both how artists work and how scientists work, whilst the advent of digital platforms has made collaboration and the sharing of 'deep knowledge' across disciplines more possible.

Kesseler explains his fascination with using microscopes as follows: 'The complexities of nature are endless and visually can really draw you in. . . also, how something so small can be so fundamental for life' (Kesseler, 2016). The following case study illustrates how his ideas could be translated into practice to enable this 'deep knowledge' in the early years' context.

▬▬▬▬▬ Case study - Focused looks ▬▬▬▬▬

Kwame has just turned five years old and is using a plastic magnifying glass to investigate organic objects gathered during a nature walk that morning; leaves, twigs, horse chestnut cases, lichen, moss, and all sorts of natural forms. . .. The teacher has set up her laptop and is using a miniature USB microscope to view the gathered materials in incredible detail. They discuss what they can see as the

(Continued)

imagery is projected on a huge scale onto the wall and floor using a digital projector. The children then work together to help arrange large 3D objects (cardboard tubes, boxes and cylinders) in front of the projector to create giant silhouettes and shapes in response to the patterns in nature that they can see...another teacher gives Kwame a small digital camera and is encouraging him to take photos of the most exciting parts of the environment they have created together in the room. These photos will later be printed out in black and white on paper for Kwame to annotate, write and draw on.

Reflective questions

- What learning is taking place here?
- How is the technology being used?
- What creative activities has the teacher designed that are social and interactive?
- How does the teacher help the children to reflect on their learning afterwards?

Science experiments all around the house

It is worth considering how we might provide inspiration for early years practitioners, parents/carers and children alike to continue with their research and investigations beyond the classroom when they get home. A key starting point for our family when our children were very young was Susan Martineau's book, developed closely with Kathryn Higgins, Head of Chemistry at Leighton Park School, entitled 'The Super Book of Simple Science Experiments' (2009). In it Martineau encourages children to 'be a bathroom scientist, a garden scientist, a kitchen scientist...' and provides creative starting points for projects to help young children understand the world, encourage scientific thinking, observe different phenomena, develop their own hypothesis and embed scientific language (see Table 11.1).

Table 11.1 Science experiments all around the house

What shall we explore? (subject)	What do we do? (experiment)	What do we observe? (phenomenon)	Why does this happen? (hypothesis)
'Be a Bathroom Scientist...' *Bubble Fun*	1 Half fill a wash basin or bowl with water 2 Pour in some bubble bath 3 Put a straw into the water and blow!	The blowing makes bubbles that EXPAND everywhere	The bubble bath makes the water elastic or stretchy so that it holds the AIR you are blowing into it. If you blow into water on its own it cannot hold the air

(Continued)

Table 11.1 Science experiments all around the house (Continued)

What shall we explore? (subject)	What do we do? (experiment)	What do we observe? (phenomenon)	Why does this happen? (hypothesis)
Float a Boat	1 Take two balls of modelling clay and make one into a boat shape 2 Fill a washbasin or bowl with water 3 Place the clay ball on the water 4 Now place the clay boat on the water	The ball of clay sinks to the bottom while the boat floats on the SURFACE of the water	The clay boat has air between the sides of it and is hollow which makes it light for its size, so it FLOATS. The ball has no air inside it and is SOLID which makes it heavy for its size and so it SINKS
'Be a Garden Scientist...'			
Bug Hunt	1 Take a magnifying glass, notebook and pencil outside into the garden or park 2 Choose a small area and look at the soil, under stones and in the long grass 3 When you find a bug or minibeast, draw it in your notebook. Count the legs, wings and parts of its body	Different creatures prefer different places to live and have different ways of moving Is it wriggling or crawling? Does it have different parts to its body?	The proper name for creepy crawlies is INVERTEBRATES (animals without a backbone), like worms, centipedes or snails. Not all INVERTEBRATES are INSECTS though, INSECTS have six legs and three parts to their bodies, like ants and beetles. Spiders are different again and are called ARACHNIDS – they have eight legs and two body parts
Cloud Code & Rainbow Magic	1 Go outside at different times of the day with a notebook and a pencil. Look up at the sky 2 Draw what the clouds look like. What is their shape, colour and size? 3 Describe what the weather is like and if it changes as the clouds change 4 Look outside when it is raining- can	The clouds look different on different days and bring different types of weather. Some are big and fluffy (called CUMULUS). White ones mean good weather, whilst dark ones (CUMULONIMBUS) bring heavy rain. CIRRUS clouds are streaky, wispy and high up in the sky – they can mean windy	Clouds are made of tiny WATER droplets or ice crystals. This water can fall as rain or snow, depending on the time of year. When it is raining and the sun is shining at the same time, you might be able to spot a rainbow. The colours always appear in the same order: red, orange, yellow, green, blue, indigo and violet.

Table 11.1   Science experiments all around the house (Continued)

What shall we explore? (subject)	What do we do? (experiment)	What do we observe? (phenomenon)	Why does this happen? (hypothesis)
	you see a rainbow at any time?	weather and maybe storms to come	This is because LIGHT looks white but is really made of many colours. The water droplets split the light into all these colours, and we see a rainbow
'Be a Kitchen Scientist. . .'			
Oily Stuff	1 Pour some water into a bowl 2 Add some cooking oil and stir 3 Now add some drops of washing-up liquid and stir the water	When you stop stirring the drops of oil stay on the top, or surface, of the water. They have a kind of stretchy skin around them and they like to stick together. The washing-up liquid breaks up this skin and helps mix the oil and water together	Oil and water do not mix. OIL can make things waterproof, like birds' feathers. The washing-up liquid breaks up the oil and can help you to clean greasy dishes when you are washing up!
Melting Moments	1 Break up some chocolate and put it in a glass bowl over a pan of gently simmering water 2 Stir it well as it becomes all runny and hot 3 Spoon the chocolate sauce on to some biscuits or small cakes in different patterns and let it cool	The chocolate chunks start as SOLID. As you heat them up, they change or MELT and become LIQUID. When you spoon this LIQUID on to the cakes or biscuits it cools down and becomes SOLID again	When we are cooking- heating, chopping, mixing and stirring – we are really doing experiments The ingredients change their STATE and can EXPAND, combine into something new, or even disappear completely due to a CHEMICAL REACTION

Maths and creativity

The subject of mathematics may not immediately offer the obvious potential for creativity or creative approaches, but with a little thought and an openness to cross-disciplinary methods, there are many opportunities that can be explored. For example, Marcus du Sautoy, Professor of Mathematics and the Public Understanding of Science at Oxford

University, reveals the strong connections between music and maths, including classical composers' fascination with numbers and pattern. The grammar of music (as discussed in Chapter 6) and key ideas such as rhythm and pitch, have mathematical foundations and like music, mathematics is about structure and pattern. Du Sautoy expands on these parallels explaining that mathematics involves a lot of choice, and it is the process that matters most. 'Just as music is not about reaching the final chord, mathematics is about more than just the result. It is the journey that excites the mathematician...' (2011). He gives the example of the organic sense of growth found in the **Fibonacci sequence** of numbers (1, 2, 3, 5, 8, 13, 21...) which could offer an attractive framework for any number of activities using sound, art materials, natural objects or musical instruments to explore pattern in mathematics.

Du Sautoy makes clear the strong connections that exist, stating that 'rhythm depends on arithmetic, harmony draws from basic numerical relationships, and the development of musical themes reflects the world of symmetry and geometry' (2011). He quotes Igor Stravinsky, composer of 'The Firebird' Suite (for Diaghilev's famous ballet company) and pioneer of rhythm in the twentieth century, who was said to have declared of his music, 'mathematics swims seductively just below the surface' (2011).

Maths and play

Play-based learning activities can be an especially powerful way to engage children at a very young age with the basic principles of mathematics. Gripton and Williams (n.d.) have stated that number sense, pattern and spatial reasoning are all key predictors of later mathematics achievement. These skills and abilities can be developed through the use of 'loose parts' (see Chapter 3); a particularly creative and perhaps more importantly, cost-effective way to enable all children in a setting to have access to materials that they can take home to continue their learning. The following case study shows how this can be put into practice and comes courtesy of Lillian de Lissa Nursery, Birmingham.

■■■■■■ Case study – Maths boxes ■■■■■■

Caitlin, along with all the four- to five-year-old children at her nursery, has been given a special box of materials to take home. When she opens it later with her grandmother, she is fascinated to see it contains pieces of wood, metal, plastic, corks, buttons and fabrics to invite her to explore different elements of mathematics in an interactive way. There are multiples of certain objects to encourage pattern making and sequencing and visuals to inspire and initiate this. The different scale and weight objects, geometric shapes, natural formations, grids and number lines have been included to support her in a play-based learning investigation. She spreads the items out on the floor of her grandmother's living room and is immediately engrossed in arranging them. Together they start grouping certain objects, counting and re-arranging...

- What mathematical skills are being developed here?
- How do the materials help with number sense, pattern and spatial reasoning?
- Why is the role of the adult so important do you think?

Natural maths

Lorna Rose, artist in residence at Lillian de Lissa Nursery School (part of the Birmingham Federation of maintained Nursery Schools), explains that 'maths in our school is unavoidable as each environment, inside and out, provides visual invitations to engage with size, weight, shape, patterns, positioning, balancing and all aspects of mathematical learning'.

Using a pedagogy of play-based learning ensures that a wide range of maths opportunities are always available for the children to explore and investigate. There are written numbers and sizes on view in text and picture form in the learning environments for teachers and children to reference, and staff use multiples of the same material to initiate discussions and play around amounts; role-play often requires these materials to act as money or food. The range and variety of approaches mean every child is actively engaged. Rose explains how they use lines and ladders to encourage the children to be physically involved, grids and geometric shapes for sequencing and pattern making, songs and nursery rhymes that mention numbers at group times and many other ways to make maths fun and understandable to each child (Figure 11.4).

This latter approach links maths to the child's everyday lived experience in a natural and unobtrusive way. In the words of Malaguzzi,

> . . .it is not an imposition on children or an artificial exercise to work with numbers, quantity, classification, dimensions, form, measurement, transformation, orientation, conservation and change, or speed and space, because these explorations belong spontaneously to the everyday experiences of living, playing, negotiating, thinking and speaking by children. (Malaguzzi, 1998, p.53)

These examples illustrate clearly the social nature of children's learning, but their efforts to communicate this learning also need careful attention. The idea of 'working theories' has been developed by early childhood practitioners in Aotearoa New Zealand and goes some way to explain what is happening, as we shall explore in the next section.

Working theories

Often described as the 'sister' of learning dispositions (Claxton and Carr, 2004), 'working theories' have emerged from the holistic approach of the *Te Whāriki* early years' curriculum from Aotearoa New Zealand (Ministry of Education, 2017) and describes how children apply previous

Figure 11.4   Natural maths: Creative and play-based approaches to learning mathematics
Source: Lillian de Lissa Nursery and Pre-school.

knowledge to new situations and start to make connections between people, places and things. According to Helen Hedges, Professor of ECE at the University of Auckland, working theories incorporate all of children's 'embodied, communicative and social efforts to learn, think and develop knowledge that enables children to participate effectively in their families, communities and cultures' (2021, p.32). The role of the 'kaiako' (Maori word for teacher or instructor) is to engage with children's working theories in 'respectful, reciprocal and responsive interactions' (Hedges, 2021, p.32); a level of respect for the child and their ideas that has echoes of the 'pedagogy of listening' that is such a central part of the Reggio Approach (Rinaldi, 2021). *Te Whāriki* empowers children as life-long learners with a framework of interwoven principles and strands, envisaging early learning settings as working in partnership with communities to realise this vision (Ministry of Education, 2017). Hedges explains that 'working theories' is an evolving area of research as international literature exploring children's cognitive development and intellectual curiosity 'are matters of global interest' (Hedges, 2021, p.32). Figure 11.5 shows the potential inter-connections between children's working theories, scientific thinking, arts-based thinking and mathematical thinking.

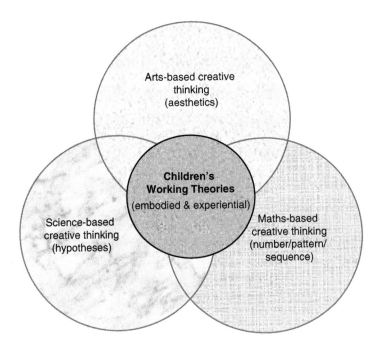

Figure 11.5 Working theories: Visualisation of the inter-connections between children's working theories, scientific thinking, arts-based thinking and mathematical thinking

Continuing this theme of thinking 'in community' and cultural knowledge, it is important to consider both the formal and informal spaces that house them; the museum, the library and the art gallery; all of these have been supporting children's intellectual curiosity for generations. The next section of this chapter explores these themes and the shared communal spaces offered by the natural world outside the classroom, all powerful arenas for learning and development.

Learning outside the classroom part 1: Formal spaces
Learning in the museum

For those of you who have ever stepped foot inside a local museum and art gallery or had the privilege of visiting one of the many national museum collections that exist up and down the country, you will know the amazing possibilities these contemporary and historic spaces hold for multimodal and multi-sensory learning (Taylor, 2020), from archaeology to zoology, science and technology to natural history, costume to music. The benefits of exposing children to different interpretations of multi-cultural objects and collections are well known (Pearce, 1994), and the educational role of the museum has been the subject of in-depth study for many years

(Hooper-Greenhill, 1994). What is less well known is that these venues often incorporate ground-breaking education programmes for all ages and abilities to access their collections, including object handling (Chatterjee, 2008), touch tours, British Sign Language (BSL) interpretation, audio description, sleep-overs (think 'Night at The Museum'!) and interactive parent and toddler sessions.

A dialogical model

My own experience working in museum and gallery education has been with community outreach, engagement and participation teams, often made up of artist educators who act as 'creative enablers' working in a spirit of collaboration, designing personalised sessions with and for a range of partners, including early years' settings (Hay and Fawcett, 2006). Rather than imparting a fixed body of 'expert knowledge', artist educators facilitate these sessions through dialogue and discussion (a dialogical model) with conversations that might generate multiple interpretations of a particular object or artwork. Learners draw on their own life experiences to make meaningful connections that are personal to each child. In this way, 'pedagogy in the gallery is concerned with generating new knowledge through a collaborative process of investigation and critical reflection' (Pringle, 2006, p.30). Museum and gallery educators might provide a context or framework for the discussion (the 'what?', 'who?' and 'when?' questions) whilst participants provide their own interpretations in answer to the 'how?' and 'why?' questions (Pringle, 2011). The 'Ways In' model, developed by Helen Charman and education staff from the TATE Gallery's Learning Team in consultation with schools, is a particularly effective way for early years' practitioners to scaffold children's learning in the museum and gallery context. Figure 11.6 shows how it might be adapted to support looking at art and objects using a co-constructed and accessible approach.

Access and inclusion

The idea of the 'participatory museum' is now embedded throughout many cultural venues around the world, with major efforts being made to engage audiences from diverse backgrounds, under-represented groups and indigenous cultures. There has been a long process of change over the last 25 years and an acknowledgement of the social role of the museum in addressing local issues, even the combating of social exclusion, although this has been problematic due to the complex nature of this area of social policy (Sandell, 1998). Exclusion and disadvantage can take many forms, and so the barriers to access are multifaceted (Taylor, 2018) and similar to many of the barriers that some children face to accessing learning itself, including social class, poverty, educational disadvantage, ethnic and cultural background, disability and an individual's own attitudes. According to David Anderson, former Head of Learning at the Victoria and Albert Museum in London, 'these factors often operate in combination, so that a successful strategy to overcome them requires a co-ordinated programme' (Anderson, 1999, p.94).

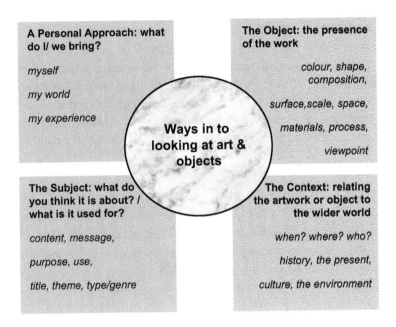

A Personal Approach: what do I/ we bring?

myself

my world

my experience

The Object: the presence of the work

colour, shape, composition,

surface,scale, space,

materials, process,

viewpoint

Ways in to looking at art & objects

The Subject: what do you think it is about? / what is it used for?

content, message,

purpose, use,

title, theme, type/genre

The Context: relating the artwork or object to the wider world

when? where? who?

history, the present,

culture, the environment

Figure 11.6 Art gallery educators learning framework
Source: Adapted from: Charman and Rose (2006).

Case study - Young at art

Rachel has taken her two pre-school children (aged four and two) to the local museum and art gallery on the high street in the town centre for the first time ever. It's a mid-week morning parent and toddler session which she hopes will be fun, despite the huge effort to get there on the bus. The publicity flyer she picked up in the local library encouraged her to 'Enjoy exploring, listening and making with your little ones' and so they have come along to join a themed art session, especially designed for under 5s. Rachel is relieved to discover there is no charge to get in and the experienced staff member welcomes them and explains that 'each week they explore clay, paint and craft materials to make something lovely, and cosy up for story time'. This friendly lady is Kate, the Learning and Communities Co-ordinator for the Museums in the County, and later, chatting over coffee Rachel is fascinated to hear about the other free sessions they run in the central library every week...

Reflective questions

- How can we develop a more democratic and inclusive approach to learning in the museum?
- What potential barriers are there for parents and children in the early years?
- Why do you think some cultural venues are still seen as inaccessible and elitist?

Pedagogy and architecture

Helen Chatterjee and Guy Noble have written extensively on understanding the health and well-being benefits of museums and libraries, through our interaction with objects and touch, but also the social role of the museum in meeting the needs of local communities in a holistic way (Chatterjee and Noble, 2017). We can see the potential for productive cross-over here between early childhood professionals and practitioners of arts in health, art therapists, care and community workers. This sentiment is echoed in the Arts Council England's new 10-Year Strategy *Let's Create* (2020):

> The pre-school years play a vital role in readying children for school, as well as helping to set the compass for future creative and cultural activity and wider success in life. We believe that it is critical to develop high-quality and affordable early years creative activity across the country, and we will support libraries and cultural organisations, community partners and the public to come together to make this available for all young children and their families. (ACE, 2020)

There is a sense that these cultural buildings themselves are not an incidental container but a source of research and experience in their own right. If we consider Malaguzzi's idea of the **environment as the third teacher** (in addition to the parent and class teacher), then in the museum, library or art gallery we can see pedagogy and architecture in dialogue, just as we might re-conceptualise space in the classroom (Strong-Wilson and Ellis, 2007). Indeed, pedagogy cannot work in isolation; it can only work in dialogue with other disciplines. Malaguzzi talked about 'the right to environment' and children having opportunities to inhabit and experience many different environments (Cagliari et al., 2016). For children nothing is neutral, they see commonalities, links and connections and look for identities within objects, places and people based on their interactions and experiences.

Learning outside the classroom part 2: Informal spaces
Outdoor learning

Being outdoors can seem such an obvious arena for learning and creativity that we might fail to see the challenges or fully grasp the limits of our understanding. For example, research has shown that some practitioners may be resistant or see learning outdoors as limited simply to a child's physical development (Bilton, 2020). In reality, outdoor activities such as running, jumping, climbing and playing can be utilised to promote all areas of learning. According to Helen Bilton, we can even go so far as to describe the outdoors as a 'complete learning environment' (Bilton, 2010, p.19) that can cater for all children's needs: their social, emotional and cognitive development, physical health and mental well-being.

Despite recommendations from health professionals that pre-school children should spend a minimum of 180 minutes (three hours) a day doing a variety of physical activities (NHS, 2022), there are valid concerns about the amount of time children are spending outdoors and the quality of the learning experiences they encounter. Parents may be concerned about the nursery or pre-school providing purposeful activities and a secure environment free from risk, but research into the Froebel-inspired **Forest Schools** of Scandinavia (originating in Denmark in the 1950s) has shown the wider benefits of a learning environment that is entirely based outdoors and encourages child-led independent learning (Knight, 2011).

Forest schools

Within Forest Schools risk is managed by the adults, but it is not an entirely risk-free environment, instead the children learn through trial and error how to find their limits and manage risk appropriately in a social group. This alternative curriculum provides important life lessons, and it could be argued that exposure to risk at an early age develops life-long skills and capabilities: problem-solving, resilience, self-regulation, confidence and sociability – all attributes that might prevent low self-esteem, poor mental health or risky behaviour at a later stage in life, typically in adolescence (Sylvester, 2011). The sensory and relational aspects of Forest School and the direct contact with art and nature can also have particular benefits for children with autism spectrum disorders (Burrows, 2011) (see also Chapter 9: SEND and creativity).

Despite these clear benefits, the Forest School movement does have its limitations. Some might say it relies too much on specialist training, thus limiting the benefits to children in certain settings that rely on key staff who are qualified. This might also limit the capacity of other settings to experiment with their outdoor curriculum beyond existing nursery, school or play sites (Knight, 2013).

'Hygge'

Other outdoor practices from Scandinavia include the Danish concept of **hygge** (pronounced 'hoogah'), which can be translated as 'cosiness' in its broadest sense. This can be used in both outdoor and indoor spaces to mean creating warm and welcoming environments and practices that address children's social and emotional needs; providing closeness and contentment in a relaxed atmosphere (Prowle and Hodgkins, 2016). Try the following creative ideas to transform your home, baby room or classroom spaces in the spirit of 'hygge':

- **Change reading corners** into cosy 'snugs' with blankets, cushions and fleeces for children to retreat to
- **Avoid electronic devices** but instead offer books and pictures for children to look at in peace
- **Use a pop-up tent** or temporary shelter, even small spaces under a stair-well or building; this works equally well inside or outside in all weathers (just provide enough hats and gloves for everyone!)

- **Low-lighting** is important – use draped fabrics or fairy lights to create an inviting, magical feel
- **Provide materials** for the children to create their own 'dens' or cosy spaces together as a group
- **Share food**: healthy eating and picnics can happen indoors or outdoors at any time of year – practice mindfulness, eating slowly, preparing food together and growing fruit and vegetables
- **Practice 'we' time**: communal reading, folklore, storytelling, singing and dancing

■■■■■■■■■   Reflective questions   ■■■■■■■■■

- What are the limitations of outdoor learning in your experience?
- How can these spaces be developed to their full potential?
- What should be the role of the adult?
- Should the activities be child-led or adult-led?

Understanding the world

As mentioned briefly earlier, learning in the outdoors offers direct contact with nature and enables children to respond using all their senses: touch, taste, smell, sight and sound, alongside other types of sensory perception; balance, weight, heat and light. The sense of touch, in particular, is related to feeling and being immersed in an environment that supports learning by inviting curiosity and amazement. Adults have a responsibility here too – we cannot and must not fake our sense of wonder; children will know. Instead, we can go about co-constructing our knowledge of the natural world together, as co-researchers undertaking fieldwork with the intention to produce questions and search for answers; 'one of the most extraordinary aspects of creativity', according to Carla Rinaldi (2021, p.80). These questions, or 'initial hypotheses' to use the language of science, offer may possible directions for children's research and many possible destinations or provisional 'landing points' for knowledge. As an adult it is important to share your own hypothesis and research with them, sharing problems and discussing strategies during the journey. In that sense, you are 'the child's travelling companion in this search for meaning...' (Rinaldi, 2021, p.80). The explanatory theories they develop in an attempt to give answers reveal the ways in which they perceive, question and interpret reality, and importantly, their relationship with it.

Dialogues with nature

The starting point should always be a question, a 'provocation' or a context for the research. For example, we might ask 'how is grass born?' or 'why do leaves change?', then, working alongside the children, we might select an area of wild grass or natural space outside for fieldwork (demarcated with string perhaps) and using the following tools for looking, encourage them to use 'more sensitive eyes':

- **Binoculars/magnifying glass** – allows children to amplify their observations of nature
- **Cardboard tube** – narrows the field of vision and enables 'focused looking'
- **Card frame/window mount** – encourages an appreciation of form, structure, light and shade
- **Microscope** – reveals details normally hidden to the human eye

If the weather is inclement or seasonal changes make these activities challenging then consider bringing the outside indoors and creating a 'winter garden' with potted plants, gathered specimens and organic materials. Alternatively, try using windows to 'collect light' from the outside garden or spaces, capturing it through natural materials or man-made items; coloured acetate sheets, reflective surfaces (e.g., recycled CDs), lenses and mirrors.

Other useful tools include **Lightboxes** – these offer many possibilities for physical interaction with organic specimens and natural materials such as leaves, flowers and petals and can reveal elements that might otherwise remain hidden within, such as:

- Colour
- Internal structure
- Transparency
- Translucency
- Form

'Simplexity'

From these simple acts of observation, looking and recording (through drawing, painting, clay modelling and digital photography) grow opportunities to re-invent the pre-school as a site for research and critical thinking. Consider 're-launching' and extending themes based on the children's ideas and interests, moving from simplicity to complexity in their thinking. Neuroscientists have developed the term 'simplexity' for this innate ability; when we are able to explore complex ideas from a very simple starting point (Berthoz, 2019; Di Paolo, 2023). The illustration in Figure 11.7 shows how we might move in eight simple steps from concrete experience to abstract thought using an embodied approach and the philosophy of phenomenology (Merleau-Ponty, 1980). Essentially, phenomenology involves examining the nature of perception and the essence of things as we experience them, often referred to as 'being in the world' (Merleau-Ponty, 1962). This example uses the simple starting point of an autumn leaf gathered by a child outside the classroom.

Recognition

This deeper thinking can be embedded by encouraging whole class discussions of what different groups of children have been researching and doing to develop more sophisticated levels of analysis. This dialogue between children should be recorded by the adults as it reveals the learning processes of each group of children and the themes of their research. Presented to a

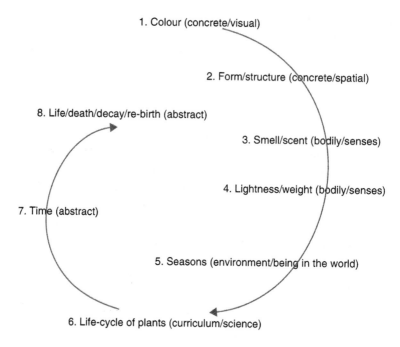

1. Colour (concrete/visual)

2. Form/structure (concrete/spatial)

8. Life/death/decay/re-birth (abstract)

3. Smell/scent (bodily/senses)

4. Lightness/weight (bodily/senses)

7. Time (abstract)

5. Seasons (environment/being in the world)

6. Life-cycle of plants (curriculum/science)

Figure 11.7 'Why do leaves change?' using 'simplexity' – A phenomenological approach

high quality this documentation can then be shared with parents as a record that tells the story of their time lived together and their shared interests. Children are aware of the challenges we all face, including ecology, our relationship with the planet, climate change and sustainability, and even education for peace in a time of war and crisis. We underestimate their ability to understand complex issues at our peril, but these challenges are also opportunities for learning, questioning and dialogue (Woolley, 2010).

Conclusion

This chapter has explored the idea that children are born researchers with a natural sense of curiosity about the world and has looked at ways in which creativity can support their research and thinking. We have seen how powerful interdisciplinary approaches can be when we combine science, technology, engineering, arts and mathematics and how creative thinking can be applied to any discipline. Digital technologies, when combined with analogue resources, are an especially powerful tool for creative inquiry and 'possibility thinking'. Cultural settings such as museums, art galleries and libraries provide rich opportunities for learning outside the classroom, and we have explored the role of architecture and the environment as 'the third teacher'. Creative spaces, both indoors or outdoors can open-up possibilities for social learning, development and the co-construction of knowledge.

Further Reading and Resources

Early Childhood Maths Group https://earlymaths.org/

The Digital Landscapes Atelier (Reggio Emilia) https://www.reggiochildren.it/en/ateliers/atelier-paesaggi-digitali-en/

Kids in Museums – working with museums, heritage sites and cultural organisations in the UK to make them more welcoming for children, young people and families: https://kidsinmuseums.org.uk/

ecARTnz – e-magazine of professional practice for early childhood educators in Aotearoa New Zealand: STEAM Special Issue, 2020 (Dr Janette Kelly-Ware, University of Waikato, provides examples from Australia, Switzerland, the Netherlands, Belgium and Germany): https://elp.co.nz/resources/ecartnz-magazine/

12
CREATIVE PEDAGOGIES
Across all areas of learning
Nicola Watson

The adult had the task of accompanying the child, of being with the child, of caring for the child. This is a kind of "leading" that often walks behind the one who is led. (Max van Manen, 2016, p.37)

━━━━━ **Chapter overview** ━━━━━

Creativity is often seen as synonymous with the arts. Like 'a horse and carriage' or 'social and emotional development', 'creativity and the arts' rolls off the tongue as though the two were one and the same. This chapter separates creativity from what we would recognise as the arts (activities covered in other chapters) and explores how creative pedagogies can inspire and support children's creative thinking across all aspects of learning. Firstly, we will define key terms in order to help identify what we mean by and what distinguishes creative pedagogies. The difference between teaching creatively (in-the-moment-planning) and teaching which supports children's creative thinking will be distinguished. Although these often act in synergy so that teachers teach creatively and teach *for* creativity (Jeffrey and Craft, 2004), they do not always do so. Pedagogies which emphasise the *learners'* rather than the teachers' creative thinking take centre stage in this chapter. The chapter concludes that creative pedagogies which embrace this principle recognise the centrality of developing children's creative thinking as essential to helping them develop problem-solving and original ideas to help them navigate the challenges and opportunities in the twenty-first century.

Defining pedagogy

The origin of the term 'pedagogy' stems from the Greek for 'child' (paidí) and for 'to lead' (ágō), so, the literal translation is 'to lead the child' (Kumar Shah, 2021). Whereas the term 'teacher' may be construed as neutral (simply one who transmits knowledge to learners), the role of the pedagogue has multiple interpretations. Thinking more deeply about what 'pedagogy' means helps to tease out some of the complex influences and orientations of the art of teaching. Firstly, there is a recognition that pedagogy is formed by its context; the socio-cultural influences of the values and ideology of the individual, the institution, community, culture and time in history (Siraj-Blatchford et al., 2002). This is perhaps more easily understood by using the analogy of the curriculum. Most of us would recognise the curriculum as relating to subject content such as Maths, English, Geography and so on. However, which subjects are seen as worthy of study depends upon the priorities of educational institutions which are governed by policies of the social and political systems of the day. For example, as part of its 'levelling up' agenda, the current government's white paper on education proposes 'payments to recruit and keep talented physics, chemistry, computing and maths teachers working in disadvantaged schools' (Department for Education, 2022a). This reflects the social and economic value currently afforded to STEM subjects. In contrast, historically, priorities were different. As we saw in Chapter 2, religious instruction was central to education for centuries and in some cultures, this remains the case today.

Whereas the curriculum relates to *what* is taught, pedagogy is concerned with *how and why* it is taught. As with curricula, this varies according to particular values but also the principles and ethics of *how* knowledge should be constructed and shared (Palaiologou, 2012, p.135).

Beghetto (2021, p.480) points out that:

> Teachers need to believe that they can support student creativity in their classroom. This has less to do with whether or not they value student creativity, as previous research indicates most generally do value creativity, and more about whether teachers have the autonomy, curricular time, and knowledge of how to support student creativity.

It is plain that what and how children learn is never neutral and an awareness of the complexities of pedagogy is essential when nurturing children's creativity. As it is a diverse concept, it is more accurate perhaps to think of *pedagogies* rather than a singular and defined philosophy of pedagogy and in this chapter, we are exploring a range of pedagogies which lend themselves to optimising creativity.

Exploring pedagogies

Pedagogies can be separated into two dominant paradigms (Kumar Shah, 2021):

- The didactic transmission of uncontested knowledge by the pedagogue to the learner (the traditional model)

- A dialogic, social process within a community of practice, whereby knowledge is constructed in partnership between the learner and pedagogue within a specific cultural context (Smidt, 2009, p.155) (the social model)

In Early Childhood Education and Care (ECEC), the traditional model broadly equates to the 'early education' approach whereby children are set goals and targets, and their progress is monitored with a view to attaining outcomes and 'school readiness' (Wall et al., 2015, p.23). This approach is informed by behaviourist theory, a dominant influence on teaching throughout most of the twentieth century. As discussed in Chapter 3, behaviourism views learning as being driven by the environment in which the learner is conditioned by rewards for what is deemed desirable behaviour. According to this theory, development is synonymous with learning and so children are viewed as passive rather than as active participants in learning. Pedagogies can stifle as well as nurture children's creativity and clearly the educator is pivotal in supporting children's early development of creative thinking (Legget, 2017, p.845). Behaviourism can be seen as at odds with developing children's creativity as it fails to address what Newman and Newman (2007, p.155) identify as the individual's 'power of competence, curiosity and mastery as motivations for learning'. Although behaviourism is still evident and influential in ECEC today (think behaviour charts and stickers for 'good' behaviour), its influence has been eroded by twentieth century theorists who have challenged its legitimacy and its allegedly simplistic view of the child as passive.

In ECEC, the social model, whereby knowledge is constructed in partnership and within a specific context is visible as the 'social pedagogy' approach which 'focuses more on the experiences and actual pedagogical practices rather than child outcomes and achievements' (Wall et al., 2015, p.23). In other words, it represents a child-centred approach where the pedagogue is attuned to the individual child, observing and reflecting upon what the child is experiencing and communicating. The social pedagogue aims to respond to the child's needs by providing appropriate opportunities for learning in a supportive environment. Evidence suggests that child-centred approaches are more likely to improve a child's motivation to learn, creativity, independence, self-confidence and initiative, and perhaps counter-intuitively have better long-term outcomes (Wall et al., 2015, p.59).

Some roots of creative pedagogies

In Chapter 1, definitions of creativity were debated, and it was acknowledged that the elements associated with creativity can be applied across the curriculum rather than confined to the arts. In aiming to foster children's creative thinking across all areas of learning, creative pedagogies seek to support children's imagination, theorising, exploration, curiosity and ingenuity. It is useful here to trace some of the historical influences which have informed social pedagogies today which place great value on the elements comprising creativity.

Socrates – Ancient Greece

Pedagogies which view learning as a social process position learners as active participants in the learning process and thereby as 'agents of their own learning' (Broström, 2017, p.4). The roots of this approach can be traced back more than two thousand years, to the Greek philosopher, Socrates (circa 470BC–399BC) who advocated posing questions rather than instruction to develop students' engagement in thinking in what became known as the Socratic Method. This method used open-ended questions and was designed to promote deeper thinking and exploration of topics, rather than to find a right answer (Crappell, 2018). Fisher (2005, p.23) points out that if a child's responses are rejected and corrected by adults, they cease inventing and speculating and instead look to the adult to supply answers to their questions. Therefore, closed questions (those with a wrong or right answer) potentially inhibit children's exploratory impulses and hypothesising whereas open-ended questions, (those without a wrong or right answer) support and encourage these dispositions.

John Dewey (1859–1952)

The influential educationalist, philosopher and founder of the progressive education movement in the twentieth century emphasised the notion of the child as an active-participant in the learning process. Indeed, he insisted that 'There is I think no point in the philosophy of progressive education which is sounder than its emphasis upon the importance of the participation of the learner in the formation of the purposes which direct his activities in the learning process' (Dewey, 1997, p.67). This made me think of my own experience in secondary school of Maths lessons. We, pupils, were given a book of Logarithms to aid our calculations and instructed on how to use them. I still have no idea what a logarithm is or its purpose although I was taught to apply them in my work and so nothing was learned.

Rousseau – The enlightenment

The eighteenth century in Europe saw the rise of philosophical ideas which emphasised reason and scepticism and challenged traditional, religious doctrines. Jean-Jacques Rousseau (1712–1778), was an influential philosopher during this period and he advocated for a 'child-centred' approach to education whereby 'expression rather than repression' was foregrounded (Johnston et al., 2018, p.19). His views were regarded as highly controversial at the time, but his ideas were influential in the early years' education and influential in the development of experiential learning, popular in the latter part of the twentieth century (Johnston et al., 2018, pp.19–20). Dewey too, believed that education should be child-centred. He asserted that education 'is a process of living and not preparation for future living', emphasising the importance of the quality of the child's experience in the processes of learning.

Lev Vygotsky

The twentieth century Russian psychologist, Lev Vygotsky (1896–1934) also advocated a child-centred approach to pedagogy, emphasising the importance of play to learning. He argued that play was inherently creative:

> A child who sits astride a stick and pretends to be riding a horse; a little girl who plays with a doll and imagines she is its mother; a boy who in his games becomes a pirate, a soldier, or a sailor, all these children at play represent examples of the most authentic, truest creativity. (Vygotsky, 2004, p.11)

Vygotsky rejected the behaviourist model of *learning as development*. Rather than regarding children as 'empty vessels' to be filled by the learned pedagogue, Vygotsky regarded learning and development as mutually dependent and interactive. He wrote that, 'Learning awakens a variety of *internal development processes* (my italics) that are able to operate only when the child is interacting with people in his environment and in cooperation with his peers' (Vygotsky, 1978, p.90). This demonstrates Vygotsky's understanding that learning takes place in collaboration with others and that knowledge is socially constructed within a specific cultural context. Like Vygotsky, Dewey also recognised learning as situated within a social context, claiming that 'education comes through the stimulation of the child's powers by the demands of the social situations in which he finds himself' (Dewey, 1897, p.229).

The twentieth century

Thanks to Vygotsky, Bruner, Dewey and others, the social constructivist view of education is well established in ECEC. The main tenet of this view is that as human beings, we construct knowledge, gradually developing a mental map of understanding about the world around us (Wilson, 2014, p.209). However, in order to develop beyond the elementary mental functions with which we are born, the development of higher mental functions must be initiated by social interaction (Keenan and Evans, 2009, p.172). Further research concurs with the idea that cognitive development is 'culturally situated', meaning that it varies according to the social environment rather than being universal across cultures (Newman and Newman, 2007, pp.152–153). This has implications for the role of the pedagogue, as their approach and consequent interactions with learners can directly impact the course and quality of learning and development. Mohammed (2014, p.114) concurs with this view, suggesting that 'A curriculum only becomes restrictive and prescriptive from how the adult views it, understands it, interprets it, and in turn implements it'.

A democratic paradigm

Thus far we have traced some aspects which have influenced the development of creative pedagogies including the use of open-ended questions, a child-centred approach and a constructivist methodology which invites the learner to be an active-participant in the learning process. These aspects coalesce to provide an approach which foregrounds the child's voice in a democratic paradigm of creative pedagogies. Building on this, exploring the work of the following theorists, we can begin to establish how we might put into practice these ideals. If we want to embrace the idea of democratic practice (which aligns with the definition of creativity as democratic rather than elite as discussed in Chapter 1), we need to be aware of where the balance of power lies. This is important because to be creative is inherently to be uncertain and uncertainty can feel uncomfortable. Davey (2012, p.99) describes the creative thinker as one who has a tolerance of ambiguity, perseverance, the courage of their own convictions and a willingness to take risks. Therefore, children need to feel that their uncertainty is valued by the adults who care for them. It's all too easy to (perhaps unknowingly), fail to acknowledge, override or impose ideas, rather than respond with sensitivity and self-awareness.

The philosopher Michel Foucault (1926–1984) suggested that in all human relationships there is a power dynamic. It might seem self-evident that in a pedagogue/learner or adult/child relationship the adult holds the power, although any teacher or parent will know from experience that the balance of power can be challenged and contested. Even so, pedagogues and learners are positioned in a fiduciary relationship, whereby authority is granted to an individual by virtue of their professional role conferred by an employer, institution, community or culture. Accordingly, pedagogues need to be conscious of the balance of power and how it is used (or perhaps inadvertently, misused). Another philosopher and educator who was concerned with the dynamics of power was Paulo Freire (1921–1997). Having worked with adult learners, Freire agreed with the idea that learners are not 'empty vessels' to be filled by more-able others but that each individual carries with them experiences and cultural knowledge which informs their understanding and ways of seeing the world. He too argued for a dialogic approach to education whereby pedagogues and learners work in partnership to co-construct knowledge. Crucially, however, Freire highlighted the idea that 'sharing knowledge is explicitly about sharing power, and may meet with resistance from more privileged groups who benefit from existing systems of education' (Yarrow and Fane, 2019, p.14); hence, his support for the dialogic approach which valued the contributions of learners in a democratic learning environment.

The idea that young children also bring to ECEC settings cultural knowledge and understanding and that this may be unacknowledged or dismissed is central to the work of Gonzales et al (2006) whose concept of 'funds of knowledge' was influenced by Vygotsky and they agreed that cultural practices act as tools and resources in the development of thinking. The premise and the findings of Gonzales and Moll's work were that, 'the education process can be greatly enhanced when teachers learn about their students' everyday lives' (Gonzales et al., 2006, p.6). This perspective positions learners as capable and as having strengths which are respected and acknowledged in the co-construction of knowledge.

The linguistic anthropologist, Shirley Brice Heath's (1983) position aligns with this strength-based approach. She sees children who are regarded as unsuccessful in formal education as underserved by their pedagogues. In the 1980s, she carried out a longitudinal study of the literacy practices of two, marginalised communities, the children from which were judged unsuccessful at school. Although both communities were working class and underprivileged, they had distinct and contrasting expectations of interactions with their children. Accordingly, when the children entered education, each group had very different needs and responded to the dominant pedagogy in different ways. This demonstrates the need for a strength-based approach which recognises and is responsive to how cultural practices shape the way in which people experience the world. Adult intervention then needs to be optimal and judicious, with a commitment to understanding the child's lifeworld orientation, and a commitment to guiding and being guided by the learner.

Lifeworld orientation

The term 'lifeworld orientation' is a concept integral to **social pedagogy** in the social work discipline which is practiced predominantly in Germany and parts of Europe and is beginning to influence the practice of social work, care and education in the UK. Put simply, to consider another person's lifeworld orientation is to put oneself in their shoes and to try appreciate the world as they experience it based upon what is known about their experiences, their cultural context, their skills and strengths. Grunwald and Thiersch (2009, p.132) suggest that the development of the concept was in response to the Second World War when German 'social work and social care took a largely repressive, disciplinary and administrative form, in accordance with the restorative rigidity of the time'. By taking a lifeworld orientation approach, the pedagogue is more able to ascertain where support is needed and crucially where it is not. Of course, the pedagogue will have their own lifeworld orientation which will impact their values, assumptions, perceptions and priorities and so should strive to be conscious of their positionality and the balance of power and its exercise.

■■■■■ Reflective questions ■■■■■

Take some time to think about your own lifeworld orientation:

- How might your experiences, cultural context, skills and strengths colour the way you position yourself as a pedagogue in relation to your learners?
- What similarities do you share with learners which may have the potential to be explored and expanded?
- Can you identify diverse lifeworld orientations in those with whom you work? How might you learn from these?

Creative pedagogies in practice

Having established *what* creative pedagogies might entail, we now focus on *how* they might be applied in practice. In Chapter 2, the benefits of creativity were considered in relation to children's well-being. Creativity and well-being are inextricably linked. Fisher (2005) confirms that creativity requires both feeling and thinking. The connections between personal fulfilment, well-being and creativity are well documented (Maslow, 1943, 1968) and so, for creativity to flourish, the learner's environment must feel emotionally safe; a space where the learner feels secure enough to 'be curious, take risks, use complex ideas and exercise the imagination' (Fisher, 2005, p.35). Claxton (2018, p.47) points out that 'how people approach learning, and how successfully they respond to novelty or difficulty, depends as much on these acquired attitudes as on any immutable kind of intelligence'. The nurturing of creative thinking then, must begin with the prioritisation of learners' well-being above all else (Ephgrave, 2018) (see case study below for a practice example).

Creative pedagogic strategies we consider here include child-led practice, in-the-moment planning and sustained shared thinking.

Child-led practice

'The most creative people are usually very motivated people. They love what they do and are intrinsically driven by the subject rather than any promised rewards or external goals' (Grigg and Lewis, 2019, p.24). This applies to everyone and in particular, to young children, who according to Winnicott (1964) begin with a belief that they own their environment and the people in it. Only as they develop socially do they become aware that there are other claims to ownership of the environment beyond themselves. Accordingly, children are most deeply engaged when they have autonomy. Ephgrave (2018) suggests that insisting children do things they don't want to, induces anxiety and actually inhibits brain development. There is evidence to support this assertion as Wall et al. (2015, p.55) confirm 'child-directed practices are likely to improve children's socio-emotional and soft skills, such as their motivation to learn, creativity, independence, self-confidence, general knowledge and initiative'. Ephgrave's (2018, p.3) stance that 'it is absolutely critical that we start with the child, be led by the child and find ways to respond which suit the child' is compelling. The following case study illustrates a child-centred approach and demonstrates several aspects of creative pedagogy.

▬▬▬ Case study - Muhammad and George ▬▬▬

This case study is an extract from a small-scale research project (Watson, 2018) which sought to support children aged 3-5 who engaged in conflicts with one another. The names of the participants have been changed.

The conflict involved Muhammad and George; boys aged five. They were playing a game of 'Peter Pan' outside with Billy, aged four. Billy ran up to Olive, the practitioner, to tell her that George had taken Muhammad's toy sword. Realising what was being reported, George shouted aggressively, 'I didn't snatch it, you liar!'.

Olive calmly asked Muhammad and George 'Could you come here please?' She then invited Muhammad and George to tell *one another* in turn their versions of what had happened. She made *no judgements* but acknowledged their feelings and in doing so mutualised their concerns; (they both wanted the 'sword'). She asked them, 'So what could we do?' This invited the children to

(Continued)

(Continued)

generate their own solutions. After some negotiation Muhammad suggested to Olive, 'I think you have to make Peter Pan costumes. One for George and one for me'. Olive suggested that they might do this together and Muhammad and George went to find the materials they thought they would need.

Deconstructing the case study

Rather than using her power and authority to bring the conflict to an end, Olive adopted a child-centred approach evidenced by:

- Focusing on the process of managing the social relationship rather than achieving an outcome.
- Inviting Muhammad and George to talk to one another and facilitating their exchange. This meant that their feelings were heard and acknowledged.
- Listening and respecting their feelings helped George calm down as the social environment was safe rather than threatening.
- Supporting George and Muhammad in approaching the problem creatively by asking open questions so that they were able to generate ideas and solve problems.
- By suggesting that George and Muhammad work together to make costumes, Olive presented an opportunity for creative collaboration with the potential to strengthen social bonds and feelings of belonging.

In-the-moment-planning

Teaching for creativity may well arise spontaneously from teaching situations in which it was not specifically intended (Jeffrey and Craft, 2004). In-the-moment-planning is a concept which recognises that relying upon pre-planned activities and desired outcomes (thereby reflecting a traditional model of ECEC), neglects the unplanned, real-time events and the spontaneous possibilities which arise in a learning environment. I suspect it is what many pedagogues do intuitively. Certainly, when I was an ECEC practitioner, I would plan ahead minimally, aware that neither I nor the children would follow an imaginary projected course of events. I would subsequently (and secretly) plan retrospectively so that my planning mirrored what had transpired. In fact, I was planning for accountability (for the prospective Ofsted Inspector or Line manager) rather than planning for learning. The concept of in-the-moment-planning was yet to be recognised but how much more vibrant could the collective pedagogical reflections have been if it was? We have Ephgrave (2018) to thank for legitimising in-the-moment planning. She explains it as 'uniquely suited to that unique child in that unique moment. The adult will be considering (either consciously or instinctively) whether they can add anything in that moment to benefit the child' (Ephgrave, 2018, p.1). This consideration demonstrates the art of adult intervention. It is not always obvious if and when to intervene in children's activity and as we have discussed, adults can stifle as well as support children's creativity. Therefore, pedagogues must reflect upon when and why to intervene in children's play and activity and attempt to optimise the benefit to the child.

Sustained shared thinking

Sustained shared thinking (SST) occurs when two or more individuals 'work together' in an intellectual way to solve a problem, clarify a concept, evaluate an activity, extend a narrative etc. Both parties must contribute to the thinking and it must develop and extend the understanding. It can occur at any time and within any activity. (Howard et al., 2020, pp.1026-1027)

The concept of SST at first glance is quite simple. It demonstrates collaboration co-construction and the opportunity for expanding learning in the learners' Zone of Proximal Development (Vygotsky, 1978). SST as a creative pedagogy offers the possibility of a bridge between learner autonomy and adult support to develop creativity. Bearing in mind accepted definitions of what constitutes creativity, i.e., it must be original and of value, SST can help support the achievement of these two elements. Beghetto (2021, p.474) explains that 'in order for a response to be considered creative, it needs to be both original and meaningfully meet the task constraints'. The constraints will vary according to the context. For example, being of value beyond its expression may be less important in dance and more important in solving a mathematical problem. SST can support the balancing of the learner's original ideas with achieving value within a meaningful context.

Together, these strategies help to minimise power imbalance by respecting the child's voice and co-constructing the learning environment whilst respecting the young child's 'intrinsically playful nature' (Legget, 2017, p.852). In combination, they can contribute to the creation of social conditions conducive to children's creative thinking.

Case study - Kira and Thalia

The following case study reflects real events in an ECEC setting. It demonstrates optimal intervention and sustained shared thinking. The names of the children have been changed.

This case study concerns Kira and Thalia, aged four, both of whom had a developing but not secure, understanding of number bonds to ten. The practitioner, Sabine, made available boxes of Cuisenaire rods; these are coloured wooden or plastic rods which can be used to support children's understanding of mathematical concepts.

Although the rods were new to the children, no explanation or introduction was given. They were simply left on a table over a period of weeks. Both children were curious about them, and the first time they encountered the rods, each explored their physical properties; their smooth texture, and variety of colours and sizes. They began to build with them, experimenting with upright structures such as 'houses' and 'bridges'. As they worked, they talked to themselves and one another, in planning and evaluating their creations. As they became more familiar with them, they used the boxes lids to make flat pictures. Over time, using the lids to contain them, the children explored the relative sizes of the rods. One day, Kira began

(Continued)

(Continued)

spontaneously to order the rods. Thalia was motivated to do the same and both children clearly gained satisfaction from their discovery as they returned to this activity many times.

At this stage, Sabine did not intervene by seeking to attribute number properties to the rods but continued to observe the children's developing sophistication in their understanding of the rods' properties. Eventually, Kira and Thalia began to attribute numbers to the rods *themselves* and at this stage, Sabine began to engage in sustained shared thinking with them. Over time, she modelled the mathematical language of addition (same, equal, more, less, etc.), posing questions and challenges; 'How can you make them all the same size?' and later 'Can you make them all ten?'. Eventually, Kira and Thalia were delighted by what they called their 'adding up machine' which demonstrated number bonds to ten. They had created their own resource which they used in other related activities.

Deconstructing the case study

Sabine adopted an optimal intervention approach evidenced by:

- Carefully observing, over time, the children's interactions with the Cuisenaire rods. This meant they were able to experiment, curate, problem-solve and make discoveries unhindered by adult intervention.
- Respecting their autonomy, shared enterprise and feelings of competence intervening only when their hypotheses about numbers were explicit whereupon she supported their thinking by modelling the language themselves had chosen to attribute to the rods.

When she did intervene, she used sustained shared thinking by

- Using open questions
- Modelling mathematical language
- Engaging in dialogue which resulted in problem-solving and extending possibilities beyond what the children had managed by themselves

---

■■■■■■ Reflective questions ■■■■■■

- How much does your practice reflect child-led practice?
- How do you decide when and if to intervene in a child's activity? Make a list of the considerations which might inform your decision.
- Analyse the list you have made. What factors underpin your reasoning?

Conclusion

Creativity can and should permeate every area of learning and the knowledge and practice of creative pedagogies supports children's creative responses and development. Respecting and valuing the voice of the child enhances the learning process and children's intrinsic motivation. It is also intrinsically rewarding for the pedagogue who is engaged with the vital work of responding to learners' needs in creative ways.

The examples from practice shared in this chapter I hope have demonstrated how creative pedagogies can be applied in areas where creativity might be less obvious or even, counter-intuitive. A child-centred approach can help us see daily routines such as mealtimes and conflicts with others as opportunities for finding new and rewarding ways of being and doing.

Creative approaches to problem-solving are essential if we are to tackle the immense challenges presented by the twenty-first century. We need our 'little scientists' to develop those attitudes to learning which enable them to dare to think original thoughts, imagine futures and share them so that we might help make them happen.

Further reading and resources

Arnott, L. and Duncan, P. (2019) Exploring the pedagogic culture of creative play in early childhood education. *Journal of Early Childhood Research, 17*(4), pp. 309–328.

Cremin, T., Glauert, E., Craft, A., Compton, A. and Stylianidou, F. (2015) Creative little scientists: Exploring pedagogical synergies between inquiry based and creative approaches in Early Years science. *Education 3–13, 43*(4), pp. 404–419.

Sefton-Green, J., Thomson, P., Bresler, L. and Jones, K. (eds.) (2012) *The Routledge International Handbook of Creative Learning.* 2nd edn. London: Routledge.

Social Pedagogy Professional Association https://sppa-uk.org/

13

THE CREATIVE AND REFLECTIVE PRACTITIONER

Creativity is how we can encounter the world, and deal with almost anything and everything. It is what makes us human and humane. Alice Kettle, Textile Artist

━━━━━━━━ **Chapter overview** ━━━━━━━━

This chapter will highlight the importance of developing oneself as a creative professional and a reflective practitioner and will encourage readers to consider their professional identity alongside the importance of research-informed professional development. This chapter explores key creative habits, reflective practice and the concept of 'praxis', the essential combination of action and reflection. We make the case for mentoring and coaching in early childhood education and argue that the sector should consider best practice as ethical practice. The numerous challenges facing the early childhood education workforce are examined, along with the importance of professional development networks.

This chapter also looks at the importance of visual metaphors and concepts such as the 'social imaginary' in developing a child's understanding of the world. It concludes by making the case for a critical pedagogy, seeing the classroom as a democratic space, valuing children's ideas, decision-making, agency and imagination in the post-modern context.

The creative professional

Throughout this book, we have explored the importance of developing oneself as a creative and critical thinker. The Centre for Real World Learning's *Five-dimensional model of creative thinking* (Lucas et al., 2013) was first introduced in Chapter 1, but here we see how it might be expanded and used to inform one's own personal philosophy, pedagogy, professional relationships at work and our approach to supporting creative habits of mind in children. These five habits are adjectives (e.g., imaginative and inquisitive) describing qualities in the individual, whilst the fifteen sub-habits are action phrases to ensure the concepts are well grounded in the everyday:

- **Imaginative:** playing with possibilities, making connections, using intuition
- **Inquisitive:** wondering and questioning, exploring and investigating, and challenging assumptions
- **Persistent:** tolerating uncertainty, sticking with difficulty, daring to be different
- **Collaborative:** sharing the product, giving and receiving feedback, co-operating appropriately
- **Disciplined:** reflecting critically, developing techniques, crafting and improving

(Lucas and Spencer, 2017, p.22)

The last dimension, 'disciplined', contains the important habit of 'reflecting critically' and reminds us that we need to spend time developing expertise and skill; a 'slow pedagogy' (Cameron and Moss, 2020) that challenges the idea that creative ideas emerge instantly. It also highlights the fact that critical thinking is not incompatible with creativity. The importance of self-reflection and thinking in a reflective way helps us to process what we have experienced, to modify our understanding of the world based on that experience and ideally to transfer that learning beyond the immediate situation (Lucas and Spencer, 2017, p.78). Self-awareness is a valuable skill for children to develop as it helps them to assess what is and is not working, and to find new ways to solve problems. Self-awareness and self-reflection are also key skills for any early years professional and the following section explores different models of reflective practice that may be of use in the nursery or pre-school setting.

Reflective practice

In the early twentieth century, progressive educator John Dewey (1938) described reflection as the hallmark of intelligent action, but it could also be argued that reflection should be seen as the hallmark of professional action in practice. We must reflect on our own learning if we are to help others learn in a spirit of co-enquiry and this approach fits well with constructivist theories of learning, as discussed previously in Chapter 3.

David Schön, writing in the 1980s, explored how teacher learning is acquired through continuous action and reflection on everyday problems. Schön (1983) identified this as reflection 'in' and reflection 'on' action, a useful approach that has been adapted since to create new frameworks for reflection (see later section on Praxis and The Creative reflective cycle) (Aguirre-Jones and Elders, 2009). Hanson and Appleby (2015) claim the importance of developing critical self-awareness can be likened to what Schön (1983) describes as 'professional artistry'. This 'artistry' is evident in the skillful way that ECE professionals work with a diverse range of people and contexts, situations that require them to be creative and divergent with their thinking and actions. The clear message for practitioners is that 'you will soon discover that every day, every child, every family and every different context in which you work will require you to use your creative professional artistry to solve the issues that arise' (Hanson and Appleby, 2015). This pro-active solving of issues is classed as 'reflective activism' (2015, p.33) whereby practitioners question, examine and challenge different positions, including their own (Hanson and Appleby, 2017). This attitude is perceived as a 'way of being' for individuals and communities of practice. It builds on a strong base of values that assume personal and professional responsibility for improving the quality of provision for children and families (Hanson and Appleby, 2017, p.156).

However, it could be also argued that the reflective practitioner should reflect on their own values and potential conflicts between the values and perspectives of others. Brookfield has suggested the use of different 'lenses' (2017) for reviewing or evaluating any situation from different viewpoints. The main ones are:

- Autobiographical: what is our own perspective?
- What is the Child's perspective?
- Colleagues, peers and other practitioners: do they have other points of view?
- Theoretical knowledge/literature/policy: what are the issues?

Hanson has proposed adding a 'fifth' lens to Brookfield's original four 'lenses' for reflection. This is the wider socio-cultural perspective, that is to say, what is the *real-world* context of the children we are working with in this situation? This might be very different from our own personal experience and assumptions about the world and so we must consider the influences impacting the lives of others so we can better understand why things might be happening (Hanson and Appleby, 2017, p.155).

Praxis

The idea of reflective practice combined with activism has synergies with Freire's model of 'praxis' which he believed should play a central role in education. Praxis is the cycle of everyday action, reflection and the re-creation of action that leads to productive changes in life trajectories (Glassman and Patton, 2014). Indeed, the democratic values that underpin this idea are so central to Freire's ideas for education that they will be discussed in more depth later in this chapter.

The importance of learning from experience is central to both Freire's concept of praxis and Kolb's (2015) experiential learning cycle; however, some creative practitioners have taken this a step further and combined it with the values and principles of the Reggio Emilia Approach, in particular the 'pedagogy of listening' (Rinaldi, 2021). An excellent example of this is the creative reflective cycle developed by Deborah Aguirre Jones and Liz Elders, for House of Imagination (formerly 5 × 5 × 5 = creativity) (Aguirre-Jones and Elders, 2009). This model combines observing and working alongside the children (reflection 'in action') with adult group reflections to revisit what has happened in each session, analyse the children's activities and evaluate how best to support their interests going forward (reflection 'on action') (see Figure 13.1).

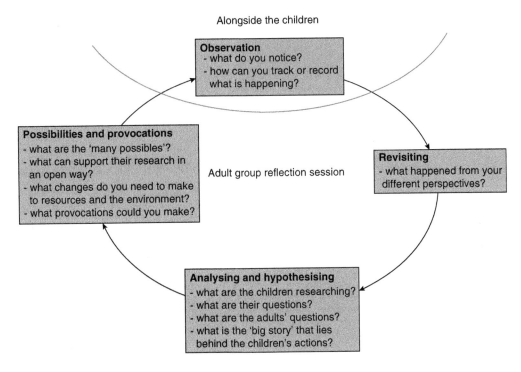

Figure 13.1 The creative reflective cycle

Source: Liz Elders and Deborah Aguirre Jones (2009) for 'House of Imagination' (formerly 5 × 5 × 5 = creativity). Published in *ReFocus Journal*, Issue 9, Sightlines Initiative, Newcastle upon Tyne.

This cycle provides the perfect model for partnership working in early childhood education and care (ECEC) settings, especially when collaborating with professionals with different specialisms or from different backgrounds, for example, artist-educators, cultural organisations and early childhood education. It can also lead to the development of new skills as the adults reflect, analyse and hypothesise together; a type of collaborative professional development that we shall explore in the next section.

Professional development

As we have discussed, there are a range of creative habits that ECE professionals can utilise, and praxis and 'reflective activism' are key to improving the quality of provision in any setting. Another key area is professional development; the role of the teacher as learner (Lucas and Spencer, 2017). In an ideal world, practitioners should be engaged in action research, personal and professional development, which is essential for effective early childhood education

(Solvason and Webb, 2022). There are many challenges facing the early years sector currently (see 'Issues and Challenges' section below) but one solution to navigating these issues is membership of professional development networks – not just focusing on individual Continuing Professional Development (CPD) but collaborative Joint Practice Development (JPD).

The following case study illustrates just such a network, with artists-in-residence and creative practitioners working alongside nursery staff and teachers in a spirit of collaboration, similar to the 'atelieristas' and 'pedagogistas' within the Reggio Approach; each acting as an advocate and mentor to other practitioners, planning, developing and disseminating best practice (Rinaldi, 2021). It also illustrates how research can be both commonplace or everyday and innovative at the same time (Solvason et al., 2021).

Case study - 'How to catch a moonbeam and pin it down'

Moonbeams is an early years' programme which focuses on arts and creativity, 'with, by and for' babies and children aged five and under. It provides a programme of action research, training and professional development, conferences and seminars, resources, interactive social networks including a Facebook community, and Podcasts to support creative and reflective practice in early years arts and creativity in the West Midlands.

Moonbeams has existed in many forms since its beginnings in 2002 when artists from different fields worked alongside educators in a wide range of settings where young children could explore creative and arts-based provocations. Each pairing of educator and artist would co-document and reflect upon the creative arts-based experiences offered, learning to understand what they were observing and participating in alongside of the children. This reflective space enabled the paring to then plan accordingly to meet with the children's own creative processes and approaches to learning.

Moonbeams (n.d.)

Reflective questions

- How might you benefit personally from joining a professional development network?
- Which creative practitioners could you collaborate with?
- What research projects might you jointly develop?

Ethical practice and the ethical practitioner

Those of you who have ever been involved in educational research with participants will be aware of the need for ethical approval and putting procedures in place to respect an individual's rights and to protect those involved, including the researcher, from harm (BERA, 2018). In this section, we make the case that the early years sector should consider best practice as ethical practice, going beyond just 'doing the right thing' in terms of safeguarding and confidentiality (Solvason, 2017). Solvason argues that we should be moving from a position of professional ethics (in research for example) to one of ethics in our professional lives, preparing ourselves, and those we work with, for the moral responsibility of early years' education (Solvason et al., 2021). Often this moral responsibility comes down to the choices we make, both on a mundane level (what to plan for this afternoon? What should the children have for lunch?) and a more profound, life-changing level (should I take that new job opportunity, even if it means re-locating?).

Carla Rinaldi (2021) reminds us that it is necessary to make choices that relate not only to pedagogy but also to ethics and values too. This act of choosing means 'having the courage of our doubts, of our uncertainties' and effectively means 'participating in something for which we take responsibility' (2021, p.128). Personal and professional development are things that we construct ourselves in relationship with others, based on shared values that may be chosen and constructed together (2021, p.100). Indeed, the term 'education' and 'values' are intrinsically linked in the sense that to educate is to transfer the intrinsic values of individuals and a culture and make these values 'extrinsic, visible, conscious and shareable' (2021, p.101). For the individual, values are those things to which we aspire or ideals by which we live. For a culture, values might be the 'norms' that help to define acceptable behaviour, social attitudes and beliefs (Hechter and Opp, 2001). However, it is a mistake to think that values are held universally, or for eternity. Instead, they evolve over time and change as they are discussed, transmitted and *created*. In actual fact, pre-schools are one of the key places where this process takes place, and it is no exaggeration to say that it is one of the biggest responsibilities they have. The critical role of the classroom as a democratic space is something that will be examined in more depth later in this chapter.

Mentoring and coaching

In the introduction to this chapter, I mentioned the importance of mentoring and coaching in early childhood education. Two key elements of this are the embedding of professional one-to-one support within a setting, and managers who can enable their staff to reach their full potential. Understanding the similarities, differences and overlap between coaching, mentoring, training and supervision is also essential in supporting reflective practice (Gasper and Walker, 2020). The main terms of reference are as follows:

- **Coaching:** usually involves an independent person who helps you identify an issue or problem in the workplace and then facilitates you to find your own creative solutions; it is *non-directive* in the sense that they are listening, asking questions and then reflecting back/summarising your own answers...

- **Mentoring:** usually involves a more senior or experienced colleague/peer from your sector who can offer advice, guidance and 'domain insight' (Cox et al., 2018); it is *dialogic* in the sense that expertise is shared and discussed in dialogue between mentor and mentee
- **Training:** usually involves a more knowledgeable tutor or teacher; it is *directive* in the sense that they are often instructing/telling you what to do and the relationship is one of expert versus novice/apprentice
- **Supervision:** the forum where all or some of the above can take place; this can take the form of weekly one-to-one meetings, monthly performance reviews or regular informal 'check-ins'

In reality, the distinction between these processes is not so simple or clearly defined and many who work in this ever-expanding field prefer to think of a sliding scale or 'coaching spectrum', from non-directive (coaching) at one end, to dialogic (mentoring) in the centre and directive (training) at the other end (Downey, 2022). There is also a wide range of theoretical approaches that can be utilised in mentoring and coaching, many based on psychology and psychotherapy techniques such as CBT (Cognitive Behavioural Therapy), Gestalt theory (a more holistic approach based on personal growth and noticing patterns of behaviour), narrative coaching, person-centred or solution-focused coaching (Clutterbuck, 2022) that, unfortunately, we do not have time to cover here.

To complicate things even further, definitions can also vary by sector, institution, country, culture and even Government initiative. One example is the recommendation from DfE (2010) for schools, that placement mentors, line managers and senior leaders can improve teaching and learning by using an approach called 'instructional coaching'; an apparent contradiction in terms as many believe coaching should never be 'instructional' but always *facilitative*.

Sound ethical practice should be central to mentoring and coaching, especially in a commercial sector that is largely unregulated (Passmore and Mortimer, 2011). Codes of Practice for coaching and mentoring are essential, but for reasons that we might not expect. Pre-agreements and 'contracting' ensure that both parties have clarity about their role (mentor/mentee or coach/client), confidentiality, the nature and duration of the relationship and the frequency of meetings. The ethical framework that is commonly used for mentoring, coaching and supervision is the Association for Coaching Global Code of Ethics (2021) that contains guidance on all these areas and other issues such as professional conduct, integrity, inappropriate interactions and potential conflicts of interest.

Finally, one further model that is relevant to all the themes we have discussed in terms of self-reflection, ethical practice, mentoring and coaching is Gibbs Reflective Cycle (1988). Originally developed by Graham Gibbs for a Further Education context, it has six main stages (see Figure 13.2) but is particularly useful to ECE practitioners in terms of its cyclical nature; it lends itself to reviewing repeated experiences in the workplace, allowing you to learn from things that either went well or didn't go well and plan accordingly. The six stages are:

- **Description** of the experience – what happened?
- **Feelings** and thoughts – how did you feel about the situation?
- **Evaluation** of the experience – what were the positives and negatives?
- **Analysis** to make sense of the situation – what different perspectives are there?
- **Conclusion** – what have you learned? what could you have done differently?
- **Action plan** – how would you deal with similar situations in the future?

(Gibbs, 1988)

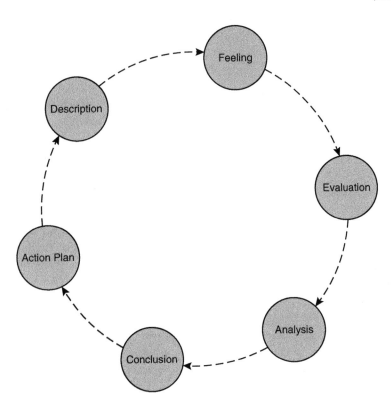

Figure 13.2 Gibbs reflective cycle (1988)
Source: University of Edinburgh (2020).

Issues and challenges within the early years' workforce

In Chapter 7, we looked at the policy context for early childhood education and heard from some outspoken critics of the current situation, such as Stephen Ball (2013, 2021) and others who claim the system of early childhood services in England remains flawed and dysfunctional, despite decades of investment and Government interference. Cameron and Moss (2020) argue that 'national discourse is dominated by the cost and availability of childcare at the expense of holistic education, while a hotchpotch of fragmented provision staffed by a devalued workforce struggles with a culture of targets and measurement' (2020). So, what exactly are the issues that are preventing this 'holistic education' that Cameron and Moss highlight in their analysis?

We might look, for example, at the impact of the pandemic on early childhood education (Sutton Trust, 2021); Government commitments to upskill and invest in training and CPD that have been abandoned in the Early Years' Workforce Strategy (DfE, 2017); the gender imbalance in the early years' workforce and the impact of this on children, even the gendered ways in which people engage with children (Josephidou and Bolshaw, 2020); or the essential role that teaching assistants played in keeping schools and nurseries functioning during lockdown (Moss et al., 2021).

Impact of the pandemic

The issue of the potentially damaging long-term effects of the coronavirus 2019 (COVID-19) pandemic on the education and development of children in the early years is only just starting to emerge in the research. A policy briefing by the Sutton Trust *Fairness First: Social Mobility, COVID and Education Recovery* (2021) was one of the first pieces of work to explore this in-depth. Polling by the Sutton Trust shows the experience of lockdown has led to huge concerns among parents about the healthy development of their children and worries on the part of schools about school readiness. Contained within the Sutton Trust's report are some important findings and recommendations. As well as highlighting its importance, the pandemic has exposed the fragility of the early years' sector; it is made up of many small and poorly funded private and voluntary providers. Pre-school age children have faced the same challenges as other children, lack of access to learning, fewer opportunities to play with their friends and less interaction with other adults. Children in this age group need more time in a high-quality educational setting and so eligibility for funded early education must be increased, particularly for those in low-income homes. There is a need for greater investment in the early years' sector to invest in and upskill the workforce, attract graduates and offer career progression (Sutton Trust, 2021, p.3). According to the authors of the report, this urgent need for investment could initially be addressed through the introduction of an Early Years' Premium, a clear example of a new policy idea that would certainly garner widespread public support in my opinion (see also Chapter 7: Policy context). This initiative could also help to develop a child's 'cultural capital'; often seen as essential for individual progression and access to privileged positions in an increasingly competitive society, as we shall continue to explore.

Cultural capital

Previously, in Chapter 10 we discussed the importance of developing children's cultural literacy (Hirsch, 1983), but in this next section we will unpack the not-unrelated idea of 'cultural capital'. The problematic issue of unequal access to positions of power in society has its origins in social class structures and familiarity with cultural codes in our early lives, according to the work of French sociologist Pierre Bourdieu (1984). Families (usually middle-class) who can afford to familiarise their children with the culture of the art gallery, theatre or museum are able to confer this distinction or social advantage upon them (Taylor, 2018). The individual is then judged as having innate good 'taste' when in actual fact it is a socio-economic advantage based on class. As Bourdieu himself stated, 'art and cultural consumption are predisposed, consciously and deliberately or not, to fulfil a social function of legitimating social differences' (Bourdieu, 1984, p.7).

In September 2019, Ofsted introduced the requirement for schools to develop pupils' cultural capital to their inspection framework in England, meaning for the first time, Ofsted began to assess schools against this criterion (CLA, 2019). Professionals across the arts sector reported increased interest from schools in working with them to deliver the new requirement for all schools to equip *pupils 'with the knowledge and cultural capital they need to succeed in life'*. This all sounds very positive, but what exactly is the 'knowledge and cultural capital' that Ofsted is referring to? Ofsted has shared its definition, derived from the wording of the National Curriculum, stating 'It is the essential knowledge that pupils need to be educated citizens, introducing them to *the best that has been thought and said* and helping to engender an appreciation of human creativity and achievement' (Ofsted, 2019) (my italics).

Many commentators have critiqued the way this narrow definition implies a hierarchy of high culture ('the best that has been thought and said') versus low or popular culture, whilst leaving out completely the cultural languages of music, dance and the visual arts. The use of the past tense also places the child in a passive position of not being able to actively contribute to this 'essential knowledge' themselves. If the definition of cultural capital remains narrow, then we run the risk of only some children gaining an advantage and this will only help to maintain the status quo:

> This leaves us in the paradoxical position that cultural education can simultaneously be a route to personal advancement, while entrenching class division at the level of society. This contention is clearly evidenced by the fact that the poorest state schools lack arts provision, while private schools invest heavily in the arts. (John Holden, CLA, 2019)

Arts Council England in its most recent strategic plan has acknowledged that for most young people, access to high-quality creative and cultural opportunities outside of the home is too dependent on their social background and their postcode (ACE, 2020, p.6). This high level of social inequality is highlighted in the book *The Spirit Level: Why More Equal Societies Almost Always Do* Better (2009) by Wilkinson and Picket. The authors show that many of society's problems, from mental illness to teenage pregnancy, anti-social behaviour and violence result from and are statistically linked with high levels of social inequality. With the widening poverty gap, some children have been left behind in terms of their access to creative opportunities and it is essential that engagement with the arts and creativity should not become merely the domain of the 'extracurricular' and determined by parents' ability to pay. A report by the Sutton Trust entitled *Parent Power* (2018) explores this in more depth and notes that children from professional households were more likely to take part in extracurricular activities. This reflects cultural capital, but also financial resources in the home, as those in lower social groups were more likely to take part in activities that didn't need to be paid for. The report concludes that

> Schools cannot be expected to rectify social problems and deep inequalities that begin from birth. But education has huge power to provide opportunity, and if the purpose of the education system is to give children the best chance of a start in life, then it is imperative that it does what it can to mitigate those inequalities. (Sutton Trust, 2018, p.52)

In this context of widening social inequality, how can we ensure that creativity, the arts and culture remain accessible to all children? Why is it important to reclaim the classroom as a democratic space? The next part of this chapter will address these and other questions.

Critical pedagogy and the classroom as a democratic space

> Education is a crucial site of power in the modern world… we teach the practice of freedom by modelling it as public intellectuals- the classroom becomes the space for how democracy works. (Henry Giroux, 2021)

Internationally renowned writer and cultural critic, Professor Henry Giroux, believes passionately in reclaiming education as a political practice to solve the many challenges that we face. His critical pedagogy is all about reclaiming matters of civic liberty and encouraging civic literacy to ensure a vibrant democracy, especially in the face of an increasingly aggressive neoliberal agenda that views the 'citizen as consumer' and where the needs of capital and the market take priority over society's needs and the needs of people. Indeed, Giroux claims that in the worst-case, social responsibility is reduced to individual choice. Instead, he argues that 'civic literacy is about learning about social problems and issues of inequality' (Giroux, 2021). Giroux defines critical pedagogy as 'thoughtful dialogue', 'learning the lessons of history' and 'to act with social responsibility'. Education is seen as a social concept – to empower individuals to be 'engaged social actors'; language especially is seen as a vehicle for critique and agency (Giroux, 2021).

Giroux's ideas are built on the pioneering work of Brazilian activist and academic, Paolo Freire (1921–1997). In his book *Education for Critical Consciousness* (1974), Freire takes the life situation of the learner as the starting point and describes the teaching of literacy to adults so they could more easily engage with the democratic process and the democratisation of culture (Freire, 1974, p.41). Freire was a fierce critic of the 'banking' concept of education and argued instead that 'knowledge emerges only through invention and re-invention, through the restless, impatient, continuing, hopeful enquiry human beings pursue in the world, with the world, and with each other' (1970, p.45). Most significantly, Freire highlighted the fact that as educators we can enable the 'practice of freedom'; 'the means by which we, teachers with learners, deal critically and creatively with reality and discover how to participate in the transformation of our world' (Freire, 1970, p.16).

This idea of 'hopeful enquiry' has strong links with the child-led pedagogy that is such a central part of the Reggio Emilia Approach to early childhood education (Rinaldi, 2021). We will continue to explore one particular element of this in the next section: the power of visual art education through children's use of visual metaphor and the 'social imaginary'.

Visual metaphor

Another very effective approach that has recently been researched by academics and early years practitioners together, is the use of metaphor and narrative, in particular visual metaphor in children's learning processes (Contini and Giuliani, 2022). Everyday objects, such as a simple kitchen utensil, a peg, a metal corkscrew, a plastic comb, or even a feather can be the starting point for children to generate imaginative stories and metaphors that reveal their understanding of the natural world. 'Children understand the world through stories' according to Malaguzzi (1998) and it is these visual metaphors, ideas and hypotheses that are an essential part of the learning process that help children to make sense of the reality around them. More precisely, visual metaphor can be understood as a poetic or symbolic language created by children that goes way beyond simple analogy and simile to reveal and make visible the mental processes that are activated in young children.

Natural phenomena such as clouds, weather, sound, light and colour are all both at the same time, scientific processes and opportunities for metaphor and innovation for young children (Contini and Giuliani, 2022, p.16). This approach links to our earlier discussions of the socially constructed nature of knowledge (see Chapter 3) and can be taken even further to help us understand how children might imagine or view themselves as part of a wider community or society, in philosophical terms; the 'social imaginary'.

Imaginaries

The imaginary or 'social imaginary' is not an easy concept to grasp but relates to the set of ideas, values and mental images that children and adults use to imagine their social selves as members of a larger group or society. It has its roots in continental philosophy and there is an important difference between the social imaginary and social theory; it is the way ordinary citizens 'imagine' their social surroundings and existence. According to Charles Taylor (2004) 'this is often not expressed in theoretical terms, but is carried in images, stories and legends' (2004, p.23), effectively, the stories that we tell ourselves about our history and identity.

Imaginaries also relate to the collaborative nature of education and children, adults, staff and parents all working together as a collective, as evidenced in the municipal nurseries and pre-schools of Reggio Emilia. This is a marked contrast to the situation in the UK, where education is taking an increasingly individualised and consumer-based approach. A recent rapid evidence review by Thomson and Maloy (2022) noted 'the absence of papers on citizenship and the small number of empirical studies which address political awareness, voice and empowerment appears to chime with critiques that the English national curriculum in particular has a strongly individualised emphasis on agency'.

The social imaginary also links to ideas about 'critical creativity' and learning through the arts (Adams and Owens, 2017); the intersection of the imaginary and the political, creativity and democracy. We might also consider the social imaginary in the light of children's working theories and interdisciplinary thinking, as we shall explore in this final part of the chapter.

Encouraging interdisciplinary thinking

In Chapter 11, we looked at children's 'working theories' (Hedges, 2021); how children revisit their own thinking in the light of new knowledge and how they might cross disciplinary boundaries between art, science, technology and maths. American academic, Danah Henriksen, has also looked at how creativity spans these different disciplines through a common set of thinking skills which she has identified as *The 7 Transdisciplinary Cognitive Skills for Creative Education* (Henriksen, 2018):

1 Observing/Perceiving
2 Patterning
3 Abstracting
4 Embodied Thinking
5 Modelling
6 Play
7 Synthesis

In the same way that Anderson and Krathwohl (2001) revised Bloom's original Taxonomy (1956) to emphasise creating (or 'synthesis') as the highest order of thinking (see Chapter 1), Henriksen defines synthesis as a form of knowledge or thinking where many or all of these skills (perceiving, patterning, abstracting, embodied thinking, modelling and play) can come together in a complex, rich and nuanced manner. 'This, we believe, is the root of true understanding' (Henriksen, 2018, pp.76–77).

Post-modern perspectives

As I mentioned in Chapter 1, some writers are very cautious about the idea of creating taxonomies or 'hierarchies of knowledge' at all. An alternative concept of knowledge, as not being linear or hierarchical, but a series of nodes and connections; 'a rhizome' (much like an organic system that grows in every direction) was first developed by French philosophers Gilles Deleuze and Felix Guattari (1999). In this concept, there is no 'tree of knowledge' with a central trunk of core ideas and associated roots and branches. Instead, we have something that shoots in all directions with no beginning or end, but always *in between*; a multiplicity of connecting thoughts and ideas. This has profound implications for teaching and learning in the sense that we should reject prescribed methods and goals and embrace uncertainty and complexity. In the words of Dahlberg et al. (1999), we should be building:

> a new pedagogical project, foregrounding relations and encounters, dialogue and negotiation, reflection and critical thinking; border crossing disciplines and perspectives, replacing either/or positions with and/also openness; and understanding the contextualised and dynamic nature of pedagogical practice...
> (Dahlberg et al., 1999, p.122)

Border crossings

According to Giroux, the student must function as a 'border crosser' – a person moving in and out of physical, cultural and social borders (Giroux, 1997), a continual process of change. As early years practitioners this means bringing in theories and concepts from different fields, not only education but also philosophy, architecture, science, literature and visual communication (Dahlberg and Moss, 2006, p.xvii). As the late bell hooks (1952–2021), American writer, academic and intellectual said in her landmark work *Teaching to Transgress* (1994), education is the practice of freedom; 'transgress those boundaries that would confine each pupil to a rote, assembly-line approach to learning' (hooks, 1994, p.13), whether they be racial, sexual or class boundaries.

Conclusion

This chapter has explored the importance of positioning oneself as a creative professional and an ethical and reflective practitioner, making the most of opportunities for networking, professional development, mentoring and coaching, in all its forms. The challenges facing the early years workforce have been examined, along with the debate around social inequality and the importance of developing cultural capital. This chapter has also made the case for a more democratic approach in the classroom, with practitioners who are not afraid to engage with critical pedagogy and encourage interdisciplinary thinking to support children's social imaginaries, visual metaphors and new forms of knowledge.

Further reading and resources

Holden, J. (2006) *Cultural Value and the Crisis of Legitimacy*. London: DEMOS.

CLA (Cultural Learning Alliance): champions a right to art and culture for every child: https://www.culturallearningalliance.org.uk/

CREC: Centre for Research in Early Childhood https://www.crec.co.uk/

House of Imagination: arts-based research and annual 'Forest of Imagination' festival of creativity: https://houseofimagination.org/

Moonbeams: professional development network supporting creative and reflective practice in early years arts https://moonbeams-ey.co.uk/

14
CONCLUSIONS AND NEXT STEPS

School is not preparation for life, it is life... Jerome Bruner (1996)

━━━━━━━━━━ **Chapter overview** ━━━━━━━━━━

This concluding chapter provides a vision for the future and includes four key questions for the creative early childhood education practitioner: how has your definition of creativity changed as a result of reading this book? What steps will you take next on your professional journey? What changes could you make to your own practice and what ideas do you hope to see developed in your setting? and finally, what recommendations would you make to the wider sector in terms of future policy and practice?

We will also examine what creative leadership might look like and the importance of connecting values, principles and relationships. Also, by examining and evaluating our own roles we can critically reflect upon ourselves as an 'agent of change'. In recognising and reflecting upon the problems we all face, we can take a holistic approach and propose potential solutions and recommendations for future practice, creating a 'pedagogy of hope'.

The pedagogy of relationships

The 'pedagogy of relations' is how Malaguzzi defined the teaching in the pre-schools of Reggio Emilia (Rinaldi, 2021, p.129), and this ethos really underpins all effective educational practice and especially managing change within a setting, or the 'art' of creative transition as he defined it (Rinaldi, 2021, p.127). Positive relationships are key to building a vision for the future and transforming practice in any setting and children's centres should really be seen as living organisms based on relationships. This relates to the theory of social pedagogy that is built on relationships, empathy and a person-centred approach, taking the time to understand the lifeworld orientation of every child (see Chapter 12).

Early childhood education practitioners can take inspiration from Rutger Bregman's ideas in his book *Human Kind* (2020). Bregman is concerned with promoting the idea that, in contrast to much established thinking in the social sciences and philosophy about the inherent selfishness and self-centred nature of human beings, more recent scientific research has shown that we are essentially collaborative creatures and want to work together for the common good. Humans have the unique ability and skill to learn from others: a capacity for social learning (Bregman, 2020). The essential values that connect this 'pedagogy of relationships' and which support and nurture it are visualised in Figure 14.1, with curiosity sitting at the very centre.

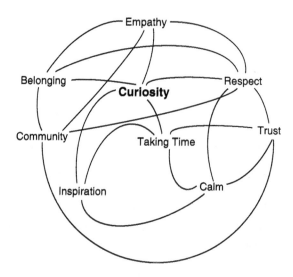

Figure 14.1 Connecting values to support a 'pedagogy of relationships'

Transformative dialogues: Becoming an agent of change

In order to be an effective agent of change, we must have buy-in and support from the whole community: practitioners, parents, staff and children. This approach sees any school or nursery as a public space, 'a place of encounter and connection, interaction and dialogue' (Dahlberg and Moss, 2006, p.xvi) with citizens, both young and old, living together in community. In this sense, it is a public space of central importance to democracy and should always be a site for ethical and political practice, offering hope for a renewed culture of childhood. The idea of the pre-school as a 'communicative system' where culture is formed (Cagliari et al., 2016) is an important one. Community should be visible, and we can engender a sense of belonging through the idea of creating a 'democratic piazza' – a public space or forum for discussion and participation where practitioners, parents, academics and children come together to explore new ideas of childhood, education and knowledge. In the Reggio Emilia Approach, the importance of this piazza or public entrance space cannot be underestimated and children understand its significance for sharing the subject of their dialogues, interests and research. This philosophy is closely aligned with the concept of 'Bildung'; the realisation of a transformative civic, moral and aesthetic education. According to Rowson (2019), 'Bildung entails a dynamic worldview that values independence of mind and spirit grounded in ecological and social interdependence' (2019, p.3). This acknowledgement of the relationship between the individual, society and learning is key to developing effective creative leadership in ECE, as we shall continue to explore in the next section.

Creative leadership

In transforming early childhood education, it is important to make the distinction between 'pedagogical leadership' and 'organisational leadership' of the managerial kind. Cathy Nutbrown, in her independent review of qualifications and training in the ECE sector stated that 'all early years practitioners can aspire to be pedagogical leaders' (2012, p.7). Her vision of a pedagogical leader was an individual with 'extensive knowledge and understanding of child development, of play, of individual needs of children and their families and how to support them all' (2012, p.56). We can go beyond this definition towards a broader vision of 'creative pedagogical leadership' and leading for creativity (Lucas and Spencer, 2017, p.96). There are a number of ways that we can nurture creativity with our teams, and Lucas and Spencer draw our attention to research with senior leaders undertaken by Stoll and Temperley (2009). This highlighted some effective approaches to unlocking creativity in staff teams, including:

- Model creativity and risk-taking: do not compromise this, even when under pressure
- Create a sense of urgency to stimulate problem-finding and creative problem-solving
- Exposure to new thinking and experiences: from other teachers, schools, settings, cultural visits
- Relinquish control: encourage staff to try out new things and share their learning
- Provide time and space: to plan and facilitate the practicalities of longer-term projects
- Promote collaborative thinking and design: with time for personal reflection and individual idea development as well
- Set high expectations: about valuing creativity and innovation
- Use failure as an opportunity for learning: value things that go wrong and give people an opportunity to put them right
- Refer back to core values: creative team efforts must have a clear common direction (see earlier section on connecting values to support a 'pedagogy of relationships')

(Lucas and Spencer, 2017, pp.97–98)

Early childhood educators Rosie Walker and Sandra Cheeseman (2019) have written extensively on different pedagogies for leading practice in ECE, bringing together experiences from professionals from around the world. They have considered various forms of collaborative working and the challenges involved in becoming a pedagogical leader and meeting the needs of the wider community but the key message is success is enabled by embedding families and community (Cheeseman and Walker, 2019).

Theory of change and evaluation

On a more practical level, in order to create effective change, whether in a leadership position or not, it is important to identify your long-term aims and then create a plan of action and ways of measuring success. Using a **Theory of Change** (TASO) (n.d.) provides a useful framework that can be developed collaboratively with colleagues and shared more widely to articulate your goals and identify the resources that will be needed to achieve those goals. The following template is worth considering as a planning tool:

1 Situation – what is the current context or situation? What are the problems or issues you are trying to address?
2 Aims – what long-term goal or change are you trying to achieve? What is your possible solution to the problem identified?
3 Outcomes – what short-term and intermediate-term goals need to be achieved for your long-term goals to be possible?
4 Impact – what is the long-term goal that relates to the original issue or problem? what result or 'measures of success' are you hoping for?
5 Activities – outline the interventions or component activities you believe will bring about the desired change
6 Outputs – what results or 'deliverables' from these activities are relevant to achieving your outcomes?
7 Inputs – what resources will you need (human, financial and organisational) and what shared values will need to be in place to achieve your desired outcomes?
8 Rationale and Assumptions – what are your assumptions? Are they supported by research? A clear rationale will strengthen your Theory of Change and increase the likelihood that your stated goals can be achieved.

(TASO, n.d.)

Making a difference in early childhood education

It is hoped that this book will help readers to make sense of the dominant discourses in education and better understand the alternative narratives in early childhood (Moss, 2019), especially around the importance of creativity that is gaining traction and starting to emerge. For example, Cameron and Moss (2020) have called for ECE provision built on democratic principles, where all learning by all children is visible and recognised, educators are trusted and respected, and a calmer approach called 'slow pedagogy' replaces outcomes-driven targets (Cameron and Moss, 2020). However, many questions remain that we might ask ourselves, for example, how can I make a difference in early childhood education? What lens should I bring to my ECE practice in terms of concepts and theories? How do we understand key terms such as aesthetics, inclusion, diversity, difference and the rights of all children in my particular setting?

This book has promoted the importance of developing a more democratic approach to education, one that values multiple voices, plurality and pluralism, a political and cultural approach that sees the value 'of differences and dialogue between differences' (Rinaldi, 2021, p.167); an approach that can lead to growing layers of understanding over time. However, this 'dialogue between differences' is not without its challenges. In Chapter 12, Nicola Watson touched on the ideas of Michel Foucault and the potentially complex nature of power dynamics between adults (parent or teacher) and children. According to British artist Bob and Roberta Smith (real name Patrick Brill), 'the arts make children powerful' and they explain how this works in very specific ways:

> ...if you develop your voice, learn to draw, learn to make things, feel that you can construct the future, you have a hand in the world and that you could contribute to that world- that makes you powerful... (Bob and Roberta Smith, NSEAD, 2022)

Towards a creative education of the future

I shall leave you with the words of French philosopher Edgar Morin and his 'seven thoughts necessary to the education of the future' (1999). Here, he highlights the importance of embracing uncertainty, being open to challenge and feeling insecure. Often we look for certainty in our thinking but rather than succumbing to the temptation to provide easy answers, Morin suggests 'replacing a thought that isolates and separates with a thought that distinguishes and invites; a thought about the complex' (Morin, 1999). Morin's book offers seven 'complex lessons' that are worth considering for a moment, especially in the context of early childhood education and care:

1 Critical thinking – the importance of interrogating knowledge (e.g. misinformation and 'fake news') and detecting errors of reason, whilst also embracing the unexpected and 'uncertain knowledge' (1999, p.11)
2 Pertinent knowledge – acknowledging the complex and multidimensional nature of knowledge
3 Teaching the human condition – unity and diversity
4 Earth identity – awareness of the planetary crisis and hope for the future
5 Confronting uncertainties – reality, knowledge and the 'ecology of action' (see 'regenerative culture' in Chapter 10)
6 Understanding each other – awareness of human complexity, tolerance and the ethics of understanding
7 Human Ethics – the individual and democracy, teaching 'earth citizenship' for the survival of our species...

These themes are echoed in the work of Zachary Stein (2022), a philosopher of education who urges us to see the current planetary crisis as a 'species-wide learning opportunity'. Indeed, Stein argues that we need to re-define the very word 'education' so it becomes transformative, and our understanding is more about the intergenerational transmission of cultural virtues, knowledge, skills and social renewal; in his words, 'the fundamental matter of how society maintains, renews and transforms itself' (2022, p.4). In that sense, 'education is the metacrisis' of our age, also known as the Anthropocene – an era of profound human-made and irreversible impact on the world that threatens ecosystems and triggers climate change (Polman and Vasconcellos-Sharpe, 2019).

Bringing it all together

This book has covered a multitude of different perspectives on the complex subject of creativity in the early years, even some that may seem at odds with each other, but there are some core themes that it is important to highlight as Connecting Principles and Relationships (see Figure 14.2). It is my hope that these will help ECE practitioners, artists and teachers develop a more holistic approach. Again, you will see that 'curiosity', that essential component of creativity, sits at the centre of these interconnected elements.

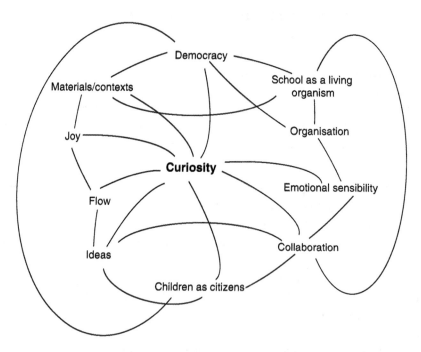

Figure 14.2 Connecting principles and relationships to support creativity in the early years

A manifesto for creativity

The way in which you go about interpreting and connecting the principles and relationships mentioned above is entirely up to you. Margaret Brooks, early childhood educator, artist and co-founder of the *International Art in Early Childhood* network recommends creating your own 'manifesto'; not a heavy political statement but a declaration of intent that can be shared with parents, staff and colleagues to provide a common framework. In her book *Authentic Art with Children* (2021), Brooks describes her approach as 'braiding'; a weaving together of contemporary visual art practice with socio-cultural theory from the likes of Vygotsky (1978) to produce a more responsive pedagogy. The resulting visualisation is entitled *An Incomplete Manifesto: Pedagogical Practices for the Visual Arts in Early Childhood Education* (see Figure 14.3) and Brooks' document provides a series of inspiring prompts, adapted from Bruce Mau's *Incomplete Manifesto for Growth* (1998), produced in answer to the question: how does one sustain a creative life? Like Mau, Brooks' version contains helpful patterns for living and working, such as:

- 'Begin anywhere!' (advice from composer John Cage)
- 'Listen'
- 'Notice and wonder'
- 'Go deeper'
- 'Encourage meaning making and expression' and
- 'Be pedagogically active' (sustained shared thinking, for example, see Chapter 12)

Reflective questions

Next Steps:
　　In order to move forward in your career journey, consider these five questions:

- How can you make a difference in early childhood education and care?
- Where does creativity sit within your personal philosophy and values?
- What ideas do you have to enable positive change?
- Who needs to be involved in the decision-making process?
- How will you know you have achieved what you set out to do?

A pedagogy of hope

It is hoped this book will empower individuals as they become early childhood education professionals who are socially responsible and culturally aware global citizens, not only with key attributes such as ethical awareness, but with the confidence to speak up for the value of creativity to the individual child, local communities and to society as a whole. As advocates for

Figure 14.3 'An incomplete manifesto: Pedagogical practices for the visual arts in early childhood education' (2021) by Margaret Brooks
Source: Adapted from Bruce Mau (1998).

creativity in the early years, collectively we can promote a culture in which children can become, in the spirit of democracy, 'agents in the transformation of society through a pedagogy of hope' (Giroux, 1997).

Reflective questions

Consider how has this book impacted upon:

- Your core values and principles?
- Your professional relationships (with colleagues, staff and parents)?
- The children in your care?
- Your institution, school or setting?

Further reading and resources

Brooks, M. (2021) *Authentic Art with Children*. Pademelon Press

Perspectiva: an international network of educational philosophers and thinkers re-imagining the future of education for society and the planet, hosts of the Transformative Education Alliance (TEA): www.systems-souls-society.com

Reboot The Future: a registered charity whose purpose is to explore how a compassionate approach to business, finance, the environment and politics can transform our world: www.rebootthefuture.org

References

AccessArt (2021) *Sharing Visual Arts Inspiration*. Available at: https://www.accessart.org.uk/ (Accessed 15 December 2021).

Acer, D. and Ömeroðlu, E. (2007) A study on the effect of aesthetic education on the development of aesthetic judgment of six-year-old children. *Early Childhood Education Journal*, 35, pp. 335–342. doi: 10.1007/s10643-007-0193-4

Action for Children (2023) *Early Years*. Available at: https://www.actionforchildren.org.uk/our-work-and-impact/children-and-families/early-years/ (Accessed 10 January 2023).

Adams. E. and Baynes, K. (2003) *Drawing on Experience: Museums, Galleries and Science Centres*. Hove: Drawing Power, The Campaign for Drawing.

Adams, J. and Owens, A. (2017) *Creativity and Democracy in Education: Practices and Politics of Learning through the Arts*. London: Routledge.

Afzal, U. (2018) *Mindfulness for Children: Help Your Child to Be Calm and Content from Breakfast to Bedtime*. London: Kyle.

Aguirre Jones, D. and Elders, E. (2009) Reflecting on the reflective cycle. *ReFocus Journal*, 8, pp. 12–13.

Ainsworth, M. (1969) Object relationships, dependency, and attachment: A theoretical review of the infant-mother relationship. *Child Development*, 40, pp. 969–1026.

All Party Parliamentary Group on Arts, Health and Wellbeing Inquiry Report (2017) *Creative Health: The Arts for Health and Wellbeing*, 2nd ed. Available at: www.artshealthandwellbeing.org.uk (Accessed 18 June 2022).

Altman, A. and Esber, J. (1995) Lego therapy. *Journal of Psychosocial Nursing and Mental Health Services*, 33(8), pp. 48–49.

Anderson, D. (1999) *A Common Wealth: Museums in the Learning Age*. London: DCMS.

Anderson, L. and Krathwohl, D. (eds.) (2001) *A Taxonomy for Learning, Teaching and Assessing: A Revision of Bloom's Taxonomy of Educational Objectives*. New York: Longman.

AnjiPlay.com (n.d.) AnjiPlay. Available at: https://www.anjiplay.com/ (Accessed 6 November 2023).

Aotearoa—Early Childhood Curriculum. New Zealand Government. Available at: https://www.education.govt.nz/early-childhood/teaching-and-learning/te-whariki/ (Accessed 15 May 2023)

Arday, J., Belluigi, D. Z. and Thomas, D. (2021). Attempting to break the chain: Reimaging inclusive pedagogy and decolonising the curriculum within the academy. *Educational Philosophy and Theory*, 53(3), pp. 298–313.

Arnold, M. (1908) Revised code of minutes and regulations of the committee of the Privy Council on education, 1862. In Martin, F. S. (ed.) *Reports on Elementary Schools 1852–1882*. London: HMSO, pp. 331–382.

Arts Council England (2000) *Year of the Artist*. London: ACE.

Arts Council England (2020) *Let's Create, 10 Year Strategy*. London: ACE.

Ashiabi, G. and O'Neal, K. (2015) Child social development in context: An examination of some propositions in Bronfenbrenner's Bioecological Theory. *SAGE Open*, April–June 2015, pp. 1–14.

Attané, I. (2022) China's new three-child policy: What effects can we expect? *Populations & Societies*, *596*(1). Available at: https://www.cairn-int.info/journal-population-and-societies-2022-1-page-1.ht m#:~:text=In%202021%2C%20China%20amended%20its,of%20strict%20coantrol%20over%20 births (Accessed 15 February 2023).

Bakapuolou, I., Triggs, P. and Novak, T. (2021) *The Impact of Covid-19 on Early Years Transition to School*. School of Education: University of Bristol.

Baker, K. (2022) My silver bullet for education. *The Times*. Available at: https://www.thetimes.co. uk/article/my-silver-bullet-for-education-79bplghw3 (Accessed 14 November 2022).

Baldock, P. (2010) *Understanding Cultural Diversity in the Early Years*. London: SAGE.

Ball, D., Gill, T. and Yates, A. (2020) Covid 19 and children's play. Available at: https://www.play england.org.uk/ (Accessed 16 June 2021).

Ball, S. (2013) *Education, Justice and Democracy: The Struggle over Ignorance and Opportunity*. Policy Paper for CLASS (Centre for Labour and Social Studies). Available at: http://classonline.org.uk/ docs/2013_Policy_Paper_-_Education,_justice_and_democracy_(Stephen_Ball).pdf (Accessed 14 November 2022).

Ball, S. (2021) *The Education Debate*. Bristol: Policy Press.

Bancroft, S., Fawcett, M. and Hay, P. (2008) *Researching Children Researching the World*. Stoke on Trent: Trentham.

Bandura, A. (1977) *Social Learning Theory*. New Jersey: Prentice Hall.

Bandura, A. (2001) Social cognitive theory: an agentic perspective. *Annual Review of Psychology, 52*, pp. 1–26.

Bartlett, S. and Burton, D. (2020) *Introduction to Education Studies*, 5th ed. London: SAGE.

Basford, J. (2019a) The early years foundation stage: Whose knowledge, whose values? *Education 3-13, 47*(7), pp. 779–783.

Basford, J. (2019b) Being a graduate professional in the field of Early Childhood Education and Care: Silence, submission and subversion. *International Journal of Primary, Elementary and Early Years Education, 47*(7), pp. 862–875.

Bateson, G. and Bateson, M. (2000) *Steps to an Ecology of Mind*. Chicago: University of Chicago Press.

Bateson, G. (1982) Difference, double description and the interactive designation of self. In Hanson, F. (ed.) *Studies in Symbolism and Cultural Communication*. Manhattan: University of Kansas.

Bateson, M. (1999) Ordinary creativity. In Montouri, A. and Purser, R. (eds.) *Social Creativity (Vol. 1*, pp. 153–171).

Beghetto, R. A. (2021) Creative learning in education. In Kern, M. L. and Wehmeyer, M. L. (eds.) *The Palgrave Handbook of Positive Education*. Palgrave MacMillan, pp. 477–489. Available at: http://creativecommons.org/licenses/by/4.0/ (Accessed 12 December 2022).

Bennett, C. (2011) China's little emperors. *The Guardian Weekly*. Available at: https://www.theguar dian.com/guardianweekly/story/0,12674,1383770,00.html (Accessed 15 February 2023).

BERA (2018) *Ethical Guidelines for Educational Research*, 4th ed. British Educational Research Association. Available at: https://www.bera.ac.uk/publication/ethical-guidelines-for-education al-research-2018 (Accessed 27 June 2023).

Berger, J. (1972) *Ways of Seeing*. London: BBC and Penguin Books.

Berthoz, A. (2019) *Simplexity: Simplifying Principles for a Complex World*. Paris: Odile Jacob.

Bhopal, K. (2018) *White Privilege: The Myth of a Post-racial Society*. London: Policy Press.

Bilton, H. (2020) Values stop play? Teachers' attitudes to the early years outdoor environment. *Early Child Development and Care*, *190*(1), pp. 12–20.

Bilton, H. (2010) *Outdoor Learning in the Early Years: Management and Innovation*, 3rd ed. London: Routledge.

Bloem, B. R., Pfieijffer, I. L. and Krack, P. (2018) Art for better health and well-being. *The BMJ*, *363*, pp. 1–6. doi:10.1136/bmj.k5353

Bloom, B. (1968) *Taxonomy of Educational Objectives: The Classification of Educational Goals*. London: Longmans.

Bob and Roberta Smith (2023) *Art Makes People Powerful*. London: Wide Eyed.

Bockman, J. (2011) *Markets in the Name of Socialism: The Left-Wing Origins of Neoliberalism*. Stanford: Stanford University Press.

Bockman, J. (2013) Neoliberalism. *Contexts*, *12*(3), pp. 14–15.

De Bono, E. (1992) *Serious Creativity: Using the Power of Lateral Thinking to Create New Ideas*. London: Harper Collins.

De Bono, E. (2000) *Six Thinking Hats*. London: Penguin.

De Bono, E. (2015) *Lateral Thinking: Creativity Step by Step*. London: Harper Perennial.

Borkett, P. (2018) *Cultural Diversity and Inclusion in Early Years Education*. Abingdon: Routledge.

Bottrill, G. (2018) *Can I Go and Play Now? Re-thnking the Early Years*. London: SAGE.

Bourdieu, P. (1984) *Distinction: A Social Critique of the Judgement of Taste*. Cambridge: Harvard University Press.

Bower, L. (2005) Everyday learning about imagination. *Everyday Learning Series*, *3*(4), p. 3.

Bowlby, J. (1969) *Attachment and Loss*. New York: Basic Books.

Boyd, D. and Bee, H. (2014) *The Developing Child*, 13th ed. Boston: Pearson Education.

Bracken, B. (2004) *The Psychoeducational Assessment of Pre-school Children*. London: Taylor and Francis.

Bracken, S. and Novak, K. (2019). *Transforming Higher Education through Universal Design for Learning: An International Perspective*. London: Routledge.

Bregman, R. (2020). *Human Kind: A Hopeful History*. London: Bloomsbury.

Brice Heath, S. (1983) *Ways with Words, Language, Life and Work in Communities and Classrooms*. Cambridge: Cambridge University Press.

British Educational Research Association [BERA] (2016) Reviewing the potential and challenges of developing STEAM education. Available: https://www.bera.ac.uk/event-series/research-commis sion-reviewing-the-potential-and-challenges-of-developing-steam-education (Accessed 14 April 2021).

Bronfenbrenner, U. (1979) *The Ecology of Human Development: Experiments in Nature and Design*. Cambridge: Harvard University Press.

Brookfield, S. (2017) *Becoming a Critically Reflective Teacher*, 2nd ed. San Francisco: Jossey-Bass.

Brooks, M. (2021) *Authentic Art with Children*. Pademelon Press.

Broström, S. (2017) A dynamic learning concept in early years' education: A possible way to prevent schoolification. *International Journal of Early Years Education, 25*(1), pp. 3–15.

Brown, F. (2003) Compound flexibility: The role of the playwork in child development. In Brown, F. (ed.) *Playwork Theory and Practice*. Buckingham: Open University Press.

Brown, F. (2019) Playwork. In Brock, A, Jarvis, P. and Olusogo, V. (eds.).*Perspectives in Play Learning for Life*. Abingdon: Routledge.

Brownell, M. D. (2002) Musically adapted social stories to modify behaviours in students with autism: Four case studies. *Journal of Music Therapy, 39*(2), pp. 117–144.

Bruce, T. (2011) *Cultivating Creativity: For Babies, Toddlers and Children*, 2nd ed. Oxford: Hodder Education.

Bruner, J. (1960) *The Process of Education*. Cambridge: Harvard University Press.

Bruner, J. (1962) The conditions of creativity. In Gruber, H. E., Terrell, G. and Wertheimer, M. (eds.) *The Atherton Press Behavioral Science Series. Contemporary Approaches to Creative Thinking: A Symposium Held at the University of Colorado*. Atherton Press, pp. 1–30.

Bruner, J. (1986). *Actual Minds, Possible Worlds*. Cambridge: Harvard University Press.

Bruner, J. (1996) *The Culture of Education*. Cambridge: Harvard University Press.

Bruner, J. S. (2004) Reggio: A city of courtesy, curiosity and imagination, *Children in Europe, 6*, p. 27.

Bugaj, K. and Brenner, B. (2011) The effects of music instruction on cognitive development and reading skills: An overview. *Bulletin of the Council for Research in Music Education, 189*(2).

Burke, N. (2018) *Musical Development Matters in the Early Years*. Watford: The British Association for Early Childhood Education.

Burrows, K. (2011) Autism, art and nature as relational aspects of forest school. In Knight, S. (ed.) *Forest School for All*. London: SAGE.

Buzan, T. (2009) *The Mind Map Book: Unlock Your Creativity, Boost Your Memory, Change Your Life*. London: BBC Active.

Cagliari, P., Castegnetti, M., Giudici, C., Rinaldi, C., Vecchi, V. and Moss, P. (2016) *Loris Malaguzzi and the Schools of Reggio Emilia: A Selection of His Writings and Speeches 1945–1993*. London: Routledge.

Callow, J. (2008) 'Show me: Principles for assessing students' visual literacy. *The Reading Teacher, 61*(8), pp. 616–626.

Cameron, C. and Moss, P. (2020) *Transforming Early Childhood in England towards a Democratic Education*. London: UCL Press.

Cameron, L., Erkal, N., Gangadharan, L. and Meng, X. (2012) Little emperors: Behaviour impacts of China's one-child policy. *Science, 339*(6122), pp. 953–957.

Campbell, C. (2019) China's aging population is a major threat to its future. Available at: https://time.com/5523805/china-aging-population-working-age/ (Accessed 6 November 2023).

Carey-Jenkins, D. (2015) Whose curriculum is it anyway? In Reed, M. and Walker, R. (eds.) *A Critical Companion to Early Childhood*. London: SAGE.

Cattan, S., Fitzsimons, E., Goodman, A., Phimister, A., Ploubidis, G. B. and Wertz, J. (2022). *Early Childhood and Inequalities*. IFS Deaton Review of Inequalities. Available at: https://ifs.org.uk/inequality/early-childhood-inequalities-chapter/ (Accessed 16 June 2023).

Chang, H., Ai, P. and Fran, D. (2017) The provision and utilization of early child care and education programs in in Chinese rural regions. *Xueqian Jiaoyu Yanjiu*, 3(3).

Charles, M. and Boyle, B. (2014) *Using Multiliteracies and Multimodalities to Support Young Children's Learning*. London: SAGE.

Charman, H. and Rose, K. (2006) *The Art Gallery Handbook: A Resource for Teachers*. London: TATE.

Chatterjee, H. (ed.) (2008) *Touch in Museums: Policy and Practice in Object Handling*. London: Routledge.

Chatterjee, H. and Noble, G. (2017) *Museums, Health and Well-Being*. London: Routledge.

Cheesemen, S. and Walker, R. (2019) (eds.) *Pedagogies for Leading Practice*. Abingdon: Routledge.

Chen, X. (1985) The one child population policy, modernization, and the extended Chinese family. *Journal of Marriage and Family*, 47(1), pp. 193–202.

Chitty, C. (2014) *Education Policy in Britain*, 3rd ed. Basingstoke: Palgrave Macmillan.

Chong, W. S. (2022) *Rhythm Circle Games Project*. Available at: https://rhythmcircleblog.azurewebsites. net/index.php/2021/01/27/graphic-scores-accessible-and-inclusive-music-notation/ (Accessed 17 May 2022).

Christer, B. (2021) *SENsory Atelier: Year 2 Interim Report*. University of Leicester.

Churchill Dower, R. (2020) *Creativity and the Arts in Early Childhood: Supporting Young Children's Development and Wellbeing*. London: Jessica Kingsley Publishers.

Clark, A. and Moss, P. (2001) *Listening to Young Children: The Mosaic Approach*. Bath: National Children's Bureau and Joseph Rowntree Foundation.

Claxton, G. and Lucas, B. (2010) *New Kinds of Smart: How the Science of Learnable Intelligence Is Changing Education*. Maidenhead: Open University Press.

Claxton, G. (2018) Deep rivers of learning: Get below surface-level knowledge to help students build attitudes and habits that will stay with them for a lifetime. *Phi Delta Kappan*, 99(6), pp. 45–48. doi:10.1177/0031721718762422

Claxton, G. and Carr, M. (2004) A framework for teaching learning: The dynamics of disposition. *Early Years*, 24(1), pp. 87–97.

Clutterbuck, D. (2022) *Coaching and Mentoring: A Journey through the Models, Theories, Frameworks and Narratives of David Clutterbuck*. London: Routledge.

Coffino, J. R. and Bailey, C. (2019) The Anji Play ecology of early learning. *Childhood Education*, 95(1), pp. 3–9. doi:10.1080/00094056.2019.1565743

Colebatch, H. (2009) *Policy*. Maidenhead: Open University Press.

Compton, A., Johnston, J., Nahmad-Williams, L. and Taylor, K. (2010) *Creative Development*. London: Continuum.

Conkbayir, M. (2017) *Early Childhood and Neuroscience: Theory, Research, and Implications for Practice*. London: Bloomsbury Academic.

Contini, A. and Giuliani, A. (2022) Metaphor and metaphoric processes. In *A Festive Thought: Visual Metaphor in Children's Learning Processes*. Reggio Emilia: Reggio Children.

Cooper, P. (2005) Literacy learning and pedagogical purpose. *Journal of Early Childhood Literacy*, 5(3), pp. 229–251.

Cox, E., Bachkirova, T. and Clutterbuck, D. (2018). *The Complete Handbook of Coaching*. London: SAGE.

Craft, A. (2001) Little c creativity. In Craft, A., Jeffery, B. and Leibling, M. (eds.) *Creativity in Education*. London: Continuum, pp. 45–61.

Craft, A. (2006) *Creativity in Schools: Tensions and Dilemmas*, 2nd ed. Oxford: Routledge.

Crappell, C. (2018) Discovering best practices by studying generational learning preferences, part 1. *The American Music Teacher; Cincinnati, 67*(5), pp. 42–44.

Centre for Race, Education and Decoloniality (CRED) (n.d.) Available at: https://www. leedsbeckett.ac.uk/research/centre-for-race-education-and-decoloniality/ (Accessed 16 January 2023).

Crenshaw, K. (2017). *On Intersectionality: Essential Writings*. New York: The New Press.

Csikszentmihalyi, M. (1990) *Flow: The Psychology of Optimal Experience*. London: Harper Collins.

Csikszentmihalyi, M. (1997) *Creativity: Flow and the Psychology of Discovery and Invention*. New York: Harper Collins.

Cultural Learning Alliance (2019) *What Is Cultural Capital?* Cultural Learning Alliance News. Available at: https://www.culturallearningalliance.org.uk/what-is-cultural-capital/ (Accessed 28 June 2023).

Cultural Learning Alliance (2022) *Briefing Paper 6 Early Years and the Arts: Why an Arts-Rich Early Years Matters*. London: CLA.

Cultural Learning Alliance (2023) *20 Year Policy Timeline*. Available at: https://www.culturallea rningalliance.org.uk/evidence/20-year-policy-timeline/ (Accessed 11 January 2023)

Cultural Learning Alliance and NESTA (2017) *STEAM: Why STEM Can Only Take Us So Far*. CLA Briefing Paper No. 1. Available at: www.culturallearningalliance.org.uk/briefings (Accessed 18 March 2020).

Dahlberg, G. and Moss, P. (2006) Introduction to the First Edition: Our Reggio Emilia. In Rinaldi, C. (ed.) (2021) *Dialogue with Reggio Emilia: Listening, Researching and Learning*, 2nd ed. Oxon: Routledge.

Dahlberg, G., Moss, P. and Pence, A. (1999) *Beyond Quality in Early Childhood Education and Care: Postmodern Perspectives*. London: Falmer Press.

Dalton, L., Rapa, E. and Stein, A. (2020) Protecting the psychological health of children through effective communication of COVID-19. *The Lancet, 4*, p. 346.

Daly, L. and Beloglovsky, M. (2015) *Loose Parts: Inspiring Play in Young Children*. St Paul: Redleaf Press.

Davey, C. S. (2012) *The Socratic Classroom: Reflective Thinking through Collaborative Inquiry*. Rotterdam: BRILL.

DCMS (2012) *Review of Cultural Education in England: An Independent Review by Darren Henley for the Department for Culture, Media and Sport and the Department for Education*. London: HMSO.

DCSF (2008) *Practice Guidance for the Early Years Foundation Stage*. Available at: https://www.early yearsmatters.co.uk/wp-content/uploads/2011/01/Practice-Guidance-for-the-Early-Years-Found ation-Stage-EYM.pdf (Accessed 1 February 2023).

Debroy, A. (2018) *How Is China Developing Creativity Among the Chinese Students?* Available at: https:// www.edtechreview.in/trends-insights/insights/china-developing-creativity-among-chinese-stud ents/ (Accessed 15 February 2023).

Deci, E. and Ryan, R. (2000) Self-determination theory and the facilitation of intrinsic motivation, social development and well-being. *American Psychologist, 55*(1), 68–78.

Deci, E. L. and Ryan, R. M. (2008) Facilitating optimal motivation and psychological well-being across life's domains. *Canadian Psychology, 49*(1), pp. 14–23.

Deleuze, G. and Guattari, F. (1999) *A Thousand Plateaus: Capitalism and Schizophrenia*. London: Athlone Press.

Denscombe, M. (2021) *The Good Research Guide: Research Methods for Small-Scale Social Research Projects*, 7th ed. London: OU Press.

DfE (2010) *Coaching for Teaching and Learning: A Practical Guide for Schools*. Available at: https://www.gov.uk/government/publications/coaching-for-teaching-and-learning-a-practical-guide-for-schools (Accessed 28 June 2023).

Department for Education (2014a) *Guidance on Promoting British Values in Schools*. GOV.UK. Available at: https://www.gov.uk/government/news/guidance-on-promoting-british-values-in-schools-published (Accessed 28 July 2023).

Department for Education (2014b) *National Curriculum*. Available at: https://www.gov.uk/government/collections/national-curriculum (Accessed 6 June 2023).

Department for Education (2014c) *The National Curriculum in England: Key Stages 1 and 2 Framework Document*. Available at: https://www.gov.uk/government/collections/national-curriculum (Accessed 12 January 2023).

DfE (2017) *Early Years Workforce Strategy*. Available at: https://www.gov.uk/government/publications/early-years-workforce-strategy (Accessed 27 June 2023).

Department for Education (2020) *Relationships and Sex Education (RSE) and Health Education*. Available at: https://www.gov.uk/government/publications/relationships-education-relationships-and-sex-education-rse-and-health-education (Accessed 30 June 2021).

Department for Education (2021a) *Statutory Framework for the Early Years Foundation Stage*. Available at: https://www.gov.uk/government/publications/early-years-foundation-stage-framework–2 (Acccessed 1 February 2023).

Department for Education (2021b) *Sustainability & Climate Change: A Draft Strategy for the Education & Children's Services Systems*. London: DfE.

Department for Education (2022a) *Opportunity for All: Strong Schools with Great Teachers for Your Child*. Available at: https://www.gov.uk/government/news/schools-white-paper-delivers-real-action-to-level-up-education (Accessed 6 March 2023).

Department for Education (2022b) *The Power of Music to Change Lives: A National Plan for Music Education*. London: DfE.

Department for Education (2023a) *SEND and Alternative Provision Improvement Plan: Right Support, Right Place, Right Time*. Available at: https://www.gov.uk/government/publications/send-and-alternative-provision-improvement-plan (Accessed 2 June 2023).

DfE (2023b) *Statutory Framework for the Early Years Foundation Stage*. Available at: https://assets.publishing.service.gov.uk/government/uploads/system/uploads/attachment_data/file/1170108/EYFS_framework_from_September_2023.pdf (Accessed 1 October 2023).

Department for Education and Department of Health (2014) *Special Educational Needs and Disability Code of Practice: 0-25 Years: Statutory Guidance for Organisations Which Work with and Support Children and Young People Who Have Special Educational Needs and Disability*. Available at: https://assets.publishing.service.gov.uk/government/uploads/system/uploads/attachment_data/file/398815/SEND_Code_of_Practice_January_2015.pdf

Department for Education and Employment (2000) *Curriculum Guidance for the Early Years Foundation Stage*. London: Qualifications and Curriculum Authority.

Department for Education and Science and the Welsh Office (1989) *The National Curriculum*. London: Her Majesty's Stationery Office.

Department for Education (2012) *Statutory Framework for the Early Years Foundation Stage: Setting the Standards for Learning, Development and Care for Children from Birth to Five*, London: DfE Publications.

Devarakonda, C. (2012) *Diversity and Inclusion in Early Childhood: An Introduction*. London: SAGE.

Dewey, J. (1897) My pedagogic creed. *School Journal: A Weekly Journal of Education*, 54(3), pp. 77–80.

Dewey, J. (1900) The school and society. Available at: http://www.gutenberg.org/files/53910/53910-h/53910-h.htm. (Accessed 9 August 2021).

Dewey, J. (1934) *Art as Experience*. New York: Penguin.

Dewey, J. (1938/1997) *Experience and Education*. New York: Free Press.

DfES (2003) *Every Child Matters*. London: HMSO.

DIALLS (2020) *Dialogue & Argumentation for Cultural Literacy Learning in Schools*. Available at: https://dialls2020.eu/# (Accessed 5 March 2021).

DIALLS (2021) *Scales of Progression for Cultural Literacy Learning*. Available at: http://dialls2020.eu/spcll/ (Accessed 14 April 2021).

Di Paolo, A. (2023) Metacognition and colours for inclusion: Results of an explorative activity in a simplexity approach. *International Journal of Business and Applied Social Science*, (9), pp. 32–42.

Dormer, P. (1994) *The Art of the Maker: Skill and Its Meaning in Art Craft and Design*. London: Thames & Hudson.

Downey, M. (2022) *The Enabling Manager: How to Get the Best Out of Your Team*. LID Publishing.

Duffy, B. (1998) *Supporting Creativity and Imagination in the Early Years*. Buckingham: Open University Press.

Dweck, C. (2017) *Mindset: Changing the Way You Think to Fulfil Your Potential*. London: Robinson.

Early Arts (2021) *Creativity in Early Brain Development*. Available at: https://earlyarts.co.uk/blog/creativity-in-early-brain-development (Accessed 15 December 2021).

EarlyArts (2021) *How Young Children Learn*. Available at: https://earlyarts.co.uk/blog/how-young-children-learn (Accessed 28 June 2022).

Education Endowment Fund (2020). *Education Evidence: Guidance Reports: Special Educational Needs in Mainstream Schools*. Available at: https://educationendowmentfoundation.org.uk/education-evidence/guidance-reports/send (Accessed 6 June 2023).

Edwards, C., Gandini, L. and Forman, G. (eds.) (2011) *The Hundred Languages of Children: The Reggio Emilia Experience in Transformation*, 3rd edn. ABC-CLIO.

Eisner, E. (2002) *The Arts and the Creation of Mind*. New Haven & London: Yale University Press.

Ellyatt, W. (2010) A science of learning: New approaches to thinking about creativity in the early years. In Tims, C. (ed.) *Born Creative*. London: DEMOS.

Engel, S. (1993) Children's bursts of creativity. *Creativity Research Journal*, 6(3), pp. 309–318.

Ephgrave, A. (2018) *Planning in the Moment with Young Children, a Practical Guide for Early Years Practitioners and Parents.* London: Routledge. doi:10.4324/9781315113500

Ereaut, G. and Whiting, R. (2008) *What Do We Mean by 'wellbeing'? And Why Might It Matter?* Department for Children and families CSF Research Report DCSF-RW073. Available at: https://dera.ioe.ac.uk/8572/1/dcsf-rw073%20v2.pdf (Accessed 14 July 2021).

European Union (2006) Recommendation of the European Parliament and of the Council of 18 December 2006 on key competences for lifelong learning. *Official Journal of the European Union. L394,* pp. 10–18. Available at: https://eur-lex.europa.eu/legal-content/EN/TXT/PDF/?uri=CELEX:32006H0962 (Accessed 16 June 2023).

Fawcett, M. (2009) *Learning through Child Observation,* 2nd ed. London: Jessica Kingsley Publishers.

Feng, X. (ed.) (2016) *Series on Chinese Education Reform: Volume on Kindergarten Education.* Wuhan: Hubei Education Publisher.

Fisher, R. (2005) *Teaching Children to Think.* Cheltenham: Nelson-Thomas.

Fox, C. (1993) *At the Very Edge of the Forest: The Influence of Literature on Storytelling by Children.* London: Cassell.

Fox, D. and Liu, L. (2012) Building musical bridges: Early childhood learning and musical play. Min-Ad: Israel Studies in Musicology Online, 1057, p. 67.

Fox, D. (1991) Music, development and the young child. *Music Educators Journal, 77*(5), pp. 42–46.

Freire, P. (1970) *Pedagogy of the Oppressed.* London: Continuum.

Freire, P. (1974) *Education for Critical Consciousness.* London: Continuum.

Gamble, N. and Yates, S. (2002) *Exploring Children's Literature: Teaching the Language and Reading of Fiction.* London: Paul Chapman.

Gardner, H. (1982) *Art, Mind and Brain: A Cognitive Approach to Creativity.* New York: Basic Books.

Gardner, H. (1999) *Intelligence Reframed: Multiple Intelligences for the 21st Century.* New York: Basic Books.

Gasper, M. and Walker, R. (eds.) (2020) *Mentoring and Coaching in Early Childhood.* London: Bloomsbury.

Gibbs, G. (1988) *Learning by Doing: A Guide to Teaching and Learning Methods.* Oxford: Oxford Polytechnic.

Gibbs, L. and Gasper, M. (2019) *Challenging the Intersection of Policy with Pedagogy.* Abingdon: Routledge.

Gibson, J. (1979) *The Ecological Approach to Visual Perception.* Boston: Houghton Mifflin.

Giddens, A. (1998) *The Third Way: The Renewal of Social Democracy.* Cambridge: Polity Press.

Gillard, D. (2018) *Education in England: A History.* Available at: www.educationengland.org.uk/history (Accessed 8 June 2021).

Gillard, D. (2021a) *Plowden Report (1967).* Available at: http://www.educationengland.org.uk/documents/plowden/plowden1967-1.html (Accessed 14 July 2021).

Gillard, D. (2021b) *Hadow Report (1933).* Available at: http://www.educationengland.org.uk/documents/hadow1933/hadow1933.html (Accessed 14 July 2021).

Gillard, D. (2021c) *Warnock Report (1967).* Available at: http://www.educationengland.org.uk/documents/warnock/warnock1978.html (Accessed 14 July 2021).

Gillard, D. (n.d.) *Revised Code (1862).* Education in the UK. Available at: https://www.education-uk.org/documents/cce/revised-code.html (Accessed 28 July 2023).

Giroux, H. (1997) *Pedagogy and the Politics of Hope: Theory, Culture, and Schooling*. Oxford: Westview Press.

Giroux, H. (2021) 'Critical Pedagogy, fascist Culture and Hope in Dark Times' Keynote Address at Hybrid Spaces: Re-imagining Pedagogy, Practice and Research. In iJADE Annual Conference 2021. Available at: https://www.nsead.org/ (Accessed 26 March 2021).

Glassman, M. and Patton, R. (2014) Capability through participatory democracy: Sen, Freire and Dewey. *Educational Philosophy and Theory*, 46(12), pp. 1353–1365.

Glăveanu, V. P. (2011) Children and creativity: A most (un)likely pair? *Thinking skills and creativity*, 6(2), pp. 122–131.

Gluschankof, C. and Kenny, S. (2011) Music literacy in an Israeli Kindergarten. *General Music Today*, 25(1), pp. 45–49.

Goldschmied, E. and Jackson, S. (2004) *People under Three: Young Children in Day Care*, 2nd ed. London: Routledge.

Goleman, D. (1996) *Emotional Intelligence*. Cambridge: Harvard University Press.

Gonzales, N., Moll, L. C. and Amanti, C. (2006) Theorising practices. In Gonzales, N., Moll, L. C and Amanti, C. (eds.) *Funds of Knowledge Theorizing Practices in Households, Communities, and Classrooms*. London: Lawrence Erlbaum Associates.

gov.uk (2023) Explore education statistics: Education, health and care plans. Available at: https://explore-education-statistics.service.gov.uk/find-statistics/education-health-and-care-plans/2023 (Accessed 14 June 2023).

Gray, C. and MacBlain, S. (2012) *Learning Theories in Childhood*. London: SAGE.

Greenhalgh, Z. (2018) *Music and Singing in the Early Years: A Practical Guide*. London: Routledge.

Grigg, R. and Lewis, H. (2019) *Teaching Creative and Critical Thinking in Schools*. London: SAGE.

Gripton, C. and Williams, H. J. (n.d.) The principles for appropriate pedagogy in early mathematics: Exploration, apprenticeship and sense-making. Research Review for the Early Childhood Maths Group. Available at: https://earlymaths.org/ (Accessed 19 May 2023).

Grunwald, K. and Thiersch, T. (2009) The concept of the 'lifeworld orientation' for social work and social care. *Journal of Social Work Practice*, 23(2), pp. 131–146.

Gu, M. (2010) A blueprint for educational development in China: A review of the "National Guidelines for medium- and long-term educational reform and development (2010–2020)." *Education China*, 5(3), pp. 291–309.

Guidici, C., Rinaldi, C. and Krechevsky, M. (eds.) (2001) *Making Learning Visible: Children as Individual and Group Learners*. Reggio Emilia: Project Zero and Reggio Children.

Hahn, A. (1987) *Policy Making Models and Their Role in Policy Making Education*. New York: Cornell University.

Haigh, G. (2006) Flutterings from the Tyndale affair. *TES Magazine*. Available at: https://www.tes.com/magazine/archive/flutterings-tyndale-affair (Accessed 21 November 2022).

Hall, E. (2014) Unique ways of seeing: Five children's approaches to observational drawing. *International Art in Early Childhood Research Journal*, 1, pp. 1–16.

Hall, E. (2022) Issues-based art education and its usefulness to primary teachers. In Pavlou, V. (ed.) *Enhancing Visual Arts Education with Education for Sustainable Development; A Handbook for Teachers*. Cyprus: Frederick University.

Hallam, S. (2014) *The Power of Music: A Research Synthesis of the Impact of Actively Making Music on the Intellectual, Social and Personal Development of Children and Young People*. London: International Music Education Research Centre (iMerc), University College London.

Hallsworth, M., Parker, S. and Rutter, J. (2011) *Policy Making in the Real World: Evidence and Analysis*. London: Institute for Government.

Hamilton, P. (2021) *Diversity and Marginalisation in Childhood: A Guide for Inclusive Thinking 0-11*. London: SAGE.

Hanna, W. (2014) A Reggio-inspired music atelier: Opening the door between visual arts and music. *Early Childhood Education Journal, 42*(4), pp. 287–294.

Hansen, K. and Appleby, K. (2015) 'Reflective practice'. In Reed, M. and Walker, R. (eds.) *A Critical Companion to Early Childhood Studies*. London: SAGE.

Hanson, K. and Appleby, K. (2017) 'Becoming a reflective practitioner'. In Musgrave, J., Savin-Baden, M. and Stobbs, N. (eds.) *Studying for Your Early Years Degree: Skills and Knowledge for Becoming an Effective Practitioner*. St. Albans: Critical Publishing.

Harvell, J. and Ren, L. (2019) It's a new dawn, it's a new day … developing an Early Years workforce for a 21st century China. In Pence, A. and Harvell, J. (eds.) *Volume 3 - Thinking about Pedagogy in Early Education: Pedagogies for Diverse Contexts*. London: Routledge.

Harvell, J. (2013) The same …. Or different? A comparative study of kindergarten policy and practises in China and England. Available at: https://eprints.worc.ac.uk/5904/ (Accessed 11 January 2023).

Hay, P. and Fawcett, M. (2006) 5x5x5 = Creativity: Researching children researching the world. *Engage 18: Research*, pp. 61–64.

Heaton, R. (2021) Cognition in art education. *British Educational Research Journal, 47*(5), pp. 1323–1339.

Hechter, M. and Opp, K-D. (2001) *Social Norms*. New York: Russel Sage Foundation.

Hedges, H. (2020) The place of interests, agency and imagination in funds of identity theory. *Mind, Culture, and Activity*. doi:10.1080/10749039.2020.1833931 (Accessed 10 June 2021).

Hedges, H. (2021) Working theories: Current understanding and future directions. *Early Childhood Folio, 25*(1), pp. 32–37.

Henrikson, D. (2018) *The 7 Transdisciplinary Cognitive Skills for Creative Education*. Cham: Springer.

Hewison, R. (2014) *Cultural Capital: The Rise and Fall of Creative Britain*. London: Verso.

Hirsch, E. (1983) Cultural literacy. *American Scholar, 52*(2), 159–169.

Hirsh-Pasek, K., Zosh, J., Golinkoff, R. et al. (2015) Putting education in "educational" apps: Lessons from the science of learning. *Psychological Science in the Public Interest, 16*(1), pp. 3–34.

Hodges, D. A. and O'Connell, D. S. (2005) *The Impact of Music Education on Academic Achievement*. Greensboro: The University of North Carolina.

Holden, J. (2006) *Cultural Value and the Crisis of Legitimacy*. London: DEMOS.

Home Office (2011) *Prevent Strategy*. Available at: https://www.gov.uk/government/publications/prevent-strategy-2011 (Accessed 17 June 2023).

hooks, b. (1994) *Teaching to Transgress: Education as the Practice of Freedom*. London: Routledge.

Hooper-Greenhill, E. (1994) *The Educational Role of the Museum*. London: Routledge.

House of Imagination (2023) *Forest of Imagination Case Study*. Available at: https://houseofimagination.org/ (Accessed 3 June 2023).

Howard, S. J., Siraj, I., Melhuish, E. C., Kingston, D., Neilsen-Hewett, C., de Rosnay, M., Duursma, E. and Luu, B. (2020) Measuring interactional quality in pre-school settings: Introduction and validation of the Sustained Shared Thinking and Emotional Wellbeing (SSTEW) scale. *Early Child Development and Care*, *190*(7), pp. 1017–1030.

Howlin, P. (2004) *Autism and Asperger Syndrome: Preparing for Adulthood*. London: Routledge.

Hoy, A. W., Hughes, M. and Walkup, V. (2013) *Psychology in Education*, 2nd ed. Harlow: Longman.

Huang, P. and Szente, J. (2014) Helping Chinese children become more creative. *Contemporary Issues in Early Childhood*, *15*(3).

Hui, A. N. N. and Lau, S. (2010) Formulation of policy and strategy in developing creativity education in four Asian Chinese societies: A policy analysis. *Journal of Creative Behavior*, *44*(4). doi:10.1002/j.2162-6057.2010.tb01334

InSEA (n.d.) *The InSEA Manifesto*. Available at: https://www.insea.org/our-manifesto/ (Accessed 14 June 2023).

Isaacs, B. (2018) *Understanding the Montessori Approach: Early Years Education in Practice*. Abingdon: Routledge.

Isaacs, N. (1969) Froebel's educational philosophy in 1952. In Lawrence, E. (ed.) *Friedrich Froebel and English Education*. London: Routledge & Kegan Paul, pp. 179–34.

Jack, C. and Higgins, S. (2019) What is educational technology and how is it being used to support teaching and learning in the early years? *International Journal of Early Years Education*, *27*(3), pp. 222–237.

James, A. (2009) Agency. In Qvortup, J., Corsaro, W. and Honig, M. (eds.) *The Palgrave Handbook of Childhood Studies*. Palgrave Macmillan, pp. 34–45.

Jeffrey, B. and Craft, A. (2004) Teaching creatively and teaching for creativity: Distinctions and relationships. *Educational Studies*, *30*(1), pp. 77–87. doi:10.1080/0305569032000159750

Jewitt, C., Bezemer, J., Jones, K. and Kress, G. (2009) Changing English? The impact of technology and policy on a school subject in the 21st century. *English Teaching: Practice and Critique*, *8*(3), pp. 8–20.

Jingnan, C. (2018) Parents plead with government to give kids more homework. Available at: https://www.sixthtone.com/news/1002084/parents-plead-with-government-to-give-kids-more-homework (Accessed 14 February 2023).

Johnston, J., Nahmad-Williams, L., Oates, R. and Wood, V. (2018a) *Early Childhood Studies Principles and Practice*, 2nd ed. London: Routledge.

Johnston, K., Highfield, K. and Hadley, F. (2018b) Supporting young children as digital citizens: The importance of shared understandings of technology to support integration in play-based learning. *British Journal of Educational Technology*, *49*(5), pp. 896–910.

Josephidou, J. and Bolshaw, P. (2020) *Understanding Gender and Early Childhood: An Introduction to the Key Debates*. Oxford: Routledge.

Katz, L. G. and McClellan, D. E. (1997) *Fostering Children's Social Competence: The Teacher's Role*. Washington, DC: NAEYC.

Keenan, T. and Evans, S. (2009) *Introduction to Child Development*, 3rd ed. London: SAGE.

Kesseler, R. (2016) *Art, Science and the Artisan: An Introduction by Rob Kesseler, UAL Chair of Arts, Design and Science.* Available at: https://www.youtube.com/watch?v=skVuCvWxTGM (Accessed 15 April 2023).

Kingston University (2022) *Future Skills for Innovation.* London: Kingston University. Available at: https://d68b3152cf5d08c2f050-97c828cc9502c69ac5af7576c62d48d6.ssl.cf3.rackcdn.com/documents/user-upload/kingston-university-3bfff097ef8-kingston-university-d2606ad3a3d.pdf (Accessed 14 November 2022).

Klein, N. (2014) *This Changes Everything: Capitalism vs. The Climate.* London: Penguin Random House.

Knight, A. (2017) Social and cultural capital of childhood. Available at: https://www.oxfordbibliographies.com/display/document/obo-9780199791231/obo-9780199791231-0143.xml#:~:text=Social%20capital%20refers%20to%20social,shown%20through%20posture%20or%20gestures (Accessed 9 January 2023).

Knight, S. (2011) *Forest School for All.* London: SAGE.

Knight, S. (2013) *Forest School and Outdoor Learning in the Early Years,* 2nd ed. London: SAGE.

Koestler, A. (1964) *The Act of Creation.* New York: Macmillan.

Kolb, D. (2015) *Experiential Learning: Experience as the Source of Learning and Development,* 2nd ed. New Jersey: Pearson Education.

Kress, G. (1997) *Before Writing: Rethinking the Paths to Literacy.* London: Routledge.

Kress, G. (2003) *Literacy in the New Media Age.* London: Routledge.

Kress, G. (2010) *Multimodality: A Social Semiotic Approach to Contemporary Communication.* London: Routledge.

Kress, G. and van Leeuwen, T. (1996) *Reading Images: The Grammar of Graphic Design.* New York: Routledge.

Kress, G., Jewitt, C., Ogborn, J. and Tsaterellis, C. (2001) *Multimodal Teaching and Learning.* London: Continuum Press.

Kudryavtsev, V. (2011) The phenomenon of child creativity. *International Journal of Early Years Education, 19*(1), pp. 45–53.

Kumar Shah, R. (2021) Conceptualizing and defining pedagogy. *Journal of Research and Method in Education, 11*(1), pp. 6–29.

Kupers,E., Lehmann-Wermser, A., McPherson, G. and van Geert, P. (2019) Children's creativity: A theoretical framework and systematic review. *Review of Educational Research,* February 2019, *89*(1), pp. 93–124.

Ladson-Billings, G. (1995) But that's just good teaching! The case for culturally relevant pedagogy. *Theory into Practice, 34*(3), pp. 159–165.

Laevers, F. (2015) Making care and education more effective through wellbeing and involvement. An introduction to Experiential Education. In Early Education Annual National Conference. Oxford, February 2016. Huddersfield: Early Excellence, pp. 1–11. Available at: https://www.early-education.org.uk/handouts-and-resources-previous-conferences (Accessed 23 June 2021).

Langsted, O. (1994) Looking at quality from the child's perspective. In Moss, P. and Pence, A. (eds.) *Valuing Quality in Early Childhood Services: New Approaches to Defining Quality.* London: Paul Chapman.

Legget, N. (2017) Early childhood creativity: Challenging educators in their role to intentionally develop creative thinking in children. *Early Childhood Education Journal, 45*, pp. 845–853. doi: 10.1007/s10643-016-0836-4

LeGoff, D. et al. (2014) *Lego-based Therapy: How to Build Social Confidence through Lego-Based Clubs for Children with Autism and Related Conditions.* London: Jessica Kingsley.

Leunig, T. (2016) *Why Real Creativity Is Based on Knowledge.* TEDxWhitehall. Available at: https://www.youtube.com/watch?v=vajIsWwHEMc (Accessed 21 November 2022).

Lewis, A. and Norwich, B. (2004) *Special Teaching for Special Children? Pedagogies for Inclusion.* London: McGraw Hill.

Lewis, J. (2011) From sure start to children's centres: An analysis of policy change in English early years programmes. *Journal of Social Policy, 40*(1), pp. 71–88.

Lillian de Lissa Nursery School (2021) *Instagram Account.* Available at: https://www.instagram.com /lilliandelissa/ (Accessed 24 June 2021).

Lilly, F. R. and Bramwell-Rejskind, G. (2004) The dynamics of creativity. *Journal of Creative Behavior, 38*, pp. 102–124.

Lilly, F. R. (2014) Creativity in early childhood. In *Encyclopedia of Primary Prevention and Health Promotion.* Available at: https://www.researchgate.net/publication/ 304094642_Creativity_in_Early_Childhood (Accessed 9 January 2023).

Lindström, L. (2012) Aesthetic learning about, in, with and through the Arts: A curriculum study. *International Journal of Art and Design Education, 31*(2), 166–179.

Lockette, K. F. (2012) Creativity and Chinese education reform. *International Journal of Global Education, 1*(4).

Longfield, A. (2021) *Building Back Better; Reaching England's Left behind Children.* 17 February. Available at: https://www.childrenscommissioner.gov.uk/2021/02/17/building-back-better-reaching-englands-left-behind-children/ (Accessed 7 June 2021).

Lonie, D. (2010) *Early Years Evidence Review: Assessing the Outcomes of Early Years Music Making,* London: Youth Music, p. 13.

Lucas, B. and Spencer, E. (2017) *Teaching Creative Thinking: Developing Learners Who Generate Ideas and Can Think Critically.* London: Crown House.

Lucas, B., Claxton, G. and Spencer, E. (2013) *Progression in Student Creativity in School: First Steps towards New Forms of Formative Assessments.* OECD Education Working Paper No. 86. Paris: OECD.

Lyotard, J-F. (1984) *The Postmodern Condition: A Report on Knowledge.* Manchester: Manchester University Press.

Macdonald, A. (2014) Human nature and participatory virtues in art education for sustainability. In *Relate North: Art, Heritage and Identity.* Rovaniemi: University of Lapland Press.

Maine, F. (2015) *Dialogic Readers Children Talking and Thinking Together about Visual Texts.* London: Routledge.

Malaguzzi, L (1998) History, ideas and basic philosophy. In Edwards, C., Gandini, L. and Forman, G. (eds.) *The Hundred Languages of Children: The Reggio Emilia Approach-Advanced Reflections,* 2nd ed. London: JAI Press.

Manen, M. (2016) *The Tact of Teaching.* Oxon: Taylor & Francis.

Van Manen, M. (2016) *The Tact of Teaching: The Meaning of Pedagogical Thoughtfulness.* Oxon: Routledge.

Maria Montessori Institute (2022) *Why Montessori?* Available at: https://www.mariamontessori. org/about-us/why-montessori/ (Accessed 6 November 2022).

Martineau, S. (2009) *The Super Book of Simple Science Experiments*. Surrey: B Small Publishing Ltd.

Maslow, A. (1943) A theory of human motivation. *Psychological Review, 50*(4), pp. 370–396.

Maslow, A. (1968) *Toward a Psychology of Being*. New York: Van Nostrand.

Mau, B. (1998) *An Incomplete Manifesto for Growth*. Available at: https://brucemaustudio.com/proj ects/an-incomplete-manifesto-for-growth/ (Accessed 25 June 2023).

Mayo, W. (2023) Student perceptions of glover/Curwen hand signs in the elementary music classroom. *Applications of Research in Music Education*. https://doi-org.apollo.worc.ac.uk/10. 1177/87551233231176218

Meador, K. (1992) Emerging rainbows: A review of the literature on creativity. *Journal for the Education of the Gifted, 15*(2), pp. 163–181.

Merleau-Ponty, M. (1962) *Phenomenology of Perception*. London: Routledge and Kegan Paul.

Merleau-Ponty, M. (1980) The nature of perception. *Research in Phenomenology, 10*, pp. 9–20.

Meyer, A. et al. (2014) *Universal Design for Learning: Theory and Practice*. Wakefield: CAST professional publishing.

Ministry of Education (2017) *Te Whāriki Early Childhood Curriculum*. Available at: https://educati on.govt.nz/assets/Documents/Early-Childhood/ELS-Te-Whariki-Early-Childhood-Curriculum-ENG-Web.pdf (Accessed 21 June 2021).

MoE (1996) *Ministry of Education Standards for Kindergarten Education*.

MoE (2010) *China's National Plan for Medium and Long-Term Education Reform and Development (2010–2020)*. Available at: https://planipolis.iiep.unesco.org/2010/outline-chinas-national-plan-medium-and-long-term-education-reform-and-development-2010-2020 (Accessed 2 July 2023).

MoE (2012) *Early Learning and Development Guidelines for Children Aged 3 to 6 Years*. Available at: https://www.unicef.cn/sites/unicef.org.china/files/2018-10/2012-national-early-learning-deve lopment-guidelines.pdf (Accessed 15 February 2023).

Mohammed, R. (2014) *Creative Learning in the Early Years, Nurturing the Characteristics of Creativity*. Abingdon: Routledge.

Moll, L. C., Amanti, C., Neff, D. and Gonzalez, N. (1992) Funds of knowledge for teaching: Using a qualitative approach to connect homes and classrooms. *Theory into Practice, 31*(2), pp. 132–141.

Montessori, M. (1949) *The Absorbent Mind*. Madras: The Theosophical Publishing House. Available at: https://archive.org/stream/absorbentmind031961mbp/absorbentmind031961mbp_djvu.txt (Accessed 7 June 2021).

Morin, E. (1999) *Seven Complex Lessons in Education for the Future*. Paris: UNESCO.

Morris, J. and Woolley, R. (2017) *Family Diversities Reading Resource*, 2nd ed. Lincoln: Bishop Grosseteste University.

Morrow, L. M. (2002) *Literacy Development in the Early Years: Helping Children to Read and Write*, 4th ed. New York: Allyn and Bacon.

Moss, P. (2019) *Alternative Narratives in Early Childhood. An Introduction for Students and Practitioners*. Abingdon: Routledge.

Moss, G., Webster, R., Harmey, S. and Bradbury, A. (2021) *Unsung Heroes: The Role of Teaching Assistants and Classroom Assistants in Keeping Schools Functioning during Lockdown*. London: UCL Institute of Education.

Moyles, J. R (1989) *Just Playing? Maidenhead*. Maidenhead: Open University Press.

Mullen, C. A. (2017a) Do Chinese students have a creativity deficit? Available at: https://ciheblog.word press.com/2017/09/22/do-chinese-students-have-a-creativity-deficit/ (Accessed 16 February 2023).

Mullen, C. A. (2017b) Creativity in Chinese schools. Perspectival frames of paradox and possibility. *International Journal of Chinese Education, 6*(2017), pp. 27–56.

Muller, L-M. and Goldenberg, G. (2021) *Education in times of crisis: Effective approaches to distance learning: A Review of Research Evidence on Supporting All Students' Learning, Wellbeing and Engagement*. Chartered College of Teaching. Available at: https://my.chartered.college/ wp-content/uploads/2021/02/MullerGoldenbergFEB21_FINAL-1.pdf

National Advisory Committee on Creative and Cultural Education (NACCCE Report) (1999) *All Our Futures: Creativity, Culture & Education*. DCMS & DfEE.

National Institute for Clinical Excellence (NICE) (2012) *Social and Emotional Wellbeing: Early Years*. Available at: https://www.nice.org.uk/guidance/ph40/resources/social-and-emotional-wellbei ng-early-years-pdf-1996351221445 (Accessed 14 July 2021).

Neenan, C. and Knight, S. (2011) Supporting emotional and social development in forest school with adolescents In Knight, S. (ed.) *Forest School for All*. London: SAGE.

Newman, B. M. and Newman, P. R. (2007) *Theories of Human Development*. East Sussex: Psychology Press.

Newton, P. M. and Salvi, A. (2020) How common is belief in the learning styles Neuromyth, and does it matter? A Pragmatic systematic review. *Frontiers in Education*, (5), p. 270. Available at: https://www.frontiersin.org/article/10.3389/feduc.2020.602451 (Accessed 1 April 2021).

NHS (2022) Physical activity guidelines for children (under 5 years). Available at: https://www. nhs.uk/live-well/exercise/exercise-guidelines/physical-activity-guidelines-children-under-five-years/#:~:text=Pre%2Dschoolers%20should%20spend%20at,The%20more%20the%20better

Nicholson, S. (1971) How not to cheat children: The theory of loose parts. *Landscape Architecture Quarterly, 62*(1), pp. 30–34.

Nilsson, M. (2010) Developing voice in digital storytelling through creativity, narrative and multimodality. *International Journal of Media, Technology and Lifelong Learning, 6*(2), pp. 1–21.

Nord Anglia (n.d.) *The Chinese Curriculum*. Available at: https://www.nordangliaeducation.com/ academic-excellence/curricula-guide/chinese-curriculum#:~:text=The%20Chinese%20Natio nal%20Curriculum%20is,secondary%20school%20(three%20years) (Accessed 14 February 2023).

Norozi, S. and Moen, T. (2016) Childhood as a social construction. *Journal of Educational and Social Research. 6*(2), pp. 75–80.

NSEAD (2021) Anti-racist art education (ARAE) resources. Available at: https://www.nsead.org/res ources/anti-racist-art-education/ (Accessed 14 June 2023).

NSEAD (2022) Bob and Roberta Smith advocacy message (video). Available at: https://www.you tube.com/watch?v=KlYOqyDTEp0 (Accessed 15 May 2023).

Nutbrown, C. (2012) Foundations for quality: The independent review of early education and childcare qualifications. Available at: https://www.gov.uk/government/publications/nutbrown-review-foundations-for-quality (Accessed 26 June 2023).

Nutbrown, C., Clough, P. and Selbie, P. (2008) *Early Childhood Education History Philosophy and Experience*. London: SAGE.

Nyland, B., Acker, A. and Deans, J. (2011) Young children and music: Participatory learning and intentional teaching. *Victorian Journal of Music Education*, 1, pp. 13–20.

Oak National Academy (2021) *Early Years Foundation Stage Music: Curriculum Map* (Version 3.0, 28 September 2021).

Ochieng, B., Nijhof, D., Ochieng, R., Owens, C., Daxini, A., & Dikwal-Bot, D. (2020) *Nurturing Babies During the COVID-19 Lockdown: Resilience, Art and Creativity*. The Talent 25 Longitudinal Sub-sample Study. Leicester: De Montfort University.

OECD (2019) *PISA 2021 Creative Thinking Framework (Third Draft)*. Paris: OECD.

OECD (2022) *PISA 2022 Creative Thinking*. Available at: https://www.oecd.org/pisa/innovation/creative-thinking/ (Accessed 2 January 2022).

Office for National Statistics (2022) *Census 2021*. Available at: https://www.ons.gov.uk/visualisations/censuspopulationchange/ (Accessed 18 June 2023).

Ofsted (2009) *Drawing Together: Art, Craft and Design in Schools*. London: Ofsted.

Ofsted (2012) *Making a Mark: Art, Craft and Design Education*. Ofsted.

Ofsted (2019) *School Inspection Handbook*. Available at: https://www.gov.uk/government/publications/school-inspection-handbook-eif (Accessed 28 June 2023).

Ofsted (2022a) *Speech Amanda Spielman at the Nursery World Business Summit 2022*. Available at: https://www.gov.uk/government/speeches/amanda-spielman-at-the-nursery-world-business-summit-2022 (Accessed 13 January 2023).

Ofsted (2022b) *Strategy 2022–27*. Available at: https://www.gov.uk/government/publications/ofsted-strategy-2022-to-2027/ofsted-strategy-2022-27#start (Accessed 7 October 2022).

Olaniyan, D. A. and Okemakinde, T. (2008) Human capital theory: Implications for educational development. *European Journal of Scientific Research*. 2(4), pp. 157–162.

Owen, K. (2021) *Play in the Early Years*. London: SAGE.

Palaiologou, I. (2012) *Ethical Practice in Early Childhood*. London: SAGE.

Paley, V. G. (1981) *Wally's Stories: Conversations in the Kindergarten*. Cambridge: Harvard University Press.

Paley, V. G. (1990) *The Boy Who Would Be a Helicopter: The Uses of Storytelling in the Classroom*. Cambridge: Harvard University Press.

Paley, V. G. (2004) *A Child's Work: The Importance of Fantasy Play*. London: University of Chicago Press.

Pascal, C., Bertram, T. and Cole- Albäck, A. (2017) *The Hundred Review: What Research Tells Us about Effective Pedagogic Practice and Children's Outcomes in the Reception Year*. Birmingham: Centre for Research in Early Childhood.

Pasden. J. (2021) Key word of the month: Jianfu. Available at https://www.sinosplice.com/life/archives/2021/09/02/key-word-of-the-month-jianfu (Accessed 25 January 2023).

Passmore, J. and Mortimer, L. (2011) Ethics in coaching. In Hernez-Broome, G. and Boyce, L. (eds.) *Advanced Executive Coaching*. San Francisco: Wileyashington.

Pavlou, V. (ed.) (2022) *Enhancing Visual Arts Education with Education for Sustainable Development; A Handbook for Teachers*. Cyprus: Frederick University.

Payne, R. (2021) *Cross Curricular Working, Cultural Capital and Craft*. London: Crafts Council. Available at: https://www.craftscouncil.org.uk/learning/education/cross-curricular-working-cultural-capital-and-craft

Pearce, S. M. (ed.) (1994) *Interpreting Objects and Collections*. London: Routledge.

Pence, A. and Harvell, J. (eds.) (2019a) *Pedagogies for Diverse Contexts*. London: Routledge.

Pence, A. and Harvell, J. (eds.) (2019b) *Volume 3 – Thinking about Pedagogy in Early Education: Pedagogies for Diverse Contexts*. London: Routledge.

Penfold, L. (2019). Vygotsky on collective creativity. Art Play Children learning. Available at: http://www.louisapenfold.com/collective-creativity-vygotsky/ (Accessed 1 February 2023).

Penfold, L. (2016) *Interview with Lorna Rose – Artist in Residence*. Birmingham: Lillian de Lissa Children's Centre. Available at: https://vimeo.com/160206410 (Accessed 25 February 2021).

Petruta-Maria, C. (2015). The role of art and music therapy techniques in the educational system of children with special problems. *Procedia-Social and Behavioural Sciences, 187*, pp, 277–282.

Piaget, J. (1952) *The Origins of Intelligence in Children*. New York: Norton.

Polman, K. and Vasconcellos-Sharpe, S. (2019) *Imaginal Cells: Visions of Transformation*. Reboot The Future.

Powell, S. and Smith, K. (2018) *An Introduction to Early Childhood Studies*, 4th ed. London: SAGE.

Power, S. and Whitty, G. (2015) Selective, comprehensive and diversified secondary schooling in England: A brief history. In de Waal, A. (ed.) *The Ins and Outs of Selective Secondary Schools: A Debate*. London: Civitas.

Pringle, E. (2005) *Learning in the Gallery: Context, Process, Outcomes*. London: Arts Council England and enquire.

Pringle, E. (2006) Researching gallery education: Recognising complexity and exploring collaboration. *Engage 18: Research*, pp. 29–35.

Pringle, E. (2011) The gallery as a site for creative learning. In Sefton-Green, J., Thomson, P., Jones, K. and Bresler, L. (eds.) *The Routledge International Handbook of Creative Learning*. London: Routledge.

Pritchard, A. and Woollard, J. (2010) *Psychology for the Classroom: Constructivism and Social Learning*. London: Routledge.

Prowle, A. and Hodgkins, A. (2016) Cosy Up! The Danish concept of 'hygge' can promote wellbeing. *Nursery World. Enabling Environments: Well Being*. 12/12/16 – 8/1/17, pp. 15–16.

Raworth, K. (2018) *Doughnut Economics: Seven Ways to Think Like a 21st-Century Economist*. London: Cornerstone.

Reggio Children (n.d.) *In the Shape of Clay Atelier*. Available at: https://www.reggiochildren.it/en/ateliers/informa-di-creta-en/ (Accessed 25 February 2021).

Reggio Children (n.d.) *Digital Landscapes Atelier*. Available at: https://www.reggiochildren.it/en/rc/ateliers/atelier-in-presenza/digital-lansdcapes-atelier/ (Accessed 19 June 2023).

Richardson, J. (2010) *A Life of Picasso*. New York: Alfred A. Knopf.

Rinaldi, C. (ed.) (2021) *Dialogue with Reggio Emilia: Listening, Researching and Learning*, 2nd ed. Abingdon: Routledge.

Robertson, J. (2000) An educational model for music therapy: The case for a continuum. *British Journal of Music Therapy, 14*(1), pp. 41–46.

Robertson, J. (2021) *Simon Nicholson and the Theory of Loose Parts – 1 Million Thanks*. Available at: https://creativestarlearning.co.uk/early-years-outdoors/simon-nicholson-and-the-theory-of-loose-parts-1-million-thanks/ (Accessed: 29 June2021).

Robertson, L. H. and Hill, D. (2014) Policy and ideologies in schooling and early years education in England: Implications for and impacts on leadership, management and equality. *Management in Education, 28*(4), pp. 167–174.

Robinson, K. (2006) *Do Schools Kill Creativity?* Available at: https://www.ted.com/talks/sir_ken_robinson_do_schools_kill_creativity/transcript?language=en (Accessed 14 July 2021).

Robinson, K. (2010) *The Element: How Finding Your Passion Changes Everything*. London: Penguin.

Robinson, K. (2016) *Creative Schools*. London: Penguin Books.

Robinson, K. (2021) *'Imagine if' Festival 2021*. Available at: https://imagine-if.com/2021-festival (Accessed 4 March 2021).

Rose, D. (2000) Universal design for learning. *Journal of Special Education Technology, 15*(3), pp. 45–49.

Rosen, M. (2010) Forward. In Tims, C. (ed.) *Born Creative*. London: DEMOS.

Rosen, M. (1 July 2014) Dear Mr Gove: what's so 'British' about your 'British values'? *The Guardian*. Available at: https://www.theguardian.com/education/2014/jul/01/gove-what-is-so-british-your-british-values (Accessed 19 June 2023).

Rossi, V. (2021) *Rear-view Mirror: Reflecting about Practice through the Lens of Universal Design for Learning Principles and Practices to Inform Learning Design*. Available at: https://include.wp.worc.ac.uk/rear-view-mirror-from-a-uk-perspective/ (Accessed 7 June 2023).

Rowson, J. (2019) *Bildung in the 21st Century: Why Sustainable Prosperity Depends upon Reimaging Education*. CUSP (Centre for the Understanding of Sustainable Prosperity). Available at: http://cusp.ac.uk/essay/m1-9 (Accessed 20 June 2023).

RSA (2021) *Learning about Culture Final Report*. London: RSA.

Ryan, R. and Deci, E. (2000) Self-determination theory and the facilitation of intrinsic motivation, social development, and well-being. *American Psychologist, 55*(1), pp. 68–78.

Saccardi, M. (2014) *Creativity and Children's Literature: New Ways to Encourage Divergent Thinking*. London: Libraries Unlimited.

Sandbrook, B. and Dower, C. (2018) *Early Years Artsmark Feasibility Study*. London: Arts Council England.

Sandell, R. (1998) Museums as agents of social inclusion. *Museum Management and Curatorship, 17*(4), pp. 401–418.

Du Sautoy, M. (27 June 2011) Listen by numbers: Music and maths. *The Guardian*. Available at: https://www.theguardian.com/music/2011/jun/27/music-mathematics-fibonacci (Accessed 15 May 2023).

Savin-Baden, M. (ed.) (2021) *Postdigital Humans: Transitions, Transformations and Transcendence*. London: Springer.

Sawyer, R. K. et al. (eds.) (2003) *Creativity and Development*. Oxford: Oxford University Press.

Schön, D. (1983) *The Reflective Practitioner: How Professionals Think in Action*. New York: Basic Books.

Seligman, M. (2018) PERMA and the building blocks of well-being. *The Journal of Positive Psychology*, *13*(4), pp. 333–335.

Seligman, M. and Csikszentmihalyi, M. (2014) Positive psychology: An introduction. In *Flow and the Foundations of Positive Psychology*. Dordrecht: Springer, pp. 279–298.

Sewell, A. and Smith, J. (2021) *Introduction to Special Educational Needs, Disability and Inclusion: A Student's Guide*. London: SAGE.

Sharp, C. (2004) *Developing Young Children's Creativity: What Can We Learn from Research?* NFER. Available at: https://futurelab.org.uk/developing-young-childrens-creativity-what-can-we-learn-from-research/ (Accessed 21 September 2022).

Silber, K. (1960) *Pestalozzi the Man and His Work*. London: Routledge and Kegan Paul.

Sims, M. (2017) Neoliberalism and early childhood. *Cogent Education*, *4*, 1–10.

Siraj-Blatchford, I., Sylva, K., Muttock, S., Gilden, R. and Bell, D. (2002) *Researching Effective Pedagogy in the Early Years*. HMSO: DfES.

Smidt, S. (2009) *Introducing Vygotsky a Guide for Practitioners and Students in Early Years Education*. Oxon: Routledge.

Smidt, S. (2013) *Introducing Malaguzzi: Exploring the Life and Work of Reggio Emilia's Founding Father*. London: Routledge.

Smidt, S. (2018) *Introducing Trevarthen: A Guide for Practitioners and Students in Early Years Education*. Oxford: Routledge.

Smolucha, F. (1992) A reconstruction of Vygotsky's theory of creativity. *Creativity Research Journal*, *5*(1), pp. 49–67.

Social Mobility Commission (2022) *State of the Nation 2022: A Fresh Approach to Social Mobility*. London: HMSO.

Solvason, C. (2017) 'Learning to be an ethical practitioner'. In Musgrave, J., Savin-Baden, M. and Stobbs, N. (eds.) *Studying for Your Early Years Degree: Skills and Knowledge for Becoming an Effective Practitioner*. St. Albans: Critical Publishing.

Solvason, C., Elliott, G. and Cunliffe, H. (2021) Preparing university students for the moral responsibility of early years education, *Journal of Education for Teaching*. doi:10.1080/0260 7476.2021.1989982

Solvason, C. and Webb, R. (eds.) (2022) *Exploring and Celebrating the Early Childhood Practitioner: An Interrogation of Pedagogy, Professionalism and Practice*. London: Routledge.

Sousa, D. (2006) *How the Arts Develop the Brain*. Arlington: School Superintendents Association.

Sprat, J. (2016) Childhood wellbeing: What role for education? *British Educational Research Journal*, *42*(2), pp. 223–239. doi:10.1002/berj.3211

Statham, J. and Chase, E. (2010) Childhood wellbeing: A brief overview. Available at: https://assets.publishing.service.gov.uk/government/uploads/system/uploads/attachment_data/file/183 197/Child-Wellbeing-Brief.pdf (Accessed 14 July 2021).

Stein, Z. (2022) Education is the Metacrisis: Why it's time to see the planetary crises as a species-wide learning opportunity. Perspectiva. Available at: https://systems-souls-society.com/education-is-the-metacrisis/ (Accessed 29 June 2023).

Stirrup, J., Evans, J. and Davies, B. (2017) Learning one's place and position through play: Social class and educational opportunity in early years education. *International Journal of Early Years Education*, *25*(4), pp. 343–360.

Stoll, L. and Temperley, J. (2009) Creative leadership: A challenge of our times. *School Leadership & Management*, 29(1), pp. 63–76.

Strong-Wilson, T. and Ellis, J. (2007) Children and place: Reggio Emilia's environment as third teacher. *Theory into Practice*, 46(1), pp. 40–47.

Sturrock, G. and Else, P. (1998) *The Playground as Therapeutic Space: Playwork as Healing (The Colorado Paper) Leigh-on-Sea*. Ludemos Press.

Sue, D. W., Alsaidi, S., Awad, M. N., Glaeser, E., Calle, C. Z. and Mendez, N. (2019) Disarming racial microaggressions: Microintervention strategies for targets, White allies, and bystanders. *American Psychologist*, 74(1), pp. 128–142.

Sustainable Development. *A Handbook for Teachers*. Cyprus: Frederick University. Available at: http://care.frederick.ac.cy/docs/CARE_IO6.pdf (Accessed 11 June 2023).

Sutton Trust (2018) *Parent Power*. Available at: https://www.suttontrust.com/our-research/parent-power-2018-schools/ (Accessed 28 June 2023).

Sutton Trust (2021) *Fairness First: Social Mobility, COVID and Education Recovery*. Policy Brief. Available at: https://www.suttontrust.com/wp-content/uploads/2021/05/Fairness-First-Social-Mobility-Covid-Education-Recovery.pdf (Accessed 28 June 2021).

Sutton Trust Policy Briefing (2021) *Fairness First: Social Mobility, COVID and Education Recovery*. London: Sutton Trust.

Swain, J. and French, S. (2000) Towards an affirmation model of disability. *Disability & Society*, 15(4), pp. 569–582.

Sylva, K., Melhuish, E., Sammons, P., Siraj-Blatchford, I. and Taggart, B. (2004) The effective provision of pre-school education (EPPE) project: Findings from pre-school to end of Key Stage 1. Available at: https://dera.ioe.ac.uk/18189/2/SSU-SF-2004-01.pdf (Accessed 10 June 2021).

Sylvester, R. (2011) Learning from working with disaffected year 10 pupils. In Knight, S. (ed.) *Forest School for All*. London: SAGE.

Tarnowski, S. (1999) Musical play and young children. *Music Educators Journal*, 86(1), pp. 26–29.

Taylor, C. (2004) *Modern Social Imaginaries*. London: Duke University Press

Taylor, S. (2020) Harnessing the power of the white cube: The contemporary art gallery as a liminal space for multi-sensory learning. In Campbell, L. (ed.) *Leap into Action: Critical Performative Pedagogies in Art and Design Education*. New York: Peter Lang.

Taylor, S. (2018) Inclusion and the arts. In Woolley, R. (ed.) *Understanding Inclusion: Core Concepts, Policy, Practice*. London: Routledge.

Taylor, S. and Payne, R. (2013) Skills in the making. In Ravetz, A., Kettle, A. and Facey, H. (eds.) *Collaboration through Craft*. London: Bloomsbury, pp. 142–156.

Taylor, S., Elders, L. and Hay, P. (2022) *Thinking Differently Project Evaluation Report, Meadow Arts*. Available at: https://meadowarts.org/learning/thinking-differently-project/ (Accessed 6 June 2023).

The Big Draw (2021) The big draw talks to... Eileen Adams. Available at: https://thebigdraw.org/the-big-draw-talks-toeileen-adams (Accessed 11 November2021).

The Book Trust (2019) *Staring into Space: A Waterstones Children's Laureate Creative Resource*. Available at: https://cdn.booktrust.org.uk/globalassets/resources/childrens-laureate/lauren-child/staring-into-space/staring-into-space-all-six-resources (Accessed 3 May 2022).

The Children's Society (2020) *The Good Childhood Report 2020*. Available at: https://www.children ssociety.org.uk/information/professionals/resources/good-childhood-report-2020 (Accessed 14 July 2021).

The Lego Foundation (2020) *Creating Systems. How Can Education Systems Reform to Enhance Learners' Creativity?* Available at: https://cms.learningthroughplay.com/media/eiwhkkhu/ creating-systems-report-eng.pdf (Accessed 20 January 2023).

The National Autistic Society (2023) *What Is Autism?* Available at: https://www.autism.org.uk/ advice-and-guidance/what-is-autism#:~:text=More%20than%20one%20in%20100,and% 20children%20in%20the%20UK (Accessed 6 June 2023).

The Teaching Factor (2021) Creativity and Social Emotional Learning (SEL). Available at: https:// theteachingfactor.wordpress.com/2021/05/19/creativity-and-social-emotional-learning-sel/ (Accessed 21 January 2023).

Thomson, P. (2011) The importance of pedagogically focused leadership. In Sefton-Green, J., Thomson, P., Jones, K. and Bresler, L. (eds.) *The Routledge International Handbook of Creative Learning*. London: Routledge.

Thomson, P. and Maloy, L. (2022) *The Benefits of Art, Craft and Design Education in Schools: A Rapid Evidence Review*. School of Education: University of Nottingham.

Tickell, C. (2011) *The Early Years: Foundations for Life, Health and Learning*. An Independent Report on the Early Years Foundation Stage to Her Majesty's Government. Available at: https://asse ts.publishing.service.gov.uk/government/uploads/system/uploads/attachment_data/file/1809 19/DFE-00177-2011.pdf (Accessed 14 July 2021).

Times Education Commission (2022) *Bringing Out the Best*. London: The Times. Available at: https://lordslibrary.parliament.uk/times-education-commission-bringing-out-the-best/ (Accessed 21 February 2023).

Tims, C. (ed.) (2010) *Born Creative*. London: DEMOS.

Tisdale, L. (2017) Education, parenting and concepts of childhood in England, c.1945 to c.1979. *Contemporary British History*, *31*(1), pp. 24–46.

Tobin, J. J., Wu, T. J. H. and Davidson, D. H. (1989) *Preschool in Three Cultures*. New York: Yale University.

Torrance, P. (1969) Creative positives of disadvantaged children and youth. *Gifted Child Quarterly*, *13*(2), pp. 71–81.

Transforming Access and Student Outcomes in Higher Education (TASO) (n.d.) *Theory of Change*. Available at: https://taso.org.uk/evidence/evaluation-guidance-resources/impact-evaluation-with-small-cohorts/getting-started-with-a-small-n-evaluation/theory-of-change/ (Accessed 4 May 2023).

Trevarthen, C. and Malloch, S. (2002) Musicality and music before three: Human vitality and invention shared with pride. *Zero to Three*, *23*(2), pp. 10–18.

Trevarthen, C. (1997) Preface to Pavlecevic, M. Music Therapy. In *Context: Music, Meaning and Relationship*. London: Jessica Kingsley.

Trinick, M. (2012) Sound and sight: The use of song to promote language learning. *General Music Today*, *25*(2), pp. 5–10.

UN (1989) United Nations Convention on the Rights of the Child. Available at: https://www. unicef.org.uk/wp-content/uploads/2016/08/unicef-convention-rights-child-uncrc.pdf (Accessed 11 January 2023).

UN (2015a) Sustainable Development Goals. Available at: https://sdgs.un.org/goals (Accessed 13 June 2023).

UN (2015b) The Millennium Development Goals. Available at: https://www.un.org/millennium goals/ (Accessed 16 January 2023).

UN (2022a) Sustainable Development Goals. Available at: https://www.un.org/sustainabledevelop ment/sustainable-development (Accessed 16 January 2023).

UN (2022b) Goal 9: Industries, innovation and infrastructure. Available at: https://www.un.org/ sustainabledevelopment/infrastructure-industrialization/ (Accessed 16 January 2023).

UN (2022c) Quality education. Available at: https://www.un.org/sustainabledevelopment/education/ (Accessed 16 January 2023).

UN (2022d) Quality education: Why it matters. Available at: https://www.un.org/sustainabledeve lopment/wp-content/uploads/2017/02/4_Why-It-Matters-2020.pdf

UNESCO (2010) Seoul Agenda: Goals for the Development of Arts Education. Available at: https:// unesdoc.unesco.org/ark:/48223/pf0000190692 (Accessed 16 January 2023).

UNESCO (2020) *Global Education Monitoring Report: Inclusion and Education*. Available at: https:// en.unesco.org/gem-report/report/2020/inclusion (Accessed 11 June 2023).

UNESCO (2021) *Reimagining Our Futures Together: A New Social Contract for Education*. Paris: UNESCO.

UNESCO (2023a) *Re-Shaping Policies for Creativity*. Available at: https://www.unesco.org/reports/ reshaping-creativity/2022/en#:~:text=The%20UNESCO%20Global%20Report%2C% 20Re,the%20Diversity%20of%20Cultural%20Expressions (Accessed 14 February 2023).

UNESCO (2023b) *Education For All (EFA)*. Available at: http://www.ibe.unesco.org/en/glossary-curr iculum-terminology/e/education-all-efa#:~:text=The%20six%20goals%20are%3A%20(a,have %20access%20to%20and%20complete%2C (Accessed 11 January 2023).

UNESCO (n.d.) *International Arts Education Week*. Available at: https://www.unesco.org/en/weeks/ arts-education (Accessed 16 June 2023).

UNESCO and España. Ministerio de Educación y Ciencia (1994) The Salamanca Statement and Framework for Action on Special Needs Education at 'World Conference on Special Needs Education: Access and Quality'. Available at: https://unesdoc.unesco.org/ark:/48223/pf0000 098427 (Accessed 28 July 2023).

United Nations (2015) Sustainable Development Goals. Available at: https://sdgs.un.org/goals (Accessed 6 June 2023).

University of Edinburgh (2020) *Gibbs Reflective Cycle*. Available at: https://www.ed.ac.uk/reflect ion/reflectors-toolkit/reflecting-on-experience/gibbs-reflective-cycle (Accessed 28 June 2023).

Vickery, A. (2014) *Developing Active Learning in the Primary Classroom*. London: SAGE.

Vidal-Hall, C., Flewitt, R. and Wyse, D. (2020) Early childhood practitioner beliefs about digital media: Integrating technology into a child-centred classroom environment. *European Early Childhood Education Research Journal*, 28(2), pp. 167–181.

Viding, E. and McCrory, E. (2022) Individuals as active co-creators of their environments: Implications for prevention of inequalities. *IFS Deaton Review of Inequalities*. Available at:

https://ifs.org.uk/inequality/individuals-as-active-co-creators-of-their-environments-implicat
ions-for-prevention-of-inequalities (Accessed 14 July 2022).

Vygotsky, L. S. (1978) *Mind in Society: The Development of Higher Psychological Processes*. Cambridge:
Harvard University Press.

Vygotsky, L. S. (2004) Imagination and creativity in childhood. *Journal of Russian and East
European Psychology*, *42*(1), pp. 7–97. Available at: https://www.marxists.org/archive/vygotsky/
works/1927/imagination.pdf (Accessed 28 February 2023).

Wahl, D. C. (2016) *Designing Regenerative Cultures*. Charmouth: Triarchy Press.

Walker, R., Reed, M. and Carey-Jenkins, D. (2017) Understanding and using policy and legislation.
In Musgrave, J., Savin-Baden, M. and Stobbs, N. (eds.) *Studying for Your Early Years Degree: Skills
and Knowledge for Becoming an Effective Early Years Practitioner*. St Albans: Critical Publishing.

Wall, S., Litjens, I. and Taguma, M. (2015) *Early Childhood Education and Care Pedagogy Review
England*. Organisation for Economic Cooperation and Development (OECD). Available at:
https://www.oecd.org/unitedkingdom/early-childhood-education-and-care-pedagogy-review-
england.pdf (Accessed 28 February 2023).

Watson, N. (2018) A unique child: By choice. *Nursery World*, *2018*(1), pp. 30–31.

Weare, K. and Gray, G. (2003) *What works in developing children's emotional and competence and
wellbeing?* Research Report No 456. Crown Printers: University of Southampton, Health
Education Unit, Research and Graduate School of Education.

Wearmouth, J. (2017) *Understanding Special Educational Needs and Disability in the Early Years:
Principles and Perspectives*. Abingdon: Routledge.

Weitzman, E. and Greenberg, J. (2002) *Learning Language and Loving It: A Guide to Promoting
Children's Social, Language, and Literacy Development in Early Childhood Settings*, 2nd ed.
Toronto: The Hanen Centre.

Wenger, E. (1998) *Communities of Practice: Learning, Meaning, and Identity*. Cambridge: Cambridge
University Press.

West, A. (2020) Legislation, ideas and pre-school education policy in the twentieth century: From
targeted nursery education to universal early childhood education and care. *British Journal of
Educational Studies*, *68*(5), pp. 567–587.

Western Sydney University (n.d.) *What Is Cultural Literacy?* Available at: https://www.westernsyd
ney.edu.au/studysmart/home/cultural_literacy/what_is_cultural_literacy (Accessed 15 June
2023).

Whitty, G. (2016) *Research and Policy in Education: Evidence, Ideology and Impact*. London: Institute
of Education.

Williams, L. (1992) Determining the multicultural curriculum. In Vold, E. B. (ed.) *Multicultural
Education in Early Childhood Classrooms*. Washington, DC: NEA.

Wilson, A. (2014) *Creativity in Primary Education*, 3rd ed. London: SAGE.

Winnicott, D. W. (1964) *The Child, the Family and the outside World*. Harmondsworth: Penguin.

Wood, E. (2013) *Play, Learning and the Early Childhood Curriculum*. London: SAGE.

Wood, E. and Attfield, J. (2005) *Learning and the Early Childhood Curriculum*, 2nd ed. London: Paul
Chapman.

Woollard, J. (2010) *Psychology for the Classroom: Behaviourism*, 1st edn. London: Routledge.

Woolley, R. (2010) *Tackling Controversial Issues in the Primary School: Facing Life's Challenges with Your Learners*. London: Routledge.

Woolley, R. (2021) *Facing Children's Difficult Questions*. Available at: https://www.worc.ac.uk/about/news/academic-blog/facing-children's-difficult-questions.aspx (Accessed 29 June2021).

World Health Organisation (WHO) (1986) *The Ottawa charter for Health Promotion*. Available at: https://www.who.int/teams/health-promotion/enhanced-wellbeing/first-global-conference. (Accessed 9 August 2021).

World Population Review (2023) *Suicide Rate by Country*. Available at: https://worldpopulationreview.com/country-rankings/suicide-rate-by-country (Accessed 16 February 2023).

Wright, S. (2010) *Understanding Creativity in Early Childhood: Meaning-Making and Children's Drawing*. London: SAGE.

Wu, K. B., Young, M. E. and Cai, J. (2012) *Early Child Development in China*. Washington, DC: World Ban, p. 13.

Wyness, M. (2012) *Childhood and Society*, 2nd ed. Basingstoke: Palgrave Macmillan.

Yarrow, A. and Fane, J. (2019) *The Sociology of Early Childhood, Young Children's Lives and Worlds*. Abingdon: Routledge.

Ye, W. (2021) China's harsh education crackdown sends parents and businesses scrambling. Available at: https://www.cnbc.com/2021/08/05/chinas-harsh-education-crackdown-sends-parents-businesses-scrambling.html (Accessed 14 February 2023).

Zhu, J. (2009) Early childhood education and relative policies in China. *International Journal of Child Care and Education Policy*, 3(1), pp. 51–60.

Index